Praise for *Making Sense of Adolescence* ...

"This book is yet another attempt to encourage parents of teens to persist: the rewards are worth the pain. The authors have done a thorough job, and I can recommend this book as a source of much wisdom and experience. Kids say the darndest things...and kids do the darndest things — and always will! I think you'll find a message of hope in these pages."

—Art Linkletter
Author of *Drugs at My Doorstep* and
founder of the Diane Linkletter Fund

"Somebody said that when children are between the ages of twelve and sixteen, the average parent ages thirty-five years. John Crudele and Dick Erickson clearly point out why it doesn't have to be that way. This is a genuine 'why you should' and 'how you can' approach to dealing with adolescence. It's chock-full of analogies, examples, illustrations, stories, and common sense, and it's reinforced with even more truth in real-life experiences. You'll enjoy and benefit from the counsel of these men."

—Zig Ziglar
Chairman, the Zig Ziglar Corporation
Author, *See You at the Top*

"John Crudele's passion for children and Dick Erickson's clinical expertise have created a valuable resource for anyone who wants to help today's troubled, confused, and often misguided adolescents find the hope and courage to create the meaningful and fulfilling lives they deserve."

—Jack Canfield
President, the Foundation for Self-Esteem
Co-author, *Chicken Soup for the Soul*

"Reviewing this book as a father, grandfather, and professional with thirty-five years experience in working with adolescents, I can comfortably say that this work is a refreshing approach to a complicated issue. I would highly recommend this book for future parents, in addition to those who work daily with this age group, such as educators, social workers, probation officers, youth workers, counselors, and the clergy."

—Patrick T. Davis, A.C.S.W., Ph.D.
President, Human Dynamics Group

"In *Making Sense of Adolescence,* the authors blend head, heart, research, and pragmatic experience. Again and again the wisdom of scholarship is personalized by true-life stories. I laughed. I cried. I found myself recollecting, reflecting, and rejoicing. The authors mince no words; the challenges of adolescence are enormous. But they also kindle hope and share perspective, pragmatism, and patience. This book is a perfect fit for our time."

—DR. DONALD R. DRAAYER
Superintendent, School District #276
Minnetonka, Minnesota
Honored as National Superintendent of Schools 1990–91

"I could not put it down once I started—took up my whole weekend. It is a powerful piece of writing without being preachy. The personal stories add a dimension that captures the heart as every family can identify with them. It will help parents realize that they are not alone in this extremely challenging role of parenthood."

—RITA WIGFIELD
Fifth-grade teacher, Hopkins, Minnesota
Honored as Minnesota Teacher of the Year, 1992

"Life isn't as much about beliefs as it is about relationships, whether with your children, your spouse, or God. Dick and John have brought to mainstream American families a great compass on the spiritual journey of life's most important relationships. Their book offers wonderful suggestions and guidelines that will help you make your family healthier. Their book will help you make sense of adolescence regardless of whether it is a present concern or a source of reflection or anticipation."

—MIKE PRITCHARD
Host of PBS-TV Family Documentaries
"Power of Choice," "You Can Choose,"
and "Big Changes, Big Choices"

"*Making Sense of Adolescence* is a refreshingly honest and well-documented approach to the challenging task of raising value-driven teenagers. John Crudele and Dick Erickson provide a scope of wisdom and experience on this subject unlike anything else I have ever reviewed at Nightingale-Conant. Be sure to keep this classic within an arm's reach."

—DAN STRUTZEL
New Product Coordinator
Nightingale-Conant Corporation

"This book underscores basic parental responsibilities and the need for a good family foundation. As the family dissolves, so go our young people and society at large. As parents we must communicate with our children and raise them properly so that they can effectively think, choose, and act responsibly. This book lays it out for all to understand. It is a commonsense approach to understanding and communicating with adolescents. Great Work!"

—DR. RONALD G. AREA
President, CEO
Oklahoma State University Foundation

"At this point on the journey of parenthood, love is not enough. What John Crudele and Dick Erickson offer is the partner to love: understanding. They offer expert guidance in understanding our children, their actions, and the effect of our reactions. Our young people are an asset for our families, our community, and our nation. *Making Sense of Adolescence* is a valuable tool for understanding and supporting their journey to adulthood."

—DR. CARL HOLMSTROM
Superintendent of Schools
St. Louis Park, Minnesota

"A terrific book, filled with inspiring ideas. It will help parents regain the joy of parenting. This book will help you learn how to pass on your treasured values to your children. I'm hoping that parents, inspired by reading this book, will take the time to develop skills that will really help them be better parents and enjoy being better parents."

—FATHER VAL J. PETER, J.C.D., S.T.D.
Executive Director, Father Flanagan's Boys' Home
Boys Town, Nebraska

"*Making Sense of Adolescence* is an analysis and an answer to the struggle of adolescence not only as a historic generational time of change and difficulty, but as an age of peculiar poignance and pain in the present generation. I am thrilled to see this book on the market. I take it as a sign of hope for all of us."

—REV. DR. ARTHUR A. ROUNER, JR.
Senior Minister Emeritus, Colonial Church of Edina, Minnesota
President and CEO, Rouner Center for Mission and Ministry
Author of several books including *How to Love* and *Healing Your Hurts*

"A wonderful, comprehensive, eminently readable book that I wish existed when I was a father coping with the teenage years. It... should be on the desk of every teacher and on the bookshelves of parents. I strongly recommend it."
—JUDGE ALLEN OLEISKY
Fourth Judicial District Court of Minnesota,
Former Chief Judge of the Juvenile Court

"*Making Sense of Adolescence* is a parenting manual and a reference book, with concise, clear directions, not just philosophy. It gives words of encouragement, empowerment, and hope. Use this as your guidebook through those difficult years of adolescence."
—CHERYL GUSTAFSON, Parent of three adolescents

"Crudele and Erickson tell us the secrets of rearing adolescents successfully while maintaining our own integrity and sanity. Most important is their invaluable advice about how to actualize our values in our parenting as we see our children through these tough but exciting years. Their book should be required reading for every parent before their children reach adolescence."
—ERNIE SWIHART, M.D., Pediatrician
Co-author, with Patrick Cotter, Ph.D., *The Manipulative Child*

"John Crudele and Dick Erickson affirm my beliefs in the godly principle of the family, the obligation and responsibility of fatherly leadership, and the values they create when surrounded in a loving, caring environment."
—CHARLES RAGUS, Founder and President of AdvoCare

"I consider John Crudele one of the most effective youth speakers in America. He knows kids. He knows their joys and he knows their hurt—he *knows what to do!* He helps us as parents to make sense out of adolescence."
—JOSH D. MCDOWELL, Communicator/author, *Right From Wrong*
and *More Than a Carpenter*

"This is a must read! It paints a picture of the many challenges and choices facing our young people today while motivating you, the parent, to learn new tools to help your youth walk the minefield of adolescence."
— JANICE FILMON, Wife of Manitoba's 19th Premier,
mother of four young adults, volunteer and popular speaker
for P.R.I.D.E. (Parents Resource Institute for Drug Education)

"*Making Sense of Adolescence* is a great book... an enormous service to parents."
—DAVID MCNALLY, Author, *Even Eagles Need a Push*

Making Sense of Adolescence

Making Sense of Adolescence

How to Parent from the Heart

JOHN CRUDELE, C.S.P.

and

RICHARD ERICKSON, Ph.D.

TRIUMPH™ BOOKS
Liguori, Missouri

For information regarding speaking engagements, seminars, audio and video tapes, or consulting, write or call:

Mr. John J. Crudele
9704 Yukon Court
Bloomington, MN 55438
   (612) 942-6207 (Office)
   (800) 899-9543
   (612) 942-7601 (Fax)

Dr. Richard A. Erickson
16587 Creekside Lane
Minnetonka, MN 55345
   (612) 949-3897 (Office)
   (800) 633-7338
   (612) 934-3635 (Fax)

Published by Triumph™ Books
Liguori, Missouri
An Imprint of Liguori Publications

Library of Congress Cataloging-in-Publication Data
Crudele, John.
   Making sense of adolescence : how to parent from the heart / John Crudele and Richard Erickson.
     p. cm.
   Includes index.
   ISBN: 0-89243-773-1
   1. Adolescence. 2. Teenagers—Family relationships. 3. Parent and teenager. I. Erickson, Richard. II. Title.
HQ793.C78 1995
305.23'5—dc20   94-41677
                                   CIP

Printed in the United States of America

First Edition 1995
9 8 7 6 5 4 3 2

*Whatever your hand finds to do,
verily do it with all your might.*

—ECCLESIASTES 9:10

Contents

Part IV
Life Beyond Adolescence

Acknowledgments

THERE ARE MANY PEOPLE to thank in a project like this. As first-time authors we have needed the guidance and support of anyone and everyone over these last couple of years. To our family and friends, we give our heartfelt thanks for their never-ending belief and patience. We are also thankful for our professional colleagues who encouraged us, challenged us, and offered their refining critiques: by phone, fax, letter, in hotel lobbies or over lunch. Each touched the final transcript, enhancing its message.

We are particularly grateful for our agent, Jeff Herman, who believed in us and the purpose of our book from the beginning and introduced us to Triumph/Liguori. We so appreciate the efforts of our editors, Kass Dotterweich and Joan Golan, and the persistent guidance of executive editor Pat Kossmann. We extend our heartfelt thanks to Kerstin Erker, our publicist, Marla Kindt, our promotions manager, Carol Meyer, general sales manager, and Ann Sudekum, copywriter. Thank you, John Eagleson, for working your typesetting and page layout magic. Here in Minneapolis we are indebted to the daily support of Jane Juetten, executive assistant to John Crudele, and Debbie Grahek, who is the marketing director for the Crudele/Erickson Communications partnership.

Also, a very special thank-you to all the kids and clients who have graced our lives. We are so deeply touched by the openness, honesty, and drama of their letters and personal stories. Without them, this book would not have been possible. By inviting us to share intimately in their life's journey, they have introduced us, and now the reader, to the answers to many of life's issues.

Introduction

THIS BOOK is a collaborative effort by two authors. We find our strengths reflected in our differences. One of us is old, one young, one married with children, the other single without children. One is a professional therapist, the other a professional speaker; both of us specialize in work with children and families. We have given equally of ourselves to this project. It is our sincere hope that as you turn the pages and discover new insights, you likewise will enjoy your journey with us.

We have joined together to make what we believe is a significant contribution toward understanding the confusing world of adolescence. While our book speaks in one narrative voice from both of us, we share anecdotes and insights from our personal experiences, using the first-person singular without identifying the speaker. Sometimes it will be obvious which of us is sharing a life lesson, and other times we leave it to the reader's imagination. What is important is that these experiences could happen to your family — perhaps some of them already have — and we can help you cope with them.

In the United States alone, 21 million teenagers and their parents struggle to cope with the mysteries of adolescence. Thousands of these parents and young people have written letters to us crying out for help, searching for answers, or just reaching out for someone who will listen and take them seriously. Their letters talk of suicide, incest, rape, alcohol and drug use, discouragement, depression, friendship, family — the list goes on and on. They are hungrily searching for direction about how to deal with life's most critical issues. They feel that no one is listening and no one understands.

I really need someone to talk to. There are a lot of things inside of me that I have never told to anyone, and I need them to be said to

1

someone. I know that you are really busy, but if you ever have a spare moment, I would really appreciate the chance to talk with you.
—TAMMY, 10th grade

Too often, in the world today, we dismiss what our teenagers are feeling and thinking. Many believe that the confusion in adolescence is just an unavoidable phase that, with time, will pass on its own.

Both of us have spent a lifetime working with adolescents and families. John brings to this book his vast experience as a youth counselor and an internationally recognized professional speaker who has addressed over a million people on the concerns of adolescents and their families. Dick brings the experience of a probation officer, school social worker, and clinical psychotherapist in private practice. We have contact with adolescents and families every day of our lives. Some come in person; others call or write letters, often in desperation, as they search for answers to their problems. Concerns are deep and serious and often reflect dangerous situations. The text we have developed includes excerpts from hundreds of letters — letters that validate these cries for help.

I get so angry that I write to myself about what's going on. I make plans to run away or how I am going to kill myself.
— AMBER, 8th grade

We know that each contact made with one of us represents thousands of individuals who don't reach out for help but who are nevertheless struggling to cope with the same kind of pain and confusion. Many young people choose suicide each year in preference to their savage loneliness, hopelessness, and endless confusion.

The breakdown of the family and societal support systems leads to a decreased sense of connectedness with the world. As a result, young people have a hard time developing a strong sense of personal identity. They cannot recognize and understand these problems. They don't have adequate life experience to mature without help. It's up to their parents and significant others to guide, love, and fill their needs as they develop and mature into adults. When adolescents feel that these basic needs are left unmet — or are even denied — they fall victim to many of life's temptations. In their vulnerability, they reach out and experiment with a variety of destructive solutions as they strive to discover and understand their specialness.

> *I had a boyfriend for about six months. I truly thought what we were feeling was love. So one day I had him over when no one was home. Actually he came over lots when no one was home. But this time was different. We started off like usual, by kissing, and one thing led to another, and normally where I would make him stop, I didn't and we ended up making love. Or at the time that's what I thought it was. Then something went wrong and he's seeing another girl. He promised he'd always be there.*
>
> — ROCHELLE, 10th grade

This book reaches out to both parents and adolescents themselves. We want you to achieve serenity by understanding that others have gone before you; and they not only survived but have created a blueprint for dealing with the complex problems of life. We will lay this blueprint before you, to be adapted to your unique circumstances. The philosophy underlying our writing has evolved both from our experiences with the issues of parents and young people and also from our study of the best psychological information available today.

> *You have encouraged me to examine some of my habits with my own children. You have given me some real insight and hope. For this I am truly grateful.*
>
> —MARK AND DIANE, parents

We ask that God bless your home, your life, and your family, as you embrace your own personal journey through the years ahead.

JOHN CRUDELE, C.S.P.
Youth Counselor and International Professional Speaker
Minneapolis, Minnesota

RICHARD A. ERICKSON, Ph.D.
Clinical Psychotherapist and Professional Speaker
Minneapolis, Minnesota

May 1, 1995

Part I

ADOLESCENCE: THE FAMILY'S BEST YEARS

Chapter 1

Smile,
It's Only Adolescence,
and It's Not Contagious

BY THE TIME we are old enough as parents to have adolescents, life has taught us much about its twists and turns. Now, suddenly, the complexity of our lives seems to increase geometrically. Sassy, argumentative aliens replace our adoring, parent-idolizing children. Even though we were expecting the turbulence, it catches us by surprise. Thoughts of running away surface, but we are too embarrassed to talk about them. Our coping mechanisms are saturated, and we lack the energy to deal effectively with a smart-mouthed teenager.

Mid-life with adolescents is particularly the time when we need to make an earnest promise to ourselves to hang in there till the end. All will be well if we rise to the challenge of adolescence with the right attitudes, values, and communication skills.

Principles of Successful Parenting

Being the parent of an adolescent and living to smile about it does require a shift in paradigms — which is a fancy way of saying we have to alter our attitudes and perception of parenting. Anyone who believes that parenting an adolescent is easy will get what we term the "wake-up call."

We believe that the parent of an adolescent who wants to enjoy the process needs to understand some basic principles of successful parenting. Seven of the principles are presented in this chapter, and others will follow. These ideas have been tested and researched and have proved reliable time and time again, so let's reflect on them and give them a try.

1. Adolescence Represents Change—for Parents and Kids

Reorganizing our attitude and accepting the fact that as parents we can't always be in control of every variable give us the opportunity to enter this challenge of parenting adolescents optimistically. Once the uncertainty and unpredictability of adolescence are embraced and accepted and we let go of our need to control, then we're well on our way to enjoying the journey. When our children were young, they would throw tantrums to test us, and the only successful response was patiently to wait them out. Now we're the ones who feel like throwing a tantrum. We're going through adolescence with our kids either way. Why fight the process?

We personally have always regarded adolescence as our favorite time. Yes, it is a time of volatility and chaos, but it's exciting, too. Kind of like hugging a lovable little porcupine — you want to, but you're never quite sure where to begin. Don't squeeze too hard, be patient, move with the critter, not against it, accept it for what it is, and pray.

2. Rebellion Is Normal During Adolescence

Adolescence is a passage through which young people have to go to mature and matriculate into the world of adulthood. This is a time of tremendous change, both physiologically and psychologically.

Adolescents can rebel healthfully only in an environment where they can internalize the fact that love and nurturance will not be withheld under any circumstance. As child psychiatrist Dr. Robert Demski states, "The instincts and drive for creativity, rebellion and individuality are widely recognized and acknowledged as necessary and even healthy strivings of youth."[1]

We meet with hundreds of parents monthly, and without exception these people want their adolescents to be compliant and cooperative. Responsiveness is the most sought-after, desirable behavior, the one that parents look for and request when the process of family counseling or individual therapy begins. Telling parents that the acting out of the adolescent is a sign of health usually elicits a smile and visible signs of relief. This is possibly the most therapeutic and significant message for the average family of an adolescent to hear.

> *I really wish my parents would do something about it when they know I've been drinking. They sometimes get mad for a couple of days, but they won't confront me about it. I wish they would simply confront me about things and tell me they love me.*
>
> —CATHERINE, 10th grade

We try our best to help parents understand that a quiet, compliant adolescent is overly afraid of the consequences of individuating — i.e., separating from his or her parents. In the midst of fearfulness, a young person may not feel able to act out or test the environment. So responsiveness is not necessarily a sign of parental competency but rather a defensive reaction to the threatening power of the parent. We must keep in mind that parental rejection is devastating to children of all ages and that teenagers often refuse to share their true feelings with parents for fear of rejection. The adolescent is often comfortable in opening up with professionals like us simply because the risk of rejection is small. They reason, "So what if the counselor blows me off or judges me! I can just quit coming," or "This guy will never be speaking in my school again, so what do I have to lose?"

> *You probably didn't really want to hear all of this, but I had to tell somebody. I guess I just figured that you wouldn't really hold it against me. Even if you do, I probably won't ever see you again because I don't think you come around here often. Everybody that I trust has turned against me when I tell them.*
>
> —STEPHANIE, 9th grade

3. Parental Influence Remains Strong During Adolescence

Regardless of adolescent reactive behavior, parents have the greatest opportunity to influence their children because children desire the love of their parents more than anything else. We hear a lot about peer pressure in adolescence, and it is real, but teens still desire parental love and approval even more than peer acceptance. Even children taken out of abusive family environments and placed in safe and peaceful foster care will spend their adolescence trying to get back into the family that was abusing them, their family of origin.

> *When you were telling the crowd how the parents are the biggest influence on children, God himself couldn't have said it any better. Sometimes people tell me that I look and act just like my mother. To me this is an insult. My mother has been married four times, and she is an alcoholic. Even though she is like this, I love her very much.*
> —SUZANNE, 9th grade

According to the "1990–91 Iowa Study of Alcohol and Drug Attitudes and Behaviors Among Youth," prepared by Dr. David Wright of the Iowa Department of Public Education, parents consistently ranked as the number-one influence in use or nonuse of mood-altering substances and as the most important source of information regarding decision-making about alcohol and other drugs. Parents ranked second to peers as a source of help.

While many people expect the school to help teens with these important issues, according to the teens, school personnel are one of the least respected sources of help. Again, we must not underestimate our opportunity to mold and influence our adolescents.

4. Coping with Turbulence Now Is Necessary and Will Not Destroy the Family

Unfortunately, teenagers in the compliant-response mode can repress their feelings for only so long; gradually, the repressed feelings begin to back up on them like a sewer. The resulting mess indicates that there is a blockage somewhere in the system. If not attended to, the mess will get worse, and most of us know what happens when the sewer backs up: The unexpected, inconvenient mess demands our immediate attention. In the course of human events, this is rarely fun. How do you spell relief? D-E-A-L W-I-T-H I-T!

> *I want to thank you for bringing up a lot of old memories for me. You forced me to deal with some things that had been kept inside of me.*
> —JANE, 9th grade

Always think in terms of consequences. Whatever is not talked out thoroughly or emotionally resolved in adolescence (e.g., anger and rebelliousness) will be acted out now or later in life.

You told me more than my parents ever did about sex and drugs. They never talked about drugs, peer pressure, sex, and other stuff like that. I guess they think that I will learn all the important stuff in school or from my friends.

—HOLLY, 10th grade

We repeat: *What is not dealt with during adolescence will have to be faced later on.* In many instances, the repressed feelings and issues will erupt during a young couple's early years of marriage. Continuing with the analogy of the sewer, without warning, old "sewage" will begin to back up and disrupt what appeared to be a fairly happy and stable marriage. These young couples won't even know what hit them.

Simply put, the greatest gift parents can give their children is the gift of a "safe" adolescence.

Human beings need to learn how to be kids first: Basic needs must be met, and then they can work toward maturity, feeling comfortable that they are ready for this important passage to the next stage in their lives: adulthood. Once frustrated parents of teenagers understand this key component of human development, they can change their paradigm about adolescence, and life will become easier in countless ways.

I wish you could have squeezed me in to talk with me after your speech. It really bothers me when people can't squeeze me in. See, my parents are divorced, and my father never has time for me.

—SERINA, 11th grade

Serina has just indicated quite clearly that she needs her parents to take the time to communicate with her and to give her physical attention, beginning with a hug. Nothing taught at school can or will replace this physical demonstration of parental affection, and the affection of a boyfriend will only be a temporary, frustrating, and empty solution.

5. *If You Expect the Best, You Will Get It*

Too often, parents anticipate adolescence with terror and anxiety. Rather than entering their children's challenge and adventure, parents often end up participating in a self-fulfilling prophesy: Their anxiety produces the very consequence they feared.

> *My dad hates me. He blames me for all of his problems. Gradually I have started to hate him. It's not that I enjoy hating him; he just doesn't respect me. He talks bad about me to everyone; he says things about my physical appearance, he hits me for no reason, and I don't like it anymore.*
>
> —GIGGLES, 8th grade

If you expect good things, you get them; the reverse is also true. Adolescence does not have to be a terrible time in the life of a family. Years ago when I was attending a Toastmasters' meeting, I heard the following message about relationships in general. Clearly, the message is appropriate for the parent/child relationship.

> If you flatter me, I may not believe you.
> If you criticize me, I may not like you.
> If you ignore me, I may not forgive you.
> If you encourage me, I will not forget you.
>
> — AUTHOR UNKNOWN

6. *Adolescents Need to be Met on Their Own Turf*

Our work with adolescents over the years has always left us predisposed to the bias that when parents realize the developmental needs of their teenage children, the entire family can venture through the teen years without fear, without hostility.

> *I was feeling down, alone, and lost — I turned to drugs, alcohol, sex, and I've been smoking for about nine months. I cry myself to sleep almost every night. Right now I'm grounded because of a school referral. I want to leave here, but I haven't anywhere to go or any money.*
>
> —JONATHAN, 8th grade

Jonathan's issues seem like an exhaustive list of challenges, but at the core is the desire to be understood. What an appropriate example of the old saying, "Seek first to understand and then to be understood," or "You have to see through Johnny before you can see Johnny through." Jonathan's wanting to run away is like an adult's desire to divorce a problem when the pain of facing it becomes too great, or a child's responding to discipline with "I hate you!"

7. It Is Best to Let the Lessons of Life Be Taught
— by Themselves

An old piece of Buddhist wisdom says, "Life is difficult. It always has been, and it always will be."

It's nice to know that even though you hardly know me, you still care. Just knowing that there is an adult that cares helps.
—JESSICA, 9th grade

Life is difficult, and Jessica's letter demonstrates the power that adults have in kids' lives. When the adolescent knows that some-one — *anyone* — is there no matter what, he or she has the courage to face life's difficulties.

Dealing With Life's Illusions

We have yet to find a family that doesn't qualify for the label of dysfunctional at some time or another. We all have an unusual aunt or uncle — even an indescribable parent or child.

We love to tell families that human perfection is an illusion, that life is rarely what you expected and anticipated. Sure, the details will vary, but the reality is the same: All families experience problems.

Myths abound in our world, and we have always been amazed by the myth that surrounds youth speakers, counselors, psychologists, and psychiatrists. It is assumed that we are perfect in every sense of the word — but we're not, and that's okay. Yet we've even had clients decide to quit coming to therapy when they discovered that we're not perfect.

My Son Kurt: University of Hard Knocks

Kurt is twenty-two. He is bright, funny, handsome, sensitive to the needs of others, unbelievably popular, a natural leader, entrepreneurial, and, most important for me, faithful to the family. He's a wonderful son.

Kurt always saw me as "Mr. Know-It-All," a label I resented. When he was seventeen, Kurt could set off a father/son fight simply by suggesting, "You really think that you have all the answers, don't you!" The ultimate insult for a therapist and a public speaker comes when your adolescent son declares at the dinner table, "I can't believe that there are actually people out there in the world willing to pay you to counsel them."

One of my biggest sources of pride today comes when Kurt asks for my advice about the development of a business he has created. As an adolescent, Kurt felt offended by my advice; as a young adult, he enthusiastically seeks my opinions on every imaginable subject.

In Kurt's eighteenth year, my wife and I returned from church to get the call that all parents of teenagers dread and fear. It was the panic-stricken mother of a friend of Kurt's. "Have you heard? The boys have been arrested for grand theft, auto." She had already contacted an attorney, and he was willing to take both cases if my wife and I wanted to share the anticipated legal fee: five thousand dollars.

When the woman gave me a chance to respond, I informed her that if Kurt was in jail because of a drinking-related incident, I was not about to bail him out. She couldn't understand my position.

Minutes later my son called and rather sheepishly told me the circumstances of his arrest and subsequent incarceration. I, in turn, explained to him that his mother and I objected to the use of mood-altering chemicals, a fact he already knew. I went on to explain that because he had been drinking prior to the offense he was being charged with, he would have to accept the responsibility of handling the situation. He said that he understood my position and asked for advice: "What would you do if you were in this situation?" Having spent a dozen years working in the court systems as an institutional family therapist, probation officer, and a juvenile center admission's officer, I could help him comprehend how the legal system works and what his options were.

I was pleased to learn that the theft incident was more a case of poor judgment than anything else. The boys had been drinking at a fraternity party, and upon leaving they thought it would be funny to move a car that someone had left warming up in the parking lot. As fate would have it, the police stumbled onto the scene, and Kurt discovered what the inside of a jail looks like.

When he arrived home about two weeks later and walked into my office, Kurt made a comment that gave me a lifelong respect for him: "Thanks, Dad, for not bailing me out. I learned my lesson well." He went on to explain that his friend's mom — the parent who had run to the rescue — was now harassing her son. She seemed to think that since she paid the bill and bailed her son out (two hours before my son was released), she had the privilege of shaming her son by harping on the inconvenience he had caused, the disgrace he had heaped on her and the family, and the overall failure he was.

For Kurt, going to jail was probably one of the best lessons he would ever learn. I'm certainly not wishing this kind of experience on your family, but often our adolescents have a valuable teacher right in the situation itself. Unfortunately, all too often we are tempted to bail them out of the lesson. Ironically, we thus cheat our children out of the opportunity to experience logical consequences and learn from the lesson.

The Courage to Be Imperfect — and Real

Popular author John Powell, S.J., gained his fame in writing his book, *Why Am I Afraid to Tell You Who I Am?* Father Powell talks about how we love to believe in myths, to be fooled by illusions. As a result, many of us feel grossly inadequate because we believe that everyone else "has it all together." Thus, we travel through life seeing ourselves as handicapped, incapable, and not "measuring up," while the rest of the crowd glides along, gifted, talented, and capable. Powell tries to help us understand how we all carry baggage from the past that somehow feels shameful. We choose to hide that baggage out of fear that others will avoid us or desert us if they see it, if they learn that we are so imperfect.

My boyfriend was the first and only person that I ever told about being raped. He was crying about as much as I was, but he listened.

He was there, and the best part is he still loved me after I told him everything. That was always a big fear of mine. I am still trying to decide about talking to my parents about this. I don't think I will ever be able to tell my daddy — I guess I am just not ready yet. I know that they will still love me, but I guess I am not ready for that side of the coping process.

—JENNIFER, 10th grade

By sharing our imperfections, we inspire and give courage to others. By having the courage to be imperfect, we become real. As the Skin Horse, in Margery Williams's classic children's tale *The Velveteen Rabbit,* so eloquently says, "Once you are real you can't become unreal again. It lasts for always." The story is delightfully simple yet profound.

The Skin Horse had lived longer in the nursery than any of the others. He was so old that his brown coat was bald in patches and showed the seams underneath, and most of the hairs in his tail had been pulled out to string bead necklaces. He was wise, for he had seen a long succession of mechanical toys arrive to boast and swagger, and by-and-by break their mainsprings and pass away, and he knew that they were only toys, and would never turn into anything else. For nursery magic is very strange and wonderful, and only those playthings that are old and wise and experienced like the Skin Horse understand all about it.

"What is Real?" asked the Rabbit one day, when they were lying side by side near the nursery fender, before Nana came to tidy the room. "Does it mean having things that buzz inside you and a stick-out handle?"

"Real isn't how you are made," said the Skin Horse. "It's a thing that happens to you. When a child loves you for a long, long time not just to play with, but really loves you, then you become Real."

"Does it hurt?" asked the Rabbit.

"Sometimes," said the Skin Horse, for he was always truthful. "When you are Real you don't mind being hurt."

"Does it happen all at once, like being wound up," he asked, "or bit by bit?"

"It doesn't happen all at once," said the Skin Horse. "You become. It takes a long time. That's why it doesn't often happen to people who break easily, or have sharp edges or who have to be carefully kept. Generally, by the time you are Real, most of your hair has been loved

off, and your eyes drop out and you get loose in the joints and very shabby. But these things don't matter at all, because when you are Real you can't be ugly, except to people who don't understand. But once you are real you can't become unreal again. It lasts for always."

Do you notice how people love bragging about their children? We would be the first to admit that it must be a thrill to tell the entire world your son or daughter was accepted into college, made the team, or received a scholarship. On the other hand, there is no thrill whatsoever in talking about a teenager's pregnancy or academic failure. Yet the downside reflects the struggle to grow, and a measure of truthfulness would help us all to cope.

Creating Hope: Reflections of an Average Family

A family is a place where you can go and feel safe. A family is a place where you can go if you are in trouble or are feeling bad. It is a place for fun. A family is a great thing to have. Be thankful you have a family.

—TOM, 6th grade

Let me share here about what life was like for my wife and me as we participated in the parenting of three children and as we're finishing that task with a fourth. All four have different personalities, and all four have at one time or another told us that they would never talk to us again as long as they lived. Interestingly, all four have survived, and they do talk to us, and three of the four have grown into the most loving, considerate, and successful human beings that one could ever meet. (The jury is still out on our youngest. He still has a few years to go.) Most significant for the present, however, is the fact that we, their parents, are blessed today with respectful, loving, and caring relationships with these adult children. Dwelling on my kids for a moment will help you in the process of reflecting on your own.

The Counselor's Kids in Crisis

Kurt, my oldest son, you've already met. My oldest child is a daughter named Kathy. She was only seventeen when a neighbor friend told me that Kathy was using cocaine. I nearly had a stroke. We are a totally drug-, alcohol-, and smoke-free family, and I had always believed that our children would do what we did. So I was stunned and thought, How can this be? We have modeled appropriately and yet this is happening. When I confronted my daughter, her excuse was, "Well, Dad, you are a drug counselor, aren't you? I just needed a little firsthand information about what you are doing and what exactly it is that you are trying to prevent in your practice."

My impulsive reaction was rage. I was embarrassed and angry and unbelievably scared about the implications of this behavior. My plan was for a perfect family. Something was drastically wrong. Defensively, I blamed Kathy's boyfriend. My wife maintained her calm nature; I was a loose canon, verbally judgmental and offensively demeaning. I immediately made an appointment for family counseling. Healing evolved, but nevertheless today, several years later, I still have some sort of post-traumatic-stress syndrome over the whole incident. I often wonder what I could have done differently in the situation. Still, we did survive, and the lesson remains there for my review: Slow down, process things, and examine the details with another adult (preferably one who is not emotionally involved) before taking action. Emergencies and crises are almost always relative, meaning that sometimes the best solution for any problem is to do nothing but wait and see what happens.

The telephone, too, has caused me no small measure of grief over the years, especially when I saw the receiver growing out of Kathy's ear. With all the wisdom that my age had brought me, I knew that phones can become major issues for parents. So, in an effort to head off unnecessary problems, I had a second line installed to keep our kids from using this issue as grounds for rebellion. But that wasn't enough; convenience didn't seem to be the issue. Still, I had to stick my nose into the matter and create a crisis. The very fact that my social butterfly daughter would talk to dozens of people every night caused me immense stress. Considering that these phone visits were all being done during homework time, I took the "Father knows best" position; I declared that this was affecting her education and therefore needed to stop — posthaste.

I smile rather sheepishly as I look back, and I beam with pride when I watch how my daughter has blossomed. She graduated from college and is almost finished with her master's program, completing it with high distinction while working — and continuing to talk on the telephone. Kathy has a thousand friends and evidently knows all their phone numbers by heart.

Peter is twenty-one, and he is probably our most industrious kid. As a parent, I frequently find it difficult to explain to my peers how successful Peter is when they ask, "What are your kids doing these days?"

Peter flunked out of college at the conclusion of his freshman year. As I recall, there were a lot of tears as we made the long trip home from the university. As I listened to Peter regret how stupid he was, I explained that success in college was more related to maturity, motivation, and perseverance than intelligence. Also I tried to explain the problems of dual careers (student and television monitor) and how it was the attraction of the television that prevented him from using his brain to successfully navigate the journey through college.

Peter works as a laborer in a glue factory at the present time. But I remain Peter's parent, and as his parent I fear that his comfortable income will diminish his motivation to return to college sometime down the road. As I think about the situation, however, and as I think about the number of college graduates who are busing dishes and waiting tables, I have to ask myself, "What is success? Is success really all about doing what your parents want you to do, or is it as simple as being happy, content to be alive and well, and pursuing your dreams?"

As you have read, from time to time our kids would get into trouble of some sort. As the years went by, I often wondered quietly to myself if my wife and I were doing any good. I would wonder what we were doing right, what we were doing wrong, what we were failing to do altogether. I figured that since I was a counselor of youth, surely I would be able to raise children with only a minimum amount of struggle. I've learned a lot since those days by watching and participating in the growth of our own kids and hundreds of other kids whom I met along the way in the counseling process. (By the way, if you are keeping track and noticed that I seem to have inadvertently left out one of my four children, the incredible story of our youngest child, Heng, will follow in a later chapter.)

Sometimes, after I have shared real-life stories with my audiences, people make comments like, "I know you were just making up those stories, but they sure were interesting." Because I am in the field of counseling and speaking, I am expected to be perfect, but I'm not — and everyone, if they are able to be honest, has a story to tell, and that's okay.

Looking Back on the Development of My Family

My wife and I have celebrated birthdays and holidays with a group of five couples since our early years of marriage. We were all members of a community service organization called the Jaycees. Eventually, we grew too old for the organization, but we have maintained those friendships over the years.

As our children got older and particularly as they got into their adolescent years, my wife and I would tell some of the downside stories about kid situations that we were experiencing. I could tell that our friends were initially shocked, but over the years they have come to understand that our stories are real stories and that we're not ashamed to be real and share them.

Sharing such stories can be fun as well as cathartic and uplifting. It's not shameful to have a problem, and it is certainly always helpful to share it. There are probably others within earshot who are going through the same thing but have chosen to protect their problems from public exposure; they simply "stuff" their situations. As a result, the inner stress level of the family is greatly intensified and added to that proverbial baggage we all carry.

My wife and I are enjoying our relationships with the three happy young adults in our lives. As we experience adolescence with our fourth child, we can sit back and smile. We have changed our attitude; we know what to expect. These will be good years — tiring, yes, but ever so good.

IOPs (Important Other People)

As you take on a mental attitude that says, "I can actually do this whole thing with a smile," the importance of IOPs (Important Other People) should never be discounted or underestimated. Since the period of adolescence is designed to test limits and authority, let the presence of other adults be a part of your family's life. Don't be afraid to let an uncle, an aunt, a longtime friend, a teacher, or even a minister get close to your child and work with you in the raising of your adolescent. Two or more adults in the life of an adolescent can only enhance the quality and depth of experience. You won't be embarrassed, either. Kids are always better down the block than they are at home. I never really understood why, but my neighbors always thought my kids were flawless.

Miss Thompson as an IOP

Let me share with you the story of Miss Thompson and one of her students. This story also points out the importance of family. When children's basic psychological needs are not adequately met at home (for whatever reason), they will attempt to satisfy those needs in another environment.

Miss Thompson was a teacher. At the beginning of every year, when she met her new students, Miss Thompson would say, "Boys and girls, I love you all the same. I have no favorites." Of course, she wasn't being completely truthful. Teachers not only have favorites; they have students they just don't like very much.

Miss Thompson didn't like Teddy Stallard, and for good reason. He didn't seem interested in school. His face wore a deadpan, blank expression, and his eyes had a glassy, unfocused appearance. When Miss Thompson spoke to Teddy, she always got monosyllabic answers. His clothes were musty, and his hair was unkempt. He wasn't an attractive boy, and he certainly wasn't likable.

Whenever she marked Teddy's papers, Miss Thompson got a certain perverse pleasure out of putting X's next to the wrong answers, and when she put an F at the top of the papers, she always did it with flair. She should have known better; after all, she had Teddy's records. The records read:

First Grade: Shows promise with his work and attitude, but poor home situation.

Second Grade: Could do better. Mother is seriously ill; receives little help at home.

Third Grade: Is a good boy, but too serious; a slow learner; mother died this year.

Fourth Grade: Is very slow, but well-behaved; father shows no interest.

At Christmas that year, students in Miss Thompson's class brought her Christmas presents, piled them on her desk, and crowded around to watch her open them. Miss Thompson was surprised to find that even Teddy had brought her a present. Teddy's gift was wrapped in brown paper and was held together with Scotch tape. On the paper, Teddy had written, "For Miss Thompson from Teddy." When she opened the present, out fell a gaudy rhinestone bracelet with half the stones missing and a bottle of cheap perfume.

The other students began to giggle and smirk over Teddy's gifts, but Miss Thompson silenced them by putting on the bracelet and splashing some of the perfume on her wrist. Holding her wrist up for the other children to smell, she said, "Doesn't it smell lovely?" Taking their cue from the teacher, the children readily agreed with "ooh's" and "ah's."

At the end of the day, when school was over and the other children had left, Teddy lingered behind. He slowly came over to her desk and said softly, "Miss Thompson... Miss Thompson, you smell just like my mother, and her bracelet looks real pretty on you, too. I'm glad you liked my presents."

When Teddy left, Miss Thompson got down on her knees and asked God to forgive her. The next day when the children came to school, Miss Thompson had become a different person. She was no longer just a teacher; she was a real human being. She was now committed to loving her students and doing for them that which would live on after her. She helped all her students, especially the slow ones — including Teddy Stallard. By the end of that school year, Teddy showed dramatic improvement. He had caught up with most of the students and was actually ahead of some.

Teddy Stallard moved on to the next grade, and Miss Thompson didn't hear from him for a long time. Then one day, she received a note that read:

Dear Miss Thompson:
I wanted you to be the first to know that I will be graduating second in my class.

Love,
Teddy Stallard

Four years later, Miss Thompson received another note from Teddy:

Dear Miss Thompson:
They just told me that I will be graduating first in my class. I wanted you to be the first to know. The university has not been easy, but I liked it.

Love,
Teddy Stallard

And, four years later:

Dear Miss Thompson:
As of today, I am Theodore Stallard, M.D. How about that? I wanted you to be the first to know. I am getting married next month, the twenty-seventh to be exact. I want you to come and sit where my mother would sit if she were alive. You are the only family I have now; Dad died last year.

Love,
Teddy Stallard

Miss Thompson went to that wedding and sat where Teddy's mother would have sat. She deserved to sit there; she had done something for Teddy that he could never forget.

Who Will Fill the Void?

The story of Miss Thompson and Teddy Stallard illustrates the importance of other people — IOPs. If we are not able to get our basic needs met at home, for whatever reason, we will move outside to an external influence.

Childhood is an apprenticeship program in life. In many ways, children are like carpenters with tool boxes, with parents in control of handing out the tools. The children don't know what tools they need and rely on the wisdom of the master craftsmen to help them fill their own tool box. If their tool boxes are well equipped with a variety of tools, almost any project can be completed. On the other hand, completion of projects declines proportionally with the lack of tools, necessary information, and available support, encouragement, and guidance.

Parents represent a vast variety of resources from which young people can draw, and it takes time to share those resources. When parents are available and nonjudgmental, young people will reach out for advice and help. When parents are not available, however, even minimally, insurmountable obstacles begin to arise. In response, young people will search their environment, trying to overcome their problems on their own. The end result, of course, is more obstacles.

> *There is something wrong with how I try to get attention. I am an A student and am involved in soccer (year round), band, jazz band, drumline, clown troupe (drug-free group), project free (also drug-free), Bible study, French club, youth group, Sunday school, chancel choir, handbells, trumpet lessons, and sign language club. I now understand that all the pressure I am putting on myself can lead to an unhealthy life. I am just trying to fill my "God space" in my heart. I am addicted to activities to keep me from seeing my bottled-up emotions.*
>
> —KIM, 10th grade

The letter from Kim demonstrates the power that adults have in a kid's life and the need for young people to have someone available to them. When a teen knows that someone is there no matter what, it gives the young person the courage to face life's difficulties. If children grow up with someone important missing from their lives, they grow up with a vacuum of sorts, a void, in their own life experience.

> *I am a fifteen-year-old. Every time I try to do something with my parents they say that they are busy. There is no time when me and my family get together, we don't even eat together. I can't remember the last time that my parents told me that they loved me, I don't think that they ever have.*
>
> —JENNY, 9th grade

Missing an important person in one's life or family can be likened to that tool box. As a person tries to complete a project or move through a phase of life, there is a struggle to cope. In the process of coping, certain skills and confidences need to be drawn upon (tools). These skills (tools) have traditionally been passed from generation to generation. In the absence of a significant person (parent, family member, teacher), completing the project becomes increasingly difficult, and in some instances impossible. Urie Brofenbrenner at Cornell University said it best: "In a study of students it was found that every successful child in this world has one thing in common, and that is they know of at least one adult in their life who, no matter what, is absolutely crazy about them."

People who are not there for kids — busy moms or dads, absent moms or dads, society, important adults of all kinds — create a situation similar to the tool box with missing tools. It is possible to survive, but life would be so much easier, and even enjoyable, if all the ingredients for happiness and success were naturally available, in a traditional sense, and functioning appropriately.

I never really knew what it felt like to be loved after my dad died, except for my sister who thought of me as a mom more than anything else.

—STACEY, 10th grade

Stacey is learning about love, not from a dad or a mom, but from a sister who is looking up to her. Stacey has fallen into the mom role, which is a different kind of love and doesn't fill her tool box. When the important tools (people) are not available or compensated for and key adults do not notice that the tools are missing, problems begin to develop.

I really do love my dad, but how do I tell him, and how do I show him, when he's so far away?

—LEIGH ANN, 8th grade

When nobody seems to notice the needs, frustrations, and pain of these kids, trouble develops. Adolescent letters cry out with, "Please, teach me what to do. I'm begging for direction."

I love my dad so much, and the most I get to see him is about three or four times a year. I think I'm in a stage right now that I need him in my life to care for me and love me and tell me who I can and can't go out with.

—SUZETTE, 9th grade

A Living Legacy

How will our children remember us? Are we able to fill their basic needs — needs that are part of every human being, needs that are especially evident during adolescence? If we're not available, compassionate, accepting, and understanding, if we don't communicate respect for our youngsters, if we don't demonstrate that our youngsters' concerns are our concerns as well, they will go someplace else to fill the void.

So often adolescence becomes such a big deal because parents and authority figures spend too much time trying to rein in the growing, insatiable energy of the adolescent.

"LETTING GO"

Letting go does not mean to stop caring;
it means I can't do it for someone else.
Letting go is not to cut myself off;
it's the realization I can't control another.
Letting go is not to enable;
but to allow learning from natural consequences.
Letting go is to admit powerlessness;
which means the outcome is not in my hands.
Letting go is not to try to change or blame another;
it's to make the most of myself.
Letting go is not to care for; but to care about.
Letting go is not to fix; but to be supportive.
It's not to judge but to allow another to be a human being.
Letting go is not to be in the middle arranging the outcome;
but to allow others to affect their own destinies.
Letting go is not to be protective;
it's to permit another to face reality.
Letting go is not to deny, but to accept.
Letting go is not to nag, scold or argue;
but instead to search out my own shortcomings and correct them.
Letting go is not to adjust everything to my own desires;
but to take each day as it comes and cherish myself in it.
Letting go is not to criticize and regulate anybody;
but to try to become what I dream I can be.
Letting go is not to regret the past;
but to grow and live for the future.
Letting go is to fear less and live more.

— AUTHOR UNKNOWN

Humor and Calm:
A Family's Greatest Resource During Adolescence

My wife and I used to attend neighborhood gatherings of couples who came together to discuss their parenting strategies. We used as a base the hottest parenting book in town: *Children: The Challenge* by Rudolf Dreikurs. Every so often, my wife and I would laugh and say, "Let's use the book by hitting them up the side of their heads just to capture their attention." We never actually did, but it was a way of venting the frustration that theory was, in fact, just theory. Practical applications never seemed to be specifically outlined in the book, or never seemed to work in our situations. We did discover, however, that the theory was a good foundation for developing strategies, and humor was a great way of developing effective coping mechanisms and achieving stress release.

It isn't uncommon for parents to get so upset with the behavior of their adolescents that they alienate themselves from their children. In one family, the father was so obsessed with being ten steps ahead of his rebellious daughter that he got stressed out and died of a heart attack. Rather than let his daughter experience some tough lessons, this man sacrificed many good years of life, which in turn, of course, had a lasting impact on his entire family.

Having a sense of humor is not laughing at our adolescents but quietly smiling to ourselves when we are confronted with one of the many adolescent issues that continually surface during this period. As an example, the next time our adolescent comes home late, we might want to smile and simply say, "You're grounded!" No further comment is necessary. Smiling is much better for the body physiologically than screaming. This is far easier to prescribe than it is to practice. Nonetheless, stress reduction can be attained using this technique.

If we are not able to call upon humor when reacting to our adolescents, let's remember that this period in their life is a time to challenge and test — all kinds of things, but particularly us. As our children continue the process of growing, the challenges will become more frequent and sometimes more outrageous.

POINT TO REMEMBER

- *Often our adolescents have a valuable teacher right in the situation itself. Let's allow them to learn from consequences.*

Chapter 2

Psychological Dynamics of the Adolescent

BEHAVIORS OF YOUTH are symptomatic. Most adolescent behaviors can be traced to an unmet need. It is the responsibility of the parent to discover what those unmet needs are.

The Family Today

Each of us is searching for love and attention from the people around us. From the beginning of time, children have wanted and demanded the attention and applause of parents and other family members. In past generations, grandparents and extended family members spent a great deal of time helping young people capture a sense of identity and connectedness, but over the last several decades the extended family has lost much of its significance and closeness. Helping children with identity and connectedness has almost completely become the responsibility of parents alone.

Family has taken on a new look. The pressures of our fast-paced society have created parents who seem to be unbelievably busy. Many families have been fragmented by divorce. Still other families have had to move forward alone as they cope with the disappearance of a father as early as during the pregnancy. The result is a void, a sense of emptiness, in children who then reach out to their surrounding environment in search of opportunities that will sufficiently fill the emptiness.

By reaching out and finding a source of affiliation, young people create their own sense of family with anyone who will provide love and attention. Unfortunately, the familial surrogate is sometimes negative and almost always insufficient. This surrogate lacks the solid and uplifting nurturance previously supplied by parents, grandparents, and extended family.

> *After you spoke, I came up and said, "I know I'm going to cry." And you said, "That's okay." The next thing I knew I was crying in your arms and you were hugging me. I had been needing that hug for a long time.*
>
> —LEASA, 8th grade

Mobility Creates a Void

Other voids are created in young people's lives by family mobility. The average family moves every three to seven years. Research has shown that families plagued by poverty move substantially more often than the average family. The frequent moving of the poverty-strapped family is often an attempt to find adequate housing with scarce financial resources. Frequent moving, regardless of the reason, leads to a loss of psychological stability and connectedness, thus creating another void for young people. The tried-and-true foundational histories shared with childhood friends are lost. Penetrating new peer groups becomes increasingly difficult, especially in junior and senior high school. As the need for peer acceptance reaches a peak and parental support tapers off, young people naturally seem to act like self-sufficient young adults. Their emotional neediness, however, remains at an all-time high.

Relocation challenges most adolescents. In an effort to fit in and achieve peer acceptance, adolescents often get themselves into compromising positions. They use alcohol and other drugs and engage in sexual behavior to "fit in." Sex is reduced to a meaningless act in their search for significance and acceptance. These are good kids, searching for affiliation as well as significance and desperate for approval.

> *Jess was drunk and high. Steve took her over to his place and while they were there they had sex. He didn't talk to her for three days. This past Friday Jess went over to his house and they did it again. Then Saturday Jess and four of my friends, all freshmen, went to a party and got buzzed. Then they all went over to Steve's with four of*

his friends and they all had sex. Two of the girls had never talked to the guys before or since. Later, one of the four girls did it again with another guy. When I asked them "Why?" they said they did it to fit in. How can I help my friends?

—JENNY, 10th grade

Parents Need to Be Parents—Not Friends

In many instances, parents have stopped being parents and have opted to be their children's friends. Rather than being loving authority figures, they have decided to ignore the wisdom of prior generations, which has clearly demonstrated that children thrive in the midst of structure and flounder without it. It is certainly much easier to have a free-floating, nonauthoritative parental style than to have the opposite, but the consequences for our children are clearly negative. Children have enough friends; what they really need are parents who are willing to accept a truly parental position with its authoritative implications.

Thanks for the hug that day. I really needed it. Would you mind if I wrote you when I just need someone to tell my feelings to?

—JENINA, 10th grade

Emotional Needs of Family Members

Family members need to be able to sense their own unique place in the family system; they need respect and validation from one another; they need people to be there for them in their life; and they need encouragement.

When I advanced to the cross-country sectionals, my coach and teammates were proud, but my parents topped the cake. They were so proud of me, they got me a special dinner; we got ice cream. I was queen of the day. That made me feel so proud and boosted my self-confidence, which is quite obvious now, how it has improved. Before, my brother was the sports god, but I became much more important, or at least I felt that way, that day.

—AMY, 11th grade

All human beings, but particularly adolescents struggling to discover their personal identity, have eight basic psychological needs, namely:

1. The need to be *loved.*

2. The need to feel a sense of *belonging.*

3. The need for *power* and *competition.*

4. The need to understand and have *purpose.*

5. The need to have a sense of *hope.*

6. The need to have freedom and *choices.*

7. The need to receive *forgiveness.*

8. The need to experience *fun* and *learning.*

The lack of fulfillment of any one of these basic needs will result in a behavioral reaction as the person attempts to access the missing need(s). We will deal with each of these psychological needs individually, but first a warning: Attempts to control family members (any family member) only cause problems. Working earnestly to understand (empathize) and meet the needs of all family members will lead to personal fulfillment on the part of the leader(s) and bring a sense of happiness to the family as a whole because everyone is working together for the benefit of the whole.

Ironically, efforts to control tend to dominate parenting styles, and it is most often a very frustrated parent who discovers that techniques designed to control have a reverse effect. A preface in William Glasser's book *The Quality School*[1] contained the following comparison of "control versus relationship" parenting:

PARENT AS LEADER AND GUIDE

A boss drives.	A parent leads.
A boss relies on authority.	A parent relies on cooperation.
A boss says, "I."	A parent says, "We."
A boss creates fear.	A parent creates confidence.
A boss knows how.	A parent shows how.
A boss creates resentment.	A parent breeds enthusiasm.
A boss fixes blame.	A parent fixes mistakes.
A boss makes work drudgery.	A parent makes work interesting.

—ANONYMOUS

Love

Love is the first and the most basic of foundational needs that a human being has. The presence of love and belonging, or the lack of them, will have an impact on absolutely everything that a person does and deals with for an entire lifetime. "A child's self-image is shaped by those who have chosen to love or not love the child and most of that is determined by age seven."[2]

My life has been filled with sadness lately. About eight weeks ago my great-grandmother died. I went to the funeral and cried and was okay. Five weeks ago my father moved out of our home for a trial separation. This was totally unexpected for me. We were always the "Cleaver" family, going on family vacations, sitting around the supper table and talking for two hours. I had absolutely no idea they (my parents) weren't getting along. Complete surprise. Two weeks ago I had an operation because the doctors thought I might have cancer. Luckily I will be fine, but it sure was scary. One week ago my grandmother died unexpectedly. Surprise, what's next? She was wonderful, the most loving, giving, and forgiving person I have ever known.

—KATIE, 11th grade

Love Is Caring Enough to Do Something

"Love" in Greek means to look for the good. To love enough to care and to care enough to do something. With love given, we feel the gift of giving, and with love received, we feel the gift of love received. We have heard it said throughout our lives that it is better to give than to receive. The paradox of that statement is that the more a person gives, the more a person receives.

Over the years, we have always heard adolescents say, particularly to their mothers, "You have to say that," when the mothers compliment them in some way. Parents love their children. Not because their children are good, but in an unconditional sense, parents love their children simply because they are their children. For the average parent of an adolescent, this concept involves loving them even when we feel they may not deserve to be loved. We love the child though we may not like the behavior.

Love Is Commitment

Love begins with a commitment to accept people for who they are no matter what. Normally, this happens pretty naturally for parents because of the special bond that comes with having children. It involves being there with them as they progress through the stages of growth — the good times and the bad times. It fulfills the responsibility of bridging the child into adolescence and then on to adulthood: not just to cheer children on to the destination of maturity, but to hold their hand, to be their safety net, and to walk with them every step of the way. The contract for bringing children into the world contains that assumption and expectation. Kids don't grow up; they are raised. As parents, we have embraced the children and the contractual fine print: "I chose the children; they did not choose me."

Love is found in the arms that rock the child to sleep and the hands that spank. Love is the whisper that consoles and the shout that scolds. Love gently pushes our children toward new experiences and growth and pulls them in from danger. The heart of love celebrates in the joys of our children's accomplishment and breaks in their failures. Love walks them around the block, to the playground, to school, to their room, and finally down the aisle. Love welcomes every child as a precious gift from God. Love is found in the creation of the person.

Love Is Often Difficult

Love is doing what is best for a person rather than responding only to what the person wants or demands. Love comes in a variety of forms and conditions. Sometimes the question is asked, "How do I love?" Sometimes the response is, "I buy you clothes, I take you to Disneyland." If you ask a child about the definition of love, most often the response will be related to the presence of parents: "They take time with me; they give me hugs; they kiss me; they tuck me in at night; they discipline me; they take me places; they show concern; they trust me."

Rarely are the responses defining love related to "They buy me things," even though this response is seen in many moderately socialized young children who have not grown out of their self-centeredness. It is sometimes also seen in the adolescent who is psychologically disturbed and needs the "things" to serve as a medication of sorts to cover the pain of poor self-worth. The two greatest fears of a child, besides the loss of a parent, are:

- to never be loved and
- to never be able to have the chance to love.

In the midst of crisis after crisis and rebellion leading almost to chaos, at the core are these two fears.

The one thing I will always remember from your speech is the four words you said, "We believe in you." You made a difference in the life of the people who heard you today. I hope I will get a chance to hear you again sometime. Thank you for touching my life and for caring about me.

—TINA, 11th grade

People Serve What They Love

People will always serve what they love. Love your job. Love your spouse. Love your kids. Love your country. Love your self. You cannot, or will not, serve what you do not love. Additionally, you cannot love something or someone that you do not know. You can, however, experience infatuation, which is nothing more than the love of a perception, love at first sight. Real love is the commitment to serve that which you have full knowledge of. Love happens in this order. Know → Love → Serve.

Love never changes, but our commitment to love does. Our ability to love is founded in the depths of our own personal security and unselfishness (or selflessness). It is the ability to selflessly give to another. Why? Just because it is right. Wanting to has nothing to do with the definition of love, but it is a reflection of seeking our own needs. Hopefully, in our relationships the reciprocal dynamic of loving someone is a warm and endearing feeling. Often a very positive result of love involves tremendous pain, and for the mother with her child it began during the pregnancy, only to be intensified during the climax of birth. The mother never tells about the pain of childbirth, but always takes us to the results, the photo of the child: "Look how beautiful."

Thanks to you my son and I will talk more. He was never aware that in my own family alone there was one suicide related to drugs and another couple of deaths related to alcohol. Hiding these facts (or at least never discussing them) doesn't help the children of today who are subject to all kinds of pressures.

— PATRICIA, parent

Love Is an Action

Love always does something. Love involves an action versus a feeling. Scriptural references abound in definitions of love. Love is patient; love is kind; love does not boast; love forgives and does not keep a record of wrongs; love is never jealous; love does not store up grievances; love perseveres; love takes stands that are inconvenient; we love until it hurts, and then we keep loving. Love worries and waits up late. Love wonders and hopes for the future. Love goes out into the night to look for a delayed child. Love says you're suspended from sports or the use of the car even though you will hate me.

Consider the paradox of hate. The degree that someone hates you is a reflection of his or her love. Hate is a love that has been hurt, and all hurt is founded in not getting one's own way. We care because we love, not the other way around. We love even though we don't feel like it. There are times when we might not like our kids, our spouse, or our siblings, but our commitment to choose to love is still a choice that is made and followed through, even when we don't feel like it.

Love nurtures the seed of becoming. All a child is destined to become is planted within that child at conception, and love fuels its development and full realization. Love displaces and compensates for all that is blocking development, such as guilt, shame, and self-doubt. We are to love with all our heart and all our mind. Love, therefore, is not a feeling as much as it is a knowing. We normally love others the same way that we love ourselves. Emotionally and spiritually, unfulfilled people have a hard time giving love and can be likened to human vacuum cleaners of love. They will give in relationships only when they know that they can receive. Pure love gives to give again. Pure selfishness or lust, when it gives, gives to get. Pure love asks only what I can give. Pure selfishness asks only what I can get. A continuum is established, and everyone is somewhere in between these benchmarks.

Belonging

It is the presence of love that creates self-worth and stabilizes that self-worth.

My parents took time out of their schedules when I was in football. It made me feel really good, because I was one of the smallest kids on the team and they encouraged me to keep playing.

—JOE, 11th grade

It is important that we as parents give our young people everything in life to live for rather than taking a materialistic position and giving them everything in life. So much of what has driven our present adolescent culture is found in the illusion that people are what they have, rather than who they are. We as parents need to work diligently to correct the breeding of misguided values. What do we place value on? Their car or their character? their clothes or their convictions? their vanity or their values? their peer group and prestige or their personality? their wealth or their worth and what their worth is founded on? Do they know? Do we know? Do they find purpose in their stuff and accomplishments or in themselves? This is, without question, a very important area of consideration for a parent. Let's examine what is driving our adolescents.

External Validation Tests Belonging

As adolescents, our children are biologically programmed to test their personal significance and worth. As our young people explore their world, they move out beyond the family in an effort to ascertain whether the feelings of love and belonging that have been their gifts in the family are also out there in the world for their personal possession. Most of our young children in their early years feel that love and attention they so badly need. Somehow that needed attention is available and freely received. At adolescence the psychology of doubt moves in and pushes the adolescent to seek that outside the family.

"Blindly groping for the way to meet their needs, young people have chosen to withdraw through drugs, drop out of a society that doesn't help them in their struggle, or turned to uncommitted sexual release. These behaviors are the symptoms. We need to focus on the real villain: the feelings, 'I am unlovable, I don't matter or belong; I am not capable of coping.'"[3] Adolescents are searching for meaning in their life. They are looking for answers about what to believe.

I wish I would have been able to talk with you personally when you visited our school. I was waiting, and then you had to go and use the telephone. I waited twenty minutes, and still you did not come back. Then I got down on myself. I was thinking that you had better people to talk to and more important things to do than sit and talk to me.

As I was walking home, I started to cry because I needed to talk to you (or someone). Then it was too late. You were gone, and I knew that I would never get a chance to talk to you again. Oh well, I bet you wouldn't have liked me anyways.

—JANA, 10th grade

The Unlovable Need Love and Belonging

The kids who are the most unlovable need love the most. As young people move out in search of validation and discover that the expected affiliation is not available, they will search out and affiliate with somebody or something that might be contrary to their family's value system. In our present culture, many young people are shouting out with their behaviors, "It's better to be wanted for murder than not be wanted at all." What a distressingly accurate yet crude description of the need for love and belonging. Many kids today are choosing misbehavior as a sign of their discouragement and their need for love and belonging.

February 5th about fourteen years ago I was adopted into a family that I now call my own. My adoption day came recently, and it seemed as though my brother was getting all the attention. You see, he was having some asthma attacks, and so he's on a lot of medicine. Now I don't want to sound selfish, but today was important to me. Not once all day did either my mother or my father say how glad they were that I was part of the family. They gave me flowers and said "Happy Adoption Day" but they could have said that they loved me, too. Maybe this was their way of doing so, but it hurts ...hurts bad. It only takes a couple of seconds to tell someone you care. I'm really confused, and I'm sorry if this doesn't make much sense.

When you said that you hadn't seen your father in sixteen years, well I never got to see mine at all, and even though I have one to replace him, I still feel rejected at times, like today.

—KELLY, 10th grade

Effective parenting becomes an exercise in bridging our children from where they are to where they need to be, while at the same time loving them unconditionally every step of the way. Boys seem to drop out of school because they reject authority and girls because they reject themselves. When girls' self-esteem goes down and they lose hope, they tend to hurt themselves; they will dig their nails into their arms in their anger, cut or color their hair in an extreme way, or smoke cigarettes; eating disorders are not uncommon symptoms of their desperation. On the other hand, as hope, purpose, and a sense of worth are diminished for boys, they tend to lash out at the environment in some way. Violence, rape, vandalism, running away from authority — all are examples we see too often.

Power and Competition

The next basic need is related to power and competition. Much of adolescent obstinacy is related to hormonal changes and growth patterns. Obstinacy also develops out of the adolescent's perception that parents have all the power, and he or she has none.

My step-mom wants everything done right all the time, but I'm not perfect. When she was growing up her dad was an alcoholic.

—MELISSA, 8th grade

Recognition is power, and that is why driving a car is such a major influence in the lives of young people. They equate the use of a car with power, and the touch of an accelerator can be an adrenaline rush so great that it is difficult to pass up the opportunity to test the capability of the car. This is particularly true in situations where adolescents have felt a sense of impotence within the family because of the strength and/or inflexibility of one or both parents.

It is power and applause that drive our athletes. The victors on the football team become heroes of sorts as they crush a team from the neighboring community. In the absence of such sanctioned activities, the adolescent moves into other arenas looking for that same kind of power and competition.

Every Monday morning in my senior homeroom class I find myself trapped in a conversation with other guys in my class related to who got drunk over the weekend and who had sex with the most chicks. I don't want to be put down and called a sissy, so I lie every week about what I did over the weekend.

—DAN, 12th grade

I heard somewhere that it takes four positives to overcome one negative. Often after a program, evaluations will be filled out. My last task of the evening is to read the evaluations. Inevitably, there will be a few evaluations in the stack that, for whatever reason, literally indicate that my presentation was despised. There could be a hundred positive evaluations in the same stack, but it is a human tendency to dwell on the two negative submissions.

Negative comments create tremendous emotional anchors, often oppositional or resentful, and these anchors frequently block the positives. In the case of a parent, because of the parent's inherent power, the effect of a negative anchor is even greater than that of anchors from external sources.

Discovering Purpose

Lacking the ability to acquire status and recognition, the adolescent will experience pain that often manifests itself in anger and sometimes in disassociation from important values. That familiar question keeps coming back, "What are my own needs?" The responses are simple but prophetic: "I can't help others until I have first filled my needs." "I've got to have a sense of conviction about why I exist — it's my purpose in life." "It's the definition of the whys of my life." "It is my understanding about what I am supposed to be doing with my life."

To discover purpose in life, we need to take three basic steps:

- Reflect on our gifts as we experience them.

- Reflect on our gifts in the context of the way other people understand them. Young people can find purpose by seeing themselves through the eyes of parents, teachers, coaches, religious leaders, scout leaders, friends, and the larger society.

- Reflect on our gifts as God reveals them to us. What do your children discover about themselves as their spiritual life develops? ("Spiritual" is defined as what's important.) The only way to know our complete purpose in life is to discover it within creation. Without a true understanding of spirituality, a person will be cut off from the ultimate source of comprehending true purpose. There are a lot of very materialistically successful but spiritually empty people in this world.

For purpose to crystallize, it must be tangible. For example, we are loved just because we exist. Love is found in our being, and purpose is found in our contribution. Purpose gives direction to our being. Achieving happiness is not the goal of life. Living out our purpose is the goal of life, and then fulfillment will result, bringing about happiness. The goal is the activity of living well, and not the feelings that accompany it.

I know it's okay to follow after what you feel is right no matter what anyone says. It feels so great to me when I am able to make a choice that will leave me free to choose again.

—CARRIE, 11th grade

Let us ask ourselves these questions constantly:

- What do our children see for themselves?
- How do they see their purpose?

Reviewing our adolescents' frame of reference can be very helpful. "If I don't care," they might think, "I cannot fail. If I don't play the game, I cannot lose." Then they join the group where it is cool not to play the game. Fear of failure often keeps our children (and us!) from trying. "If I try and fail, I am a failure, but if I don't try and fail, then I haven't really failed, because who knows what I could have accomplished or been if I had really tried?"

My dad and I talked to each other pretty seriously tonight at the supper table. He was talking about me not being able to handle constructive criticism. He's right, no doubt, but he says that's why I'll never get my license, 'cause I can't drive with him. He feels I'll never pass — maybe he's right, but it makes me feel bad because of it. It's like he has no faith in me. Do you think there is a way for me to get over not being able to handle constructive criticism and being able to handle it?

—DAVID, 9th grade

There is a direct correlation between how we perceive people and how we treat them. All too often we see adolescents in particular putting down others in their midst. From a psychological standpoint, this is a devastating activity that often has lifetime implications. If we see people as losers and then treat them as losers, those people will pick up on and mirror our beliefs and act like losers.

Misguided adolescents believe that put-downs will result in an elevation of their own personal worth. This turns out to be a very inaccurate perception. How we see others may also be a projection of how we see ourselves. It is very difficult to value or treat others better than we feel we deserve to be valued. When we are unable to discover the value in our children, it is probably because we have yet to discover it in ourselves — our own worth.

At the core of pure purpose are the attributes of love, joy, peace, patience, kindness, goodness, trustfulness, gentleness, and self-control. As an individual grows and his or her purpose in life is being refined, the desire to live out these qualities of purpose will begin to surface more and more. The opposite is also true. Living out those characteristics will introduce an individual to a better understanding of life's purpose.

I was given a strong sense of right and wrong by my parents. They taught me the importance of family. They taught me that respect, honesty, dignity, and responsibility were the keys to a happy life. I believe that with such a strong base of values and ones that the community keeps reinforcing, I am learning about human worth.

—ROXANE, 11th grade

Kids need to know why they exist and what their true purpose is. They are searching to discover why they were created. The world creates confusion for them by selling them on false happiness. Society promotes the belief that fulfillment will be found in sexuality, wealth, accomplishments, looks, relationships, instant gratification. This leads to tremendous frustration, because as teens seek to acquire these attributes, they continue to discover emptiness. Many adults are living in emptiness and wonder why. A sense of purpose is life-giving. Purpose helps to fuel hope.

Hope

Hope gives our children (and us, for that matter) the courage to move forward. It is understood that with effort things will get better. It is a time line for life; it is the fuel, the energy, the fortitude, to hang in there and to embrace the belief that a solution will surface.

My dad doesn't claim me and I've never seen him, but at least I had older brothers. I don't know how I'd be now if I had been the oldest.
—SHAWNA, 10th grade

Hope is what we can fall back on in times of mounting stress and trial. Without hope, we can fall into the use of chemicals and other mood-altering drugs as a way of medicating our pain. When young people know that the family is there, and will always be there, hope can then enter their lives.

I sit at home on weekends unless there is a home ball game — then the band plays (I'm in the band). I have a lot of friends most people would think, but there is nobody that is really close to me. I try hard to fit in, but most often I find that it is not worth it. There's no one to turn to anymore.
—NEAL, 10th grade

Almost everything is boring and a lot of work if we believe the complaining of the average adolescent. As life moves forward, however, maturity helps the young adult understand the concept of cause and effect. Unless adolescents are spoiled by always getting what they want, they learn a significant lesson related to life's opportunities. There is in fact no free lunch, so if we see something we want, we have an opportunity to work for it, and the intensity of the desire will determine whether ownership is acquired. If ownership has been acquired, the rest of the project will be perceived as fun, bringing forth hope and enthusiasm. There are very few things in life that can exceed the joy resulting from a sense of accomplishment because "I did it myself."

Freedom and Choices

The basic psychological needs referred to as "freedom" and "choice" represent a story of adolescents in a nutshell. They want, and often demand, the freedom to make their own choices, especially the freedom from adult coercion.

My mother never lets me stay out after 9:00 p.m. Nine o'clock is so early. Kids that are younger than me can stay out later. I wish my mother would be less strict and let me have more fun. Letting me have more fun doesn't mean I'm going to go do drugs and drink alcohol and turn into a nobody. I just want to be treated more like a teenager instead of a kid.

—HEATHER, 11th grade

It is a sign of maturity as well as age to be free and able to make our own decisions. This is one of the most intensely sought-after privileges that adolescents are looking for. They want the opportunity to decide for themselves whether they will have a curfew or not, go to school or not, go to a party or not, and the list can go on. They want to make all kinds of decisions, but at the same time they don't have the maturity and experience with life to truly understand which decisions are good and which are not good in relation to the long-range picture. The adolescent doesn't have the luxury of seeing life from the vantage point of an adult. As a result, decisions and particularly the desire for freedom are strictly based on immediate needs and the satisfaction of those needs.

My dad is overprotective because my parents are divorced and when I lived with my mom she didn't take good care of us. Now my dad is trying to "make up for lost time" by being really strict.

—LISE, 8th grade

Forgiveness

Regardless of input from the parent, the adolescent might make bad choices, even catastrophically bad ones. When things get fouled up, there is usually a plea and a desire for forgiveness; but later, the same offense may be repeated with some slight variation.

The principal strategy of a rationally functioning parent needs to move toward an understanding and acceptance of the concept of forgiveness. At the time of crisis — any kind of crisis — parental judgment, even though it may be shared in love, leads to shame, inducing the diminishment of self-worth.

> *One year ago I was in an accident in which we were hit head-on by a drunk driver. The accident left me in a coma for two and half months. When I finally did come out, I had no idea of who I was. You see, I didn't remember anything. Doctors weren't sure if I could ever walk, read, write, or do anything. I felt helpless. I would cry myself to sleep and pray that God would kill me. Suicide crossed my mind several times. I felt things were as low as they could go, or so I thought.*
>
> *My father, or at the time the man I called dad, seemed to blame himself for what happened, and rather than help me fight he committed suicide. To this day I blame myself for what he did. But I realize now that my accident was an excuse for what he did.*
>
> —ERIC, 10th grade

It is a natural inclination on the part of most parents to give unrequested commentaries and lessons. These are perceived by the adolescent as judgmental. The best possible scenario for effective parenting is found in leading our young people into a position in which they feel comfortable asking questions of us. As the questions surface, they will automatically ask for our guidance. Guidance given in response to a request is seen as positive and supportive.

Fun and Learning

There comes a time in life when ownership of something is acquired. Whether the ownership is of something tangible or of something intangible, such as education or a relationship, it is at that time that the concepts of fun and learning mold themselves into the life of a person. An example is the adult homeowner who needs his or her house painted. It is a big job and will require a lot of work. The opportunity can be seen as a total bore or as an opportunity to grow because of the experience of learning that goes along with the project. The homeowner may not have fun, as defined by an adolescent, but the experience can easily be translated as meaningful when we consider the sense of satisfaction and sense of accomplishment produced by the house's new appearance.

Another example is the washing of the family car. In early adolescence, the job is seen as a time-wasting chore. When the adolescent grows up and has his or her own car, the washing of the car is exciting and a source of pride.

Still another is education. Junior high, high school, and college are often experienced in either of two ways: something I *have* to do or an opportunity I *get* to do. Am I waiting to be taught or am I there to learn? Depending upon the expectations, these experiences take on completely different meanings.

The chores of life can be fun; it's all a question of attitude. Embrace and model growth and learning as at the heart of a stimulating and fulfilling life. When we teach the love of learning, our children become lifelong explorers.

POINT TO REMEMBER

- *The unlovable child needs love the most.*

Chapter 3

Adolescents: What Do They Look Like? What Makes Them Tick?

THERE ARE A NUMBER of developmental stages that the adolescent needs to move through, but generally speaking this entire period lasts from about eleven to twenty-one years of age. There are very distinct characteristics that differentiate the early stage, middle stage, and late stage of adolescence.

Anatomical, physiological, emotional, intellectual, and social factors all enter into the adolescent picture, filling it with uncertainty, frustration, and instability. Adolescence is precipitated by hormonal changes that define the onset of puberty. The relative calm of latency is replaced by the rising adolescent storm. Sexual and aggressive activities surface almost without warning. While they still act like children, adolescents demand to be treated as adults; and while they demand adult treatment, they are afraid of adulthood because of their inexperience.

Adolescents may seem impulsive and unpredictable, even to themselves. They experience rapid mood changes that neither they nor the people around them understand clearly. The body keeps changing and growing faster than the adolescent can adapt. At a time when they may be exquisitely sensitive to the opinions of others, their bodies make them clumsy and ridiculous, and they detest the attention this draws.

Sooner or later psychological and physiological changes will precipitate adolescent rebellion. Although the young adolescents need adult guidance and protection, they generally hate their dependent needs. They are afraid that the adult world will undermine their drive toward emancipation. They cannot stand being treated like children when they know very well that they are growing up. At a time when they actually need supervision, they may berate their parents for attempting to supervise them.

This is a relatively difficult period because parents often find themselves treated with indifference, coldness, scorn, or hostility by a child whom they may have always loved unselfishly, and still love. They hear themselves addressed condescendingly and their cherished values ridiculed or rudely challenged. A growing adolescent may ignore parents, avoid them, and look at them hatefully. What the heck happened? It all came on so suddenly.

Adolescents: What Do They Need?

Adolescents ultimately are a reflection of the environment in which they grow up. As parents, we bring them into the world, and as a society, we reinforce the process that the family begins. The time we have with our children determines what they will learn, what they sense, and who they are.

An old African proverb says it best: "It takes an entire village to raise a child." In America that process of raising children is carried out by the family, the school, the church, the neighborhood, and the surrounding culture. In generations past, these social institutions were significantly stronger than they are today, but even so, these institutions do exist and continue to be influential.

Need to Form a Separate Identity

Young people, in their search for significant relationships, often indicate that they don't really want to be around their parents or other significant adults. As they move away from the family, adolescents are looking for identity and independence free from the domination of their parents and family of origin. Down deep, however, they are, in fact, looking for constant attention and direction from their family. Adolescents often complain about education and guidance, but the reality is that they are looking for answers to life's daily questions — tough questions. They hunger for relevant information and someone to teach them how to find success and happiness in their present lives and in the future. As we mentioned in Chapter 1, important other people (IOPs) can be a tremendous aid in this discovery.

Need for a Sense of Security

Adolescents experience security in knowing that they can, on their own time, come back to the parents they are rebelling against. The ironic truth is that these young people can rebel and completely mature through the emotional phase of adolescence only within a loving, stable environment. The instinctive but seemingly unexplainable intuitive understanding is, "I must challenge the parent to discover who I am." The identity of the individual is nurtured in childhood, setting up the final transformation to adulthood that takes place during the necessary rebelling process of adolescence. At that time the adolescent sheds the family to embrace the full responsibilities of life and living.

Reflecting on the patterns of growth in my own childhood, I remember grasping my parents' hands, balancing between their legs as we waddled together across the living room. Eventually, I broke free and stumbled toward the end table. Plopping down on my Pampers, I looked up to their affirming gaze and could tell by the sparkle in their eyes that I had "done good." I crawled, waddled, walked, and finally ran. In my anger, I even ran away from home, only to return by lunch. I remember tricycle to training wheels to falling on the cement all afternoon, eventually finding my independence on a two-wheeler: my very own bike and ticket to the neighborhood. I remember sitting on Dad's lap to steer the station wagon, the driver's permit, and finally, at sixteen, a license to freedom and the family car. As a toddler, I had to break free from my mom and dad's loving hands to learn to walk; as an adolescent, I needed to break free once again to achieve full independence.

Parents must remember, as with every other important time in our children's development, not to take the struggles of adolescence personally. Our children need us to hold them up now, just as they have over the years. They need us to be there for them as we always have been. Most of all, our children need us to let go. Only then, in each phase of their development, will they be able to mature in a healthy way.

Adolescents can leave the nest only if they have a nest to leave, and that's a secure and stable home and an available parent who is willing to be a sparring partner they can push against, challenge, threaten, and eventually bow to in mutual respect. Just as in the childhood game of hide-and-seek, adolescents can confidently run away only from a place that they know will be there when they are ready to return, a safe home base.

Need for a Sense of Direction

Adolescents who lack instant access to success, fulfillment, and happiness are in a constant and almost never-ending search mode. They rarely understand that success and happiness are part of a process rather than end results.

If there are no reliable adults available to provide them with a sense of direction, teens may try to fill the void with success in external activities. Educational endeavors, sports, and other activities, of course, are positive involvements in and of themselves. Problems occur when these activities are pursued with the belief that participation provides the individual with value. A compelling need to achieve often reflects an unfilled hunger for love. Healthy people *want* — but do not *need* — to do and achieve. Young people cannot make this fine distinction on their own; they need patient and sensitive direction from adults who are genuinely invested in their well-being.

> *Both of my grandparents died within six months of each other. I didn't really want to believe it because they were the only people that I could really talk to. I can't really talk to my parents because they are part of the reason that I feel miserable a lot of the time. They are always so busy. I often tell them that I love them but all I hear is thanks and then they're off to some other project.*
>
> —ERIN, 9th grade

Erin's parents are missing her subtle prodding. Their daughter is trying to say, "How can I talk about my problems since *you* are my problem? If I told you, you wouldn't believe me; you'd probably just say that you love me and that I am just not noticing. If I persist, you'd tell me that I am selfish and inconsiderate of the busyness of your lives. Best that I just shut up and blame myself."

Erin may be a needy child, but isn't that okay? When our children were little, they cried when they needed us, and we responded to meet their needs. They continue to need us as much as ever today. Though they may look all grown up on the outside, though they may convey a certain distance — even hostility — they desperately need our direction as they continue to search and to mature.

> *I want my sons' lives to be completely different from the way mine was. We are affectionate and never a day goes by that I don't tell them that I love them. When I grew up my mom tried to buy a lot of things for us kids. Still, I turned to drugs and alcohol because life at home (I felt) was really the pits. You can't buy love!*
>
> —JODI, parent

Jodi's mom tried to give gifts to offset the family's problems, but that simply does not work. Jodi tried to fill that space with drugs — but that doesn't work either; it never does. There is no substitute for love. Nothing physical can fill an emotional or spiritual need. Motivational speaker and trainer Jim Rhone says, "That which you don't pay for with the pain of self-discipline will be paid for with the pain of regret." Nothing in the world will substitute for and fill the space that was created for love.

> *It's nice to know that even though you hardly know me, I feel that you care about me. Just knowing that there is an adult, any adult, out there interested in me helps.*
>
> —JESSICA, 9th grade

Adolescent Values

The Tendency Toward a Lack of Commitment

A man built a business; his son ran the business; his grandson lost the business. Unlike the business itself, the sense of commitment and ownership did not pass from generation to generation.

In the past, working in the family business naturally created a process that taught people about life. There existed a camaraderie and a shared sense of ownership in the struggle to build the business, and then a commitment to maintain that sense of ownership. When the third generation inherits ownership of the company, it often doesn't inherit the intrinsic attitudes and passions that make up the foundational commitment.

The same thing happens with life in general. The responsibilities of parents haven't changed a whole lot through the generations, but the "services" parents provide have changed dramatically. The traditional family, with a mother staying at home to nurture and care for the children, has gone by the wayside and now accounts for a mere 7 percent of American families. Either by necessity or by desire, the families of today often see the absence of both parents, as they are off working in an effort to keep the family financially stable. Going back to the analogy of the third-generation business, just going through the motions won't make the business work. Again, the nurturing and commitment that are required to develop and maintain a healthy family are inadvertently redirected or simply not understood.

So it can be said of today's young people that they have been given life, but more is required: They need a sense of commitment to themselves and their values. They look out at the world, and without commitment they assume they understand life. They look around, and they see themselves looking like everyone else. They live in a house, and they have food and clothes. Even with their basic needs met, however, there is a gnawing sense that something is missing: commitment.

There is more to loving our children than providing for their basic needs. Love in the context of commitment is the foundation. Children need to witness the many dimensions of love that only the value of commitment can display. When a couple's relationship flourishes because it is rooted in commitment, it brings life to the couple's children. When the basic foundations in the family are shallow, or important factors are missing, children, especially adolescents, will find it difficult to identify who they are, what they are. These children reach out into the environment to build their lives around things that are superficial and empty, things like grades, sports, clothes, or being in the popular group. These things develop tremendous power over kids because they are looking to external factors to fill internal voids.

In an environment where children's value is *intrinsically implanted*, because their parents are committed to each other and to the family, children feel secure without even knowing why. Because they are nurtured and loved, their sense of security and identity are natural parts of their inner spaces; there are no internal voids. In an environment that delivers the message "We are committed to you no matter what," maturity evolves naturally.

Unfortunately, young people today are not witnessing commitment. Indeed we have all been witnessing the escalating fragmentation of the family over the last three decades. Unintentionally, we are modeling for our children a belief in lack of commitment, and we don't fully understand, or embrace, the impact that this lack of commitment has on our children. (That's not to say that there are some situations where divorce and the breaking of a commitment shouldn't occur. Sometimes the quality of life is improved by separation, especially when there is abuse and counseling is ignored or rejected by one or both parties. It is our belief that divorce can usually — but not always — be circumvented if the commitment of marriage is honored by the couple seeking counseling to both understand and mediate the marriage disagreements or problems.)

The irony is that we have never found parents who don't love their children. So, even in the midst of a divorce, it is important that the parents work through their own personal pain and not use the children as a vehicle to punish a former spouse for some earlier transgression. All children have a need to love and relate to their parents, consistently. Divorce, separation, alienation, overinvolvement, cannot be allowed to interrupt the means by which that need is met.

Tragically, many parents didn't have good role models themselves, and this lack of commitment and example in itself has set the course for problems with this generation. Parents are doing the best they can with the tools they have available.

My parents are divorced and my dad has been out of my life for the past six years. Now I am sixteen, and he still hasn't made an effort to see me or anything. Sometimes I feel like crying, and sometimes I get so mad I want to scream.

— ASHLEIGH, 10th grade

Our society seems to have embraced the philosophy of change: If something isn't "going right," change it. Often we even make changes for change's sake. We don't look at what commitment means; we don't try to work at something because we believe in it; we just make a change, call it "irreconcilable differences," and go on. As kids watch this process, they are taught the concept of instant gratification. They then act out this lesson in their pre-occupation with new clothes, the latest music, widespread sexual experiences, a variety of drugs, and short-term friendships. This is different from decades past. As we model less commitment and as we suggest that commitment is an optional value, we deliver a very important, but unfortunately negative, lesson for our children.

> *I've gone through divorce three times. My mom never did anything to help us. It hurts to know that she doesn't care about me. I live with my grandparents and I haven't seen my mom for three and a half months.*
>
> —INNA, 7th grade

The Tendency to Have a Self-Centered Personality

Generally speaking, the adolescent of today is self-centered and concerned with "What's in it for me?" To a certain degree, this is age-appropriate. However, our society is allowing this age-appropriate characteristic to become a way of life. The world we live in tends to reinforce a "me-oriented" attitude rather than an "other-oriented" one, individualism versus communitarianism.

Our young people are also being taught to lean heavily on the concept that they have rights — and they do. They have the rights of *young people*, not adults, not parents. Teenagers focused on themselves will exclaim, "I deserve to be happy, to have my own way. I deserve to be what I want. Everything is owed to me. If I want an education, that's owed to me. If I want a car, it is owed to me." Yet we earn rights only as we take on responsibility.

Contrary to past generations who sought the advice of the more experienced adults, representing the wisdom of age, today's youth stress a distorted sense of fairness for everyone regardless of age, wisdom, or experience. This reinforces and empowers the self-centered rights-driven attitude, as opposed to a responsibility-driven attitude. Sadly, the world is not modeling a different value for them. Adults insist on having their own way, one way or the other: "I can finance my way through the divorce, and that's easier than dealing with the messy complications of the relationship." "I got pregnant, so what! I can get an abortion." Our kids are simply copying the adult population.

As a society, we have spent more time teaching the concept of not hurting the environment than we have in teaching strategies about how not to hurt each other. The environment seems to have become our god. We believe that it is the environment that is going to take care of us in the future. Thus, if we lose the environment, if the ozone layer goes, if the water supply disappears with the rain forests, we have nowhere to live. As researcher and environmental advocate Jacques Cousteau says so eloquently, "If we are concerned about the external pollutants that threaten our environment, we should be equally concerned about internal pollutants — like marijuana products. For sheer survival, we must defend ourselves against both kinds of pollution. I believe that we need to keep all our senses constantly at their maximum keenness if we are to take full advantage of our short participation in the miracle of life."[1]

We need to look at the structure and the importance of family with the same far-sighted sense of respect, survival, seriousness, and commitment. We cannot lose our focus on the basic dignity of life — all life, including human life — if we are to introduce to our children a healthy sense of self-value rather than a demand-based sense of entitlement. As we consider what is ultimately important within our family environment, let us consider what validates and what gives us and our children value.

Let's use a dating situation as an example. If I really love another person, by definition that means doing what's in that other person's best interest. No matter what, it means taking into consideration how my behaviors are going to affect that other person, not just tonight, but for tomorrow and for a lifetime. It is necessary to think, in a mature way, about the long-term implications rather than the short-term. It is important to think not just about yourself but about the other person. Yet young people concentrate on "What can I get?" rather than "What can I give?"

Parents provide their children a tremendous service by helping them become other-oriented. Let's help our children become accountable for their actions. If they get kicked off the team, if they get F's, if they lose their license, then we need to allow the natural consequences to occur. The lesson, and basic principle of life, is that you're not ready for the activity until you are ready for all the possible consequences. Choice-making becomes very simple when we honestly understand that we are going to be held accountable for every decision that we make. Life isn't done to us; we do to life.

Sensitivity Around Self-Esteem Issues

I never knew I could be so happy with someone, yet so miserable as well. I now realize that I was happy because I was in love with a pretty okay guy, but I was miserable with myself.

—CARRIE, 12th grade

As a society, we try to teach our children how to acquire and maintain self-esteem. We tell them, "If you love yourself, no matter what you believe or what you do, you will have value." For example, in a 1989 international comparison of industrialized nations, American students scored last in the area of math and science. South Korean students scored at the top, outperforming United States students four times over! When asked if our American students were, in fact, good in math, Bill Bennett says in *The De-valuing of America*, "Ironically sixty-eight percent of American students thought they were (the highest percentage of any country) compared to twenty-three percent of South Korean students (the lowest percentage of any country), which demonstrates that this country is a lot better at teaching self-esteem than it is at teaching math."[2]

In our country, self-esteem is becoming linked to the idea that if you think you are good at something, you are, regardless of evidence to the contrary. We have forced ourselves to be satisfied with shoddy results because we don't want to judge anyone critically.

According to Dr. Michael Carrera, founder of New York City's Adolescent Pregnancy Prevention Program, "You can't *teach* self-esteem. But if we can get kids to stay in school, get good grades, get a job, those things *produce* self-esteem."[3] In previous generations, people had worth because performance was factored into the picture, because they did things that were right, because a set of standards determined quality. People knew what the standards were, knew how to achieve them, and knew how to support others in that process. They had a barometer or standard for measurement to check out their place relative to an accepted standard of societal truth: universally embraced guiding principles. If we continue on our present course, we will lose all sense of what to value.

It seems at times that I want to die and other times I just love life. It's really strange how things work. I'm learning to like myself more now than ever, but it's just little problems like grades and my parents.

—TRENT, 11th grade

People sense that they are valued only to the extent that they value themselves. How they feel about themselves is their self-esteem. According to Dorothy Briggs in *Your Child's Self-Esteem*, "Self-concepts are learned, not inherited. This means that attitudes toward the self can be altered in a positive direction. The main requirement for change, however, is positive experiences with people and life. To feel lovable, the child must experience acceptance from those around him; to feel competent and worthwhile, he must experience success for his efforts."[4]

I always used to think that I was not so special. I've finally realized that I have what it takes to be a leader. The sad thing is that there are so many people out there who have what it takes, but are afraid to try.

—Tina, 9th grade

Naturally, our children's needs are different from ours and generally so are their interests. If we are fulfilled and complete adults, however, we are available to anticipate, recognize, draw out, understand, and nurture their uniqueness. If we have unmet love hungers from our own childhood, we may unconsciously (or consciously) try to get them fulfilled through our children. Hence we have the father who pushes his son in sports to be all that he never was, or the mother who bickers about her daughter's weight because of an unhealed resentment from her own weight problems as a young teen. This transference is a projection of the needs of parents onto their children. Children then feel judged as they get caught in a performance trap. They feel that love is conditionally controlled or determined by their performance.

Often in single-parent households, though not confined to them, a temptation exists to develop a friendship with the child, especially as the children advance into adolescence. I often hear from girls, "My mom and I are best friends." This may feel all well and good, but the child doesn't need another friend as much as she needs a parent. The friendship will naturally develop in a healthy way when the child is in her twenties or after a major rite of passage such as marriage.

In divorce, it is tempting to use the child as leverage against the other parent. In almost every situation, this represents unresolved anger that reflects many of the communication problems that led to the divorce. The axiom "Whatever we cannot talk out we will act out" is being acted out here through the child. To continue behaviors like this just perpetuates and reinforces the behaviors that led to the divorce, and this experience emotionally confuses the child. This will also come back to haunt the emotionally abusive and manipulative parent after the child becomes an adult. In the maturation process, the child will see through these behaviors and eventually resent them.

Manipulating children to meet our needs is unhealthy for both us and our children. Let us come to see our children as individuals rather than as extensions of ourselves. If we find this difficult or discover that a pattern exists, our children may be introducing us to one of our unmet childhood needs. Let's step back and explore and then assess our cravings. A counselor may be helpful in this process. Again, what we live is what we learn. If we don't figure it out in our lifetime, we will pass it on to the next generation — and they will have to deal with it.

> *I went into my room and changed to make my mother happy, so she wouldn't be angry for the entire day. It turned out she was angry all day anyway. I did yell at her when I tried to defend myself. I probably shouldn't have, but I did. I lost my temper. This time the fight got so bad that I threatened to go live someplace else.*
>
> —JACKIE, 10th grade

Emotionally satisfied and fulfilled people raise emotionally stable children. Individuals who look to their children to fill a need will gradually drain from their children that which they do not have the ability to provide. Parents simply cannot fill their children's sense of self with their own neediness. Children will doubt their own adequacy before they question a parent's expectations, whether these expectations are realistic or not.

Attraction to False Freedoms

Too many people believe that everyone has to succeed and has to be equal. As a result, society has lowered its standards to strike a semblance of equality. Along with lower standards, however, our society has lost its opportunity to learn, teach, and guide. We seem to be wasting energy on a "victim" mentality, nurturing and enabling the woundedness of the person rather than building skills and a competency to survive in a demanding world. By validating the brokenness of the individual, we empower the wounded to believe that they are okay where they are and cut them off from the tools, incentives, and pathways to growth and real fulfillment.

There are basic moral truths that exist as tenets in successful societies. These doctrines lend power and objectivity to our lives and are irrefutable rules of conduct. Simply stated, these time-tested truths are the values and building blocks of society, family, and the individual.

When a society strives to create a perceived utopia where all values and choices are equal or value-free, that society eliminates comparisons between right and wrong, good and bad, wise and unwise. This results in today's adolescents and young adults exclaiming, "Why do you think my lifestyle is messed up? You're judging me. Don't impose your religion on me. You have your rights and I have mine. I can believe whatever I want, and what I do with my life is my business." When we accept such arguments, we allow our young people to sever themselves from loving correction. Their resulting defensiveness protects their views from being challenged.

This form of enslavement is the result of separation: separation from God and separation from self. The great journalist and author G. K. Chesterton said it so well: "The danger when men stop believing in God is not that they believe in nothing, it's that they will believe in anything." This separation naturally leaves people vulnerable to the programming of society, specifically through the temptations of false freedoms. The outcome is always the same: In their frustration, these people rebel, and the resulting consequences take the form of emotional or physical violence.

Real freedom, on the other hand, involves the exercise of personal choice to do what is already defined as a true good. Exercising personal choice, however, involves three components: an informed moral conscience, a commitment to being responsible, and a mature regard for the good of others. The result of not living out these criteria is to run the risk of becoming enslaved by society's temptations. Sounds a lot like adolescence, doesn't it?

I respect people who don't drink alcohol, but what I don't like is people who don't respect me for drinking. I don't care if they don't do it, but I still have a right to do it—I just don't get caught.

—DEAN, 11th grade

I tell the students during my talks that freedom is not found in what they can say yes to but in what they are able to say no to. Their yeses are meaningless unless they are able to say no. If they are not strong enough to set down the drink of alcohol, there is no way that they are strong enough to pick it up. If they are not strong enough to get out of the relationship that they are in, then they are not ready for the relationship. Anything or anyone that they are unable to say no to or walk away from can use them. Our adolescents are ready to date when they can look someone in the eye who is challenging their values and say, "Next!" If they can't, then they are not *wanting* to be there, they are *needing* to be there. Adolescents are thereby looking outside themselves to fill an internal void, a hunger for love.

This is where we find ourselves today. Subjective morality ("If it feels good, do it") is the cry of the age; blame and victimization ("Someone made me who I am, so I am not responsible") are the topics of the talk shows; and narcissism and self-centeredness ("I have my rights") are the pathologies of our teens. Should we expect anything else?

Many parents go to the school to demand their children's "rights." "Our kid is a good kid, no matter what he did." Parents sue schools for suspending their child from activities, especially athletics, for alcohol consumption — even after they've signed discipline policy contracts at the beginning of the school year. Incredible! Extracurricular activities are a privilege, not a right, and they come with specific, agreed-upon expectations. The focus needs to be changed from "rights" to being held accountable and responsible.

The walls that teens put up to keep other people out are often the same walls that keep them in. Their claim to a "right" to any belief or behavior is no more than a layer of insulation to protect them from criticism. Unfortunately, those who don't admit to their problems are unable to do anything about them. To face those problems feels like failure. Thus, young people are protected from criticism and failure — and have no opportunity to learn and grow. There have been many times in my life when I locked onto a view of myself that I held for years only to discover that these self-perceived views were, in fact, false. Looking back, I always found that others were lovingly trying to tell me otherwise. I was just not ready to listen.

Whose Values? Whose Philosophy? Whose Moral Vision?

Adolescents, and all of us for that matter, don't know what to do until they first know what to believe. Our society is spending much of its time dwelling on issues rather than beliefs. We can discern only when we are able to think clearly, with maturity, and then consider all the consequences — long term. We can think only when we can understand and see distinctions. Thinking means raising the question "What's the better thing to do?"

As values are eliminated from the decision-making process, the distinction between right and wrong, good and bad, is obscured, and the distinction between pleasure and pain is emphasized. "What gives me the most pleasure and the least pain is the best choice." "What on TV is good to watch? Well, what do I want to watch?" "How can I get money? Well, how do I want to get money?" These choices are supposed to give happiness, so if we can control these choices while creating the least amount of discomfort to ourselves, we are going to have success. The notion of right and wrong has been reduced to a message of consensus, and truth has been reduced to a message of personal choice. This is the standard our young people are seeing modeled and are adopting.

> *In today's society I feel that many people have compromised their values either to fit into a group, for their own personal pleasure, or to avoid the consequences of their actions. If we can learn to stand up for ourselves and learn from other people's mistakes, then maybe we can improve our society by establishing better values ourselves.*
>
> —BRIAN, 12th grade

The world we presently live in has chosen to ignore the message that patience is a virtue. We want things instantly, and if we don't get our own way, we have a tendency to flare up with anger. All too often that anger results in our own personal destruction and humiliation or the destruction of others.

Sadly, we are not passing on the truth: The difficult routes in life — not control — lead to satisfaction and fulfillment. Anything we need to control, we lose. If we try to control someone in a relationship, we will lose that relationship. If we try to control our kids, they will rebel against us. If we try to control our own life, we get depressed. Pure and simple: Though we've been led to believe the opposite, control goes against what leads to peace and happiness.

So we are left with a few simple questions. Have the values for a successful life really changed? No. Have these values been ignored? Possibly. Have they been advanced? Doubtful. The truth is much like gravity: Whether we believe in it or not, it still holds us accountable. The truth itself is not something we vote on; it is something we share.

Adolescent Development

Education and Its Importance

In past generations, we earned the right to have an education, and we cherished the opportunity. In our present society, however, the mentality seems to be that education is a "given." We may be giving today's generation of young people technological skills, but are we ignoring the basic training? As we lose sight of the basics, we build a house with a weak foundation. It looks wonderful to the world, but as pressure is leveled against the foundation, it gives way, and everything that is on top tumbles.

"We know student achievement is directly related to parent involvement," says Thomas Evans, principal of the Chesapeake Bay Middle School, Pasadena, Maryland.[5] "The high achieving Asian-American and high achieving Anglo-American students came from family backgrounds which were essentially identical. High achieving students, regardless of ethnic background, came from families which were stable and close-knit. The families ate meals together at the table and engaged in family activities at least once or twice weekly. A significantly higher percentage of Asian-American families functioned in this close knit way, thus accounting for the higher rate of academic success among Asian-American students."[6]

Perhaps if the world was better educated, we would get along better. We have the ability to learn, and we should use this resource to its fullest. The more we learn, the more we understand. Learning is a gradual process, and it can lead to open minds as well as unbiased thinking. The only way to achieve this is through extreme education.

Education can be found in schools, libraries, and by traveling. No matter what way it is found, it will prove to be valuable.

—DALE, 11th grade

Emotional Development

Increasingly, I am seeing a glazed expression in the audiences that I work with; I see more emptiness than I've ever seen before.

Lately I have been struggling to figure out the source of some un-nameable feelings. I tried to talk to someone on the phone, but I wasn't able to tell them. I wouldn't let myself get emotional, so I would just shut up every time the tears and feelings of hurt started.

—TINA, college freshman

Teenage crime has increased 150 percent during the last two decades. Part of this is because violence is being modeled for the young. When we are exposed to a constant diet of violence, we begin to assume that it is an appropriate and available means of accomplishing whatever we want.

People these days don't take responsibility for their own actions any-more. "It wasn't my fault" — that's the common phrase instead of, "Oh, my fault." Kids are learning that they can get away with crime. That's just not right. How many people can argue that it's okay to shoot someone for $75? [this refers to a boy killed over a $75 mari-juana debt].

—BRIAN, 11th grade

As our young people mature, violence becomes one of the tools in their tool boxes. They become desensitized to nonviolence as an option. It's like living close to railroad tracks; people who have become accustomed to it don't even notice the noise. If they have relatives visit overnight, however, the guests won't be able to sleep. Yet, if the noise suddenly ceased, the residents — those who live there — would wake up, startled by the quiet.

Spiritual and Psychological Development

"What's in it for me?" This is where the adolescent begins. It's like shopping with a credit card. You can buy now, but eventually you will have to pay. Youngsters, however, simply don't understand that they will have to pay for their behaviors sooner or later.

The challenge to parents and those who love and work with teenagers is to help them understand what guides their consciousness. By pulling religion (which has long been one of the guides for our spirituality) out of that process, we have lost a significant anchoring device. It's like the absolute of driving on one side of the street. As long as everyone does it, you can pass another car at sixty miles an hour and do it safely. If you remove the absolute — driving on a specified side of the street — you have highway chaos.

Previously, societies found security, standards, a reliable barometer, a measuring device in the absolutes that are today viewed as restrictive. It's like the speedometer in your car; without it, you can't tell how fast you're going. The speedometer does not restrict your speed; it only gives you reliable feedback that you can use to make cautious choices.

I really wish my parents would do something about it when they know I've been drinking. They sometimes get mad for a few days, but they won't confront me about it. I wish they would confront me about things and tell me that they love me.

—JOE, 11th grade

Students are coming to school with more and more emotional baggage. Self-esteem used to be taught by the concept that "God loves you and everything that God loves has value." We used to tell kids, "You are precious and are a special miracle of God." Today, we spend billions of dollars trying to replace those three words, "God loves you." We try to tell young people, "If you love yourself, you have value." But what about those days when they don't love themselves? What happens to their value then? If they are their own standard, then life is always insecure and in a state of flux.

Rudolph the Red-Nosed Reindeer illustrates the issue perfectly. He comes into the world and doesn't know that he is different until the other reindeer point it out. He doesn't feel like a "misfit" until his community, presumably including his parents, treat him as one. His father even tried covering up Rudolph's nose, sending the message that "there is something wrong with you." Parents naturally have power over their young, which is good when the home is a healthy one, with parents, teachers, and people in authority loving and nurturing and taking the time with young people to guide them appropriately. It used to be that way. The whole system worked together; if you heard something at church, you heard it in the family, you heard it in the classroom. There was a universal belief system that was built on and depended on a sense of common respect. Individuals in the community supported one another.

Today our culture says that we are a melting pot — but we are not really a melting pot; rather, we're a gumbo soup. We have individual components floating around in the liquid. Previous generations looked to the highest elements of everything to determine the ethics and principles that became the foundations of societal standards. Now, we have gone in the other direction. This limits the number of agreed-upon tools that we choose to share with our youth.

I'm seventeen and I have a baby. I'm scared of facing the cold, cruel world with my daughter at my side. I don't know what I'm going to do, where I'm going, anything. I'm afraid to fall in love. I'm afraid to fail. I'm afraid of making more mistakes.

—TINA, 12th grade

Parents and society often send mixed messages. Through our indifference, young people often go out into the world confused. They try to build something, like a relationship, yet few have been honest and direct with them about sexuality, for example. "They just tell me to protect myself with a condom." But even if that person uses a condom, the girl can still get pregnant and either party can get AIDS — so whom do you blame? These students cry in my arms, and they ask me, "What went wrong? I used a condom and I still got pregnant [or a sexually transmitted disease, or dumped]. I thought that's what they told me to do. I feel so used." The condom doesn't protect them emotionally, spiritually, physiologically, and barely physically.

People who are alike tend to like one another. Instead of looking at a common standard or value, however, they look at one another's behavior. And, since they are all doing the same thing, they think that they're okay, normal, acceptable. If the standard is drugs, it's okay, because everyone is taking drugs. Everyone in their peer group is having sex, so it must be okay. Enter one person who does not choose to use drugs or who is a virgin, and the group considers that person odd, dumb, wrong. Our world says that all thought is equal, so the one in the crowd whose thought is "different" should, at the very least, be seen as an equal to remain consistent, but instead that person will end up ostracized or get sucked in. Peer pressure gains power as a result of emotional neediness. Young people are hungry for friendship to fill the emotional and spiritual void — and friendship means being involved with whatever is the going thing.

> *I guess that's the way everything started, going to parties I mean, because I had to show I wasn't a goody-two shoes. But in time I went just to have a good time with my friends and socialize. When my friends and I get drunk, we do it so we can have more fun — by being stupid, etc. It loosens everyone up so it seems more fun.*
>
> —TAMI, 9th grade

Parents, teachers, and those who love and work with young people can help reverse the process by letting the "odd ones," these few young people who are trying to stand for something, understand that their way is founded in time-tested, proven truths and is right and wise. Let's share our beliefs with our children. How else will their beliefs be formed? In the midst of peer pressure, adolescents need friendships, but they also need spiritual and emotional support and direction from their parents.

Pressures, Discouragement, and Depression

> *I feel worthless, like I can't do anything right to please anyone, especially my mom. She's always coming down really hard on me for no reason. Sometimes I don't even want to open my mouth for fear of being yelled at. It's gotten to the point where we can't even sit down and have a civil conversation without screaming.*
>
> —JACKIE, 11th grade

Discouragement is founded in the frustration of not being able to get our own way, not being able to have things we believe we deserve. Children come to school discouraged because they didn't get what they wanted at home: a mom, a dad, a community that knows them. As a result, these discouraged young people begin to build walls to protect themselves from others so that they can't get hurt. By keeping others out, they keep themselves in — and they lose an opportunity to grow. They get discouraged because they can't measure up.

I can't remember one day when I haven't been insulted by someone at least once. When I moved to my new school, I started receiving compliments occasionally. I felt better about myself.

—ANGIE, 10th grade

Our society suggests, "Let's eliminate the grade system so that students won't be discouraged." But there is a better way: Let's give our students the tools they need to meet expectations and overcome discouragement. It takes a lot of time, but it is important that time is taken to nurture them through the process. Loss of any hope or control, founded in anger turned inward, is defined as depression. If people can't talk it out, vent, or somehow feel validated in what they're experiencing, they will repress the issue, and after an accumulation of experiences, they will become depressed.

Forming Identity: Who Am I, and How Can I Find Out?

Our identity is formed and fashioned at an early age by those who choose to love us and those who choose not to love us. It is formed by how we see ourselves in a family unit, in society, in a group. If I did something, was something, accomplished something, it validated my identity. Our identity is not found just because someone says we are special. Identity is always found in relationship to something or someone else. We look at the earth in relationship to the sun and at the moon in relationship to the earth. The moon is not a moon by itself; it is a moon because it circles the earth. If it was just floating around in space, it would be something else. What made the moon a moon is its relationship to the earth. What makes a man a husband is founded in his relationship to his wife. Having a child makes a woman a mother. Teenagers discover their identity in their relationship with their moms and dads. Whether those relationships are healthy and supportive or disintegrating, insecure, and fragmented, they will have a direct effect on the child. When I start to become a contributing member of something, beginning with the family, I begin to feel a sense of self-respect.

I've never really liked myself. I've never looked in the mirror and said, "I like me," because I don't. I have good days and bad days like everyone else, but even on my good days I don't feel satisfied with myself. My good days are days when I can get my hair to do what I want. On bad days I feel like just standing in the field, opening my arms, looking into the sky, and saying, "Come and get me."

—ANGIE, 10th grade

If the groups we associate with are negative groups, our identity will be dictated by the negative values of those groups. In situations where gangs are available, for example, people without identity can assimilate an identity from the gang.

No one will go out with me because I am so ugly. I am so lonely because all my friends go out and I just sit home by myself on a Saturday night.

—JENNY, 9th grade

Gangs become families — conditional families. We have to do something to become part of it and to remain part of it. The alcohol group accepts me because I show up and drink; the drug-using group accepts me because I show up and use drugs. In academics I have to be at the top of my class to be accepted. In sports I have to be good athletically to join the group. In band or music I have to be musically talented to join. In all these small "families," I have to *do* something. My real family, on the other hand, loves me no matter what.

I'm fat and ugly and it's hard trying to get a guy to go out with me without sleeping with him. I don't know what to do. I'm so confused.

—CANDY, 10th grade

Sex in relationships becomes so prevalent because the need for love is so great — and that need for love can get many people into trouble. I've discovered in my student audiences that the kids whose shells are the hardest to break through are the ones who are fighting desperately to hang on to the little that they have. They're even willing to die for the little they have, because they don't know if what's left would be worth living for.

POINT TO REMEMBER

- *Parents need to spend time trying to teach skills and reinforcing attitudes that are "other-oriented" rather than "me-oriented."*

Part II

INTRINSIC NEEDS
OF ADOLESCENTS

Chapter 4

Teen Motivation: Uncovering the Mysteries

ALL OF US are motivated in one way or another. Who among us has not experienced an unexplained spurt of energy on a weekend and been amazed at the accomplishments? Then again, who among us hasn't experienced the unexplainable lethargic lack of energy on a succeeding weekend with nothing accomplished?

Parents frequently look at their adolescents and ask, "Why isn't he motivated to take better care of himself?" "Why isn't she motivated to get better grades?" These and other questions seem to inundate the thoughts of parents who are trying our best to understand and survive the years with our adolescent children. The psychology of adolescent motivation is absolutely fascinating and unquestionably predictable.

Driving Forces Within the Adolescent

The following are basic principles that apply specifically to adolescents. They dictate to a great degree the adolescent's motivation at any given time. Let's reflect on these principles as we move into the vignettes and lessons that follow:

1. All adolescents are motivated. Defining their motivational goal is sometimes next to impossible for parents caught up in their own emotional response to the onset of new and unfamiliar behaviors.

71

2. Life at adolescence is a time of intense turbulence, reflected in hormonal changes that influence and drive an individual's motivation.

3. Growth spurts will often create exhaustion and stress.

4. Adolescence is a time of emotional instability.

5. Adolescence is a time of intense self-doubt. Our children are intermittently overwhelmed by feelings of inadequacy, inferiority, and self-consciousness.

6. Fear is often masked in bravado, rebellion, and indifference.

7. Teens are most concerned with the short term, and a sign of maturity is when a choice is made today while considering the long-term consequences.

8. All adolescents are searching for love, stability, and feelings of significance.

9. All behaviors are motivated by our own personal or individual needs and values.

10. Parental values that have been modeled faithfully over the years will be copied by the adolescent.

   - The adolescent is driven to test the validity of a parent's value system. It is important not to judge the adolescent behavior and present values as lifelong.

   - Through the process of maturity, it is inevitable that the adolescent will acquire and retain values implanted by parents.

The Motivation Behind School Adjustment

School adjustment, like the development of peer relationships, is a manifestation of self-esteem and maturity. We have seen over the years hundreds of very intelligent students who either have dropped out of school or have simply skimmed by (barely) at the last minute. These students lacked motivation more than anything else, a factor directly related to self-esteem development during childhood.

If you happen to have a child who is doing poorly in school, the last thing he or she needs is to have a parent yelling about laziness and stupidity. The adolescent who does best in school is not necessarily the brightest student in the school, but usually the hardest-working and the most persistent. As a rule of thumb, a motivated and interested student will spend ten minutes per school-grade level each day in homework trying to learn and progress adequately.

If a student experiences some sort of learning disability, that student will discover that more time needs to be allocated to compensate for the disability. For example, a poor reader will have to spend considerably more time reading and digesting material than a good reader. Both can successfully master the material, but at different speeds. One of the principal jobs of a parent is to reinforce this concept rather than let the adolescent simply back away because "I can't do it." The more we intervene with the school to make exceptions for our child, the more we handicap that student for a lifetime. We would be well advised to work with our children so that they can learn to cope with their world as it is.

We frequently read stories about people who graduate from college when they are in their eighties or nineties. These are not all people who had to give up education to work their family farms; often they are people who finally got motivated to do something for themselves. So the moral of the story is this: If you happen to be living with a "late bloomer," don't despair. Love the heck out of him or her and be patient (not overprotecting); just be patient.

I hate school and I get into battles with my parents frequently about school being a waste of time. I don't plan to go to college anyway, so I don't get what the big deal is. I have never been very good with my grades, and if I get a D or an F my parents go crazy. Sometimes I feel like running away just to avoid all the fighting that we do.
— TRACY, 10th grade

Trust the process! It is not the end of the world if your child does not go to college, and it is definitely not the end of the world if your child drops out of college. Remember the old cliché that says, "When the student is ready, the teacher will appear."

The average adolescent graduating from high school today has a maturity level about three or four years behind that of students several decades ago. Maybe this accounts for the large number of adolescents who go off to college unsure of what they want to study as well as of who they are. As with my son Peter, they may believe that college is one big party, only to receive a wake-up call — in their own time.

Let's continue to support patiently, guide lovingly, encourage gently, and to offer timely challenges, but let us remember, kids have to want to do it. Sometimes the best thing we can do for our children is be patient and wait for maturity. Rather than getting angry and upset at our children's lack of achievement as we spend thousands of dollars on college, let's wait. When they really want to go and are motivated, they will work on their own behalf rather than to satisfy us.

Adolescent Mood Swings

Much has changed over the decades, and many new influences and pressures, both negative and positive, have surfaced for families and adolescents. One of the most noticeable characteristics of adolescents that has not changed over time is the presence of mood swings. Mood swings are puzzling for parents and very frustrating for young people. In many respects, mood swings are related to hormonal changes. In other ways, the mood swings are related to the psychological response of an individual to the pressures taken on in the course of a day. Mood swings influence motivation.

Adolescence is a period of transition and experimentation. It is during this period of experimentation that the adolescent finds out, often painfully, that life has many disappointments in store for each of us. Idealistic expectations can surface during adolescence. When young people encounter roadblocks to these expectations, they sense major doom.

Most situations will rectify themselves. Alert parents can spot these situations and talk them through to the satisfaction of adolescent and parent alike. If, however, the personality of an adolescent has changed dramatically, we need to take special note. If a clinical depression is lingering, we will often see our adolescent not sleeping well, not eating well, and possibly even losing weight. He or she might be getting frequent headaches. Depression in a late adolescent can be signaled by a student dropping out of college even though there has been a history of academic accomplishment.

Adolescents will typically refuse to participate in counseling; but considering this age's characteristic unstableness, it would be in everyone's best interest to reach out, force the issue, and get an opinion and some advice from a professional therapist. Always better to be safe than sorry.

> *When I was little, my dad left me and my mom. I was only three. The one thing I do remember is the time my dad promised to take me to the zoo and said he wanted me for the weekend. My mom packed my suitcase and I sat on the porch and waited for him from 8:30 to 6:00 p.m. That was when my mom made me come in. I hate that man, but I really love him inside. It must be hard to lose your father in death, but I think it is harder to know that a father is alive and doesn't even want to be with you.*
>
> —JASON, 10th grade

Often it is hard to know what is troubling our adolescents. As with Jason, the basis for depression can be information that has been stored in the mind and ruminating for years. Jason's story reflects his interpretation of rejection. When adolescent turmoil is at full peak, young people almost always go back to memories of the past and begin to dwell on those memories to the point of sadness.

> *You mentioned that I should talk to someone. I can't do that. I'm not a very open person. Furthermore, it would bring about too many memories that I'm scared to face.*
>
> —MICHELLE, 11th grade

Ironically, Michelle shares a fear that most of us have. There is a myth about the sharing of feelings and what that sharing will feel like. It is believed that reflecting on prior bad experiences will make people angry and will do nothing but depress them. The exact opposite is the truth. The more we talk about our feelings and the more available we are to talk through things that are hidden, the healthier we become, and we soon discover that the brain finds the energy to help move beyond that problem into something new and wonderfully creative as well as exciting.

> *It's about my dad's girlfriend. She and I don't get along that well. My dad is caught between two women, and my dad can't decide what he wants. If he doesn't so something soon, he is going to lose me, and I don't think he wants that.*
>
> —KATIE, 9th grade

Much of the stress buildup is often unrecognized. Think about the last time you were anticipating the arrival of a wonderfully relaxing weekend, only to discover, for whatever reason, that you felt depressed, lethargic, and somewhat cranky. If you are like me, you have experienced situations like that, and like me you haven't been able to logically account for your blues.

Parents often misunderstand the intensity of their children's pressures, and unfortunately it is often assumed by the adult population that stress buildup and pressures are manifested only in adult life. Pressures and stress buildup are a very real part of an adolescent's life. Failure to identify and respond to adolescent stress can have disastrous effects on young people.

It is especially important to note that at early adolescence (ages 11–14), the level of pressure and insecurity is so intense that these years may well be the most difficult of a person's life. It is during this period that young people tease each other relentlessly and demand conformity. Everyone needs to look alike, dress alike, and act alike. Failure to comply results in teasing. The teasing creates significant pain, and the typical defensive response is to react with more outrageous teasing toward someone else. A person who is saturated or overwhelmed will usually withdraw or act out in some way, and that will manifest itself as a mood swing.

We share the story of Billy at this point in an effort to help clarify the concept of mood swings.

Billy — a Case History

After speaking at the junior high in my hometown several years back, I was approached by a mother who was concerned about her son and his self-esteem. His name was Billy, and at the time he was twelve years old. Billy had a brother three years younger, and both boys got along quite well and were very close, probably more so than is often the case.

Billy's mom and dad had been divorced for a couple of years, and it was the mother who had the principal custodial responsibilities for the children. Dad was around and available, and he seemed to have a good relationship with both boys and frequent contact with them.

The mother persuaded me to meet and talk with her son, who,

as she described it, had significant self-esteem problems in his life. Billy found school difficult to deal with and, even though very bright, was struggling with what appeared to be depression. His depression was related directly to school and his lack of any friendships within the school setting.

Even though bright and a computer hacker at the time, Billy found himself socially isolated in his seventh-grade setting. He attributed this isolation to the fact that "I am fat." Everywhere that Billy went, it seemed as though people would make fun of him. On the bus, fellow students would be chanting, "Fatty, Fatty, two by four, can't get through the kitchen door." It was not unusual to hear himself being referred to as "Blubber," "Minnesota Fats," and "Two-Ton Billy." These nicknames were extremely hurtful for Billy, and he wasn't able to ignore them as his mother had so often suggested. Billy would try hiding inside his jacket, or at other times he would pull his stocking hat all the way over his head and eyes, hoping that people wouldn't recognize him. They always did, and so school came to be Billy's worst and most difficult part of the day. He knew he was safe at home, and so Billy would wait until the very last moment to get on the school bus and try to be the first to get off, always hoping desperately to avoid the verbal harassment of his peers.

In an effort to counteract a dramatically falling self-esteem, Billy tried going on a diet, but it seemed that the harder he tried to diet, the more weight he would accumulate on his body. Frustration and depression became a part of his life along with the ever-present miserable feelings about his worthlessness.

After considering the request by Billy's mother to be a counselor and big brother of sorts to Billy, I finally accepted the opportunity. Over the next couple of years, I met with Billy every week. He was initially very shy with me, but after just a short period of time we became close. Eventually, it was clear that Billy did not have low self-esteem in my presence. All kids yearn for respect, and Billy was looking for respect himself. In my presence, he felt that respect, and during the short period that we spent with each other weekly, Billy learned how to like himself. Often as children grow into adolescents, they feel that their moms and dads have an obligation to be nice and say nice things. If a kid, any kid, can find just one additional source of respect from an adult outside the home, it has a powerful influence and sends the uplifting and significantly anchored message, "I'm really important in the eyes of this person." That particular belief will lift the spirits of almost all people and help them to soar like eagles.

When Billy and I were together, I could tell that he was learning to like himself and love himself regardless of what his body weight said about him. Had it not been for Billy's parents and their love of him, I am sure that Billy would have quit school at the earliest possible time.

Billy's self-esteem seemed to be rising with the recent remarriage of his mom and dad, and in the midst of their reunion, the newly structured family relocated to a lakeside home where they could start over together in a new community. Billy's school remained the same, but it seemed that he had more resilient energy as his mom and dad came back together.

Billy and I had been seeing each other for about twenty-six months when a call came into my office one afternoon. It was Billy. I asked him, "What's up?" Billy pleaded with me, "Can you come out and be with me?" I had an extremely busy schedule of appointments that afternoon, so I suggested that I could meet with him the next day. His response was quick: "Haven't you heard?" "Heard what?" I said. Billy's response shook me to the core. He told me, "My mom and dad were killed this morning in a plane crash."

What do I say to a kid who lost both parents on the same day? Not only was this the first time I had experienced something so devastating, I was really fearful about my ability to respond appropriately, not only to Billy's needs but also in some way to Billy's younger brother. My response to Billy was, "Sure, I will be out there as quickly as I can shut down my office and get there." Billy's home was about thirty minutes away from my office. I really didn't know what to do, so I first stopped at a friend's house and asked for advice. We both cried together and talked about strategies and ideas that I could use when I met with Billy. Finally I got up the courage to head out to meet with him.

I arrived at Billy's home about two hours after our phone call. By the time I got there, Billy's grandparents had arrived from North Dakota.

Billy and I went into his bedroom, talking and crying together for a couple of hours. Billy said that he wished he could have been with his parents and died with them. I stayed with Billy and his grandparents for several hours before departing for home. Between that time and the next time I met with Billy, the plane crash had generated lots of publicity in magazines and on national news programs.

Billy returned to school about two weeks after the plane crash and the death of his parents. As he returned to school, he reported being shocked by the reaction of the other kids in his school. For the first time in his life, kids treated him with dignity and respect. Kids would say, "I'm really sorry to hear about your folks, Billy." Others approached him and asked him to join them at their lunch table; some invited him to stay at their home for the weekend.

Billy hadn't lost any weight at that time and asked an important question when he next met me: "Why did it take the death of my parents before the kids at school would stop teasing me and treat me with dignity?" I found it a difficult question to answer.

Billy's story points out the psychological damage done to young people in our school system with teasing comments. This psychological damage can last a lifetime. We have been asked over and over, "Why do kids do that to each other?" It happens in all schools, public and private. We know from our work with kids that none of them would like to be teased. It seems, however, that they feel as though they are somehow elevated by their deprecating comments about others. It satisfies the basic intent of the aggressor: "Make myself look good by making all others look mediocre and deficient."

Billy's experience also points out the unseen problems and the hidden psychological burdens that almost all young kids are carrying, in one way or another, as they go to school every day. It is a natural part of the adolescent passage to feel self-conscious and pressured and sensitive about a variety of things. More than anything, the lack of empathy and understanding from peers and the difficult and varied pressures that young people face at school naturally spill over into the home setting. Conversely, the pressures, interactions, and lack of empathy and understanding from the home spill over to the school environment.

Life Really Starts at Home

On the home front adolescents should be expected to reach out for independence and test limits; this is a sign of health and a part of the natural growth process, and it is natural for young people to begin the process of distancing from the family. It is the parent's responsibility to understand this growth process so that the behaviors that surface will be seen as a natural component of age rather than as a personal attack or a personal rejection of the parents.

All of us, adult and children alike, release our stress at home — always more freely than we do anywhere else. This is a psychological dynamic related to an unconscious awareness on the part of all of us. At home we know we are safe; it's the place where we can find and hang on to "unconditional love," and so it is at home that we find the freedom to "let our hair down," regardless of how bizarre our actions may seem.

Billy experienced a delayed reaction to the phenomenon we call unconditional love, because after the death of his parents he went to live with relatives. In that new kind of home environment (the same thing happens in a divorce and remarriage situation), normal adolescent behavior has to be redefined as well as redirected. The varieties and intensities of these readjustments number in the hundreds if not the thousands. New authority figures come on the scene, disrupting previous response patterns. In both situations, divorce or new home placement, adolescence will surface as a much more difficult process for the young person as well as the family. Often the reaction is delayed, but in other situations it is not unusual to see the adolescent react immediately with behaviors that fairly resemble the workings of a pinball machine.

Billy's motivation and behavioral responses were interesting and quite different from other adolescents'. Because Billy had been living with relatives since the death of his parents, he responded to his early and middle adolescence in a relatively quiet and compliant manner. When he reached his eighteenth birthday, he inherited hundreds of thousands of dollars as a result of a lawsuit and litigation settlements from insurance companies.

Within days he bought a new $23,000 car, and after he smashed it up, he bought another, and then another, until he had gone through six cars in his first year as an adult. Along with the cars, Billy started to collect CDs, and at last count he had over a thousand. Into his home Billy brought the finest big-screen television with all fifty-six channels. Living by himself in his newly purchased home, Billy was generous to anyone who would come and be his friend. You'll recall, too, that Billy and I met several years earlier in an effort to work on self-esteem issues that manifested themselves in food consumption. Now, with Billy's possession of lots of money and no external force to monitor it, food reentered his life. As will often happen, Billy fell back into using a physical need to attempt to fill an emotional void.

Two years ago I had a very serious disease called anorexia nervosa because I kept all of my pain and feelings inside. I ended up taking it out on myself, until I was admitted into a hospital in Madison, Wisconsin. As I was going through the treatment, my nurses always wondered if I ever cried or showed any emotions. In my family I always felt that it was silly to feel the way I did and I always thought my pain would go away. So, I never talked about my feelings to anyone, not even my best friend. Until this day I am still very shy and keep most of my anger and sorrow inside.

—GINGER, 12th grade

Searching for Love, Stability, and Feelings of Significance

As we discussed in Chapter 2, satisfactory adjustment at adolescence relates very specifically to the acquisition of several qualities, including love, hope, purpose, and forgiveness. All the characteristics are tied together and build upon one another. How do we fit into our children's search to satisfy these core requirements?

Note how easy it is to entice little children to jump off some elevated object into waiting arms. The jump always involves a strong faith on the part of the child, who firmly believes that the waiting arms will, in fact, provide safety.

Slowly — and sadly — that trust and faith of early childhood disappear as children become adolescents. They have so often interpreted their parents' messages as negative, indicating that the significant adults in their life are *not* waiting to provide safety.

Well, I've taken up enough of your time with my unimportant problems and my unimportant self. I'll try not to bother you too much anymore.

—NICOLETTE, 11th grade

Stephen Glenn, author and internationally recognized child psychologist, says that "young people need three things: they need

to feel listened to, to feel taken seriously, and to feel significant."[1] Those are the key areas of dialogue in the practice of
communicating with firmness, dignity, love, and respect.

> *I need to feel listened to, Mom and Dad. Really listened to. Look
> into my eyes. I need to feel taken seriously. I know I don't have all
> the answers. I know many of my answers are immature. I know that
> you can't accept some of my answers, but please take them seriously
> because this is how I view life right now. And help me feel significant.*
> —TANYA, 11th grade

When mistakes are made, adolescents need to understand first
and foremost that we all make mistakes, and mistakes bring certain consequences. But that's not enough for adolescents; they also
need to know that their parents' love will not be withdrawn and
they will not be shamed as a result of their mistakes. They need to
be assured; they need the attentive patience of their parents to ensure that their hope will not be crushed and their sense of purpose
destroyed. It is so important that parents understand this concept
throughout the frustration and chaos of adolescence. Adolescents
need to be loved, and when mistakes happen, even with the embarrassment certain mistakes can bring to parents and families,
kids need to know that loving forgiveness is a part of the committed bond that holds families together. We don't need to love the
behavior; we must love the person.

> *You probably didn't want to hear all of this, but I had to tell someone.
> I guess I just figured that you wouldn't hold it against me. Even if
> you did, I probably wouldn't ever see you again. Everybody that I
> think I can trust has turned against me when I tell them.*
> —STEPHANIE, 10th grade

The fact is that children always want their parents to be there,
regardless of how rebellious their behavior is. Children have a natural tendency to search for ways to increase parental contact and
respect.

> *I'm not comfortable talking to my parents because I don't think they
> would take what I have to say seriously. I also don't think they would
> know how to respond. I'm almost certain my dad would make a joke
> out of the whole talk, or act like God and think he knows everything.
> I'm not comfortable talking to my mom about serious things. I can*

talk with her about fun and exciting things that happen but not serious things.

—SARAH, 9th grade

Like the rest of the world's adolescents, Sarah really wants the relationship with her parents to work, but she struggles. She looks to her parents to provide the initiative, to invite and encourage. She has so much she would like to share.

All adolescents want to please their parents. The chances of that happening 100 percent of the time, of course, are nil. So, in the midst of conflict and rebellious behavior, it is our responsibility as parents to remember this, to realize that the present tension is simply characteristic of adolescence, that this is the process by which children break away and establish their own identity. Because their self-esteem is often tied directly to their parents' reactions, fragile, budding adolescents often conclude, "I'm not a good person when my parents are not happy with me."

My handicapped mom yells at me and complains that I never help out around the house. My favorite part of the day is when I go to sleep. I wish I could go to sleep and never have to get up again.

—GINGER, 9th grade

Adolescents often interpret their parents' nonverbal communication. They read eyes, tone of voice, and set of the jaw and pick up messages that may or may not be accurate. This is why face-to-face communication with the adolescent allows both parent and child to sort through many of the emotional issues that ignite frustrations and cause unhappiness to linger for years.

We must talk to our kids. As adolescents, they may consider our attempts to "talk" as dumb — "really dumb" — but let's not permit them to intimidate us. Let's learn to talk with them. As Mother Teresa says, "Kind words can be short and sweet, but their echoes are truly endless." Let's learn to listen, too. Let's offer advice and, more important, ask for advice. Let's listen to that advice honestly and intently. We will be pleasantly surprised.

I try to stay away from the house because I get tired of being put down.

—MELISSA, 10th grade

Many parents want to believe that all their children's needs will be met if they simply love their kids. In their publication *Free to*

Be Family, the Family Research Council notes that this is not completely true. "With the exception of the child-parent bond, the most solid bond in the lives of children is the one they see between their parents. In a well-functioning family, the bond between the parents is a guarantee of a loving and supportive environment for the child. When this dissolves, children naturally conclude that there are no permanent bonds in life."[2]

Adolescence is a period of anxious experimentation with life. The degree to which adolescents experience security is directly parallel to how much they trust the love their parents have for each other. When parents love each other and have a relationship that spills over to their children, the children sense a home base that they can keep coming back to.

> *My family is very important. How could I live without my family? I need them to love and care for me and help me solve some of life's problems. There are so many things my family does for me that make me feel that I am loved and part of my small loving family.*
>
> —JOEY, 8th grade

A child's greatest fear is the loss of a parent. That used to mean an unexpected death. Now it includes divorce as well. Will my parents stay together? Can I count on my family to be there for me? Can I venture out and experience life knowing that there is a secure foundation at home? This really strikes a chord with me because of my own experience when my father committed suicide. I was haunted by questions: "Can I risk loving and not be hurt? Will other people leave me? How can abandonment be avoided in the future? Protect yourself. Stay in control. Don't risk vulnerability."

> *I miss my father so much. I don't know why. I wish I knew. Why did God take him so soon? My mother doesn't talk about him unless you ask, and then she quickly changes the subject. I feel so empty and depressed. Why can't I be happy once again?*
>
> —NICOLETTE, 11th grade

During adolescence, the level of self-esteem will determine the extent and magnitude of problems and frustrations. Problems are an inevitable part of life, but the way these problems are confronted is directly related to one's sense of value, identity, self-definition, and connectedness to life-giving resources, primarily the family. The higher the level of self-esteem, the easier it is for a person to cope with the frustrations that life presents time and time again.

Every one of us searches for love, significance, and respect. Football superstar Bo Jackson shared a recollection from years past that directly speaks to this need for love. "We never had enough food. But at least I could beat on the other kids and steal their lunch money and buy myself something to eat. But I couldn't steal a father. I couldn't steal a mother's hug when I needed one. I couldn't steal a father's whipping when I needed one."[3]

Friendships and Peer Pressure

Average adolescents find their most helpful emotional support and understanding in the close companionship of their peers. Within that intimate company, they discover that others their own age have the same problems with their parents, the same resentments, loneliness, disdain, anxiety, and guilt. They understand one another even without understanding what their rebellion involves. They feel aloof from their elders and need independence and recognition as individuals.

When adolescents attach themselves to a peer group, they experience a sense of belonging instead of feeling alone and misunderstood. Adolescents of the same sex and same basic level of maturity can share their experiences, join in deprecating their parents, and together admire certain adults while hating others.

Respect the Peer Group

Because the peer group serves a fundamental role in the development of our children, let's not fear its influence. Peer pressure does not cause children to be bad, just as it does not cause them to be good. Peer pressure is simply the behavioral response one chooses in the midst of peers. It is nothing more than a manifestation of a child's level of confidence, which is a form of maturity.

I don't know what I like or dislike, because with the friends I've got I have to do what they say or they won't like me. If one gets mad, they all do, and it doesn't take much for them to get mad at me. I don't know if I respect myself because I don't know what my real self is like. I know I hate to hurt people, but my friends are really mean to people they don't like.

> —JAMIE, 8th grade

With confidence and sufficient self-esteem, all of us — adult and child — feel comfortable making our own decisions; lacking that comfort, we will tend to let others lead us. It is impossible for anyone to "make" us do anything. Others can "make" us feel, think, and behave only to the degree that we allow them to control us.

I wish someone would have stated some of the statistics about smoking when I started, besides telling me that it was wrong. No one ever knew that I smoked, well, except for the two friends I smoke cigarettes with. Don't judge them too harshly — they didn't pressure me into it at all. I was just fascinated by smoking, so I got involved.

> —KATIE, 10th grade

Countless parents create disagreements with their children about association with peers. "That person is not good." "That person is too old." "That person is too bossy." "That person does not have proper parental supervision."

I've been miserable for about two years. I was engaged to be married this past summer. I was also valedictorian of my class, held high offices in several organizations, tutored, and had many friends, and yet there was this other side of my life that no one ever knew about. The guy I was engaged to (a junior in college) was very controlling, possessive, and jealous. I had dated him for three years. There are many things that I missed out on in high school because I let him run my life. He had a terrible temper, and I was always so scared of doing something wrong. As I got older, I was able to confide in my parents, and they have helped me to end this relationship. It wasn't easy because my boyfriend had always threatened to kill anyone who interfered in our relationship. I am really glad I had my parents to help me.

> —CHRISTY, 11th grade

Our job is not to control our children's social environment. Rather, our work is to equip our children to do that for themselves. When young people feel foolish and worthless, when they don't like themselves, when they are frightened by the threat of ridicule or rejection, they are highly vulnerable. They are at great risk of being led into any way of thinking, feeling, and acting by the influence of peers. Our job is to help them build the self-worth and personal confidence they will need to avoid such risks. When the time is right, our children will make the necessary moves by themselves — often in consultation with us.

> *I was going out with my boyfriend. He decided that we were both going to get drunk this one night. When I told him that I didn't want to drink, we broke up. For the better (I hope).*
> —CONNIE, 11th grade

Unmasking the Power of Peer Pressure

The old saying "Birds of a feather flock together" is certainly descriptive of adolescence. Young people are drawn to one another for purposes of affiliation. "We're all in the same situation. We're all reaching out for independence, and for whatever reason, we have all somehow decided to test the limits at the same time."

As we mentioned earlier, this drive to cluster, to seek "friends," is a sign of health. It is the parents' cue that the child is undergoing a rite of passage based physiologically in the hormones. This drive is extremely intense, so intense that it can drive parents crazy.

Let's keep in mind that peer pressure is essentially defined as the influence of a preferred relationship; peer pressure becomes negative only when that companionship, and its subsequent influence, is pursued or maintained for the wrong reasons. Negative peer pressure has a strong attraction for young people as they strive for control and independence. The extreme vulnerability of adolescents sets up a dynamic in which an internal drive pushes or draws them in an almost addictive way. When parents insist that a certain companion or group of companions is "forbidden" or undesirable, something in the adolescents draws them even more powerfully to the forbidden liaison.

Parents Have Peer Groups

Parents do well to remind themselves that they have peer groups, just as their children do. Human beings simply gravitate toward others as they try to fill the perceived voids in their lives. These peer groups will provide the companionship, drugs, activities, and escapes needed to fill any existing void. We and our children make our own choices in that regard.

Does this mean that peer pressure is not to blame for our adolescents' behavior? Exactly! "Peer pressure" is a term teens — and adults, especially parents — use to rationalize behavior, passing blame on to others when in reality they simply are not ready to take responsibility for their own choices and behavior. Nobody "puts pressure" on us; we put pressure on ourselves.

Adolescent Vulnerability

Adolescents are vulnerable; there is no denying that. But why? To the extent that adolescents need to feel accepted and to the extent that they need to feel significant and to fit in with a certain group, they will choose to do things that will fill those needs. The sense of pressure comes from that belief. They will, indeed, not be accepted into a certain group if they do not behave in a certain way. When we as parents fail to see our children's intentional involvement in this dynamic, we become pawns and enablers who impede our children's growth and maturation.

This is the theory that seems clearly implanted in adolescents' minds: "If I do this, I will get that." As adolescents make important decisions based on this theory and because they seek affiliation so intensely and want to fill a need so immediately, they will consider violating any and all values. For example, researchers have discovered that "kids often deliberately switch to another peer group so as to be with kids who have made the same decision as they have about using or not using alcohol/drugs."[4] As parents, therefore, we make better use of our time and energy by looking at the psychological dynamics of what is happening rather than simply declaring unilaterally that certain friends are forbidden.

Parents and Negative Friends

We are not suggesting that all our adolescent's friends are to be tolerated. Rather, we recommend trying to understand what role they play, what need they meet in our child's life. Let's look to the belief behind the behavior to understand what is driving the behavior. When the beliefs and feelings change, behavior will change.

If it's any consolation, let's simply hear that our children will "come home" to our values and beliefs as long as they have been afforded the opportunity to experiment, test, and explore their own version of ethics, limits, responsibility, and irresponsibility. It is our hope that adolescents will experience their "rite of passage" within the boundaries of what the parent deems acceptable.

Building the Power of Personal Identity

I have no girlfriend. Every time I come to really like someone, they seem to turn the other way and say, "You're not my type." Then I feel very bad and break down. I try to lift my spirits up, but it doesn't work for me.

—CHRIS, 10th grade

Chris is vulnerable. The tenor of his letter suggests that, in an effort to meet his hunger for love, he will react to external influences and compromise all sense of personal identity. The good news is that through trial and error, Chris — and most other adolescents — will mature through this time of discovery. Until then, however, the influences of his peers will be perceived as incredibly powerful. Only a sense of personal identity and self-pride will provide him with the strength he needs to make his own choices according to his own values.

In my speeches I put it this way: "I don't see me the way I see me, and I don't see me the way you see me. I see me the way I think and the way I perceive and the way I feel that you see me. I see myself through my friends' eyes, through my parents' eyes, through my priest's, pastor's, or rabbi's eyes, through my teachers' eyes, through my coach's eyes, and through the world's eyes. How I perceive and believe the way you see me is what drives who I am. As I mature through adolescence and make the transition toward adulthood, I develop autonomy and separateness to a point where I see myself through *my* eyes. At that point, I bring myself into the world versus caving in to the world."

Looking inside oneself rather than to the world for an identity is the definition of maturity and security. It is also referred to as an internal versus an external locus of control.

I want desperately to feel special. I hate when I compare myself to other people. How do I stop?

—KRISTEN, 12th grade

During my senior year of high school, I was involved in an incident that might help clarify the realities of peer pressure. We often had pep assemblies to rally around the athletes as they prepared for that week's events. The winter activities included basketball, wrestling, and swimming.

The swim team, of which I was a member, never got much attention. To turn this around, the cheerleaders came up with a spirit-building idea and asked if they could present their idea at practice one day. The coach agreed. They started with a simple, almost silly question.

"You guys swim, right?"

"Yeah, we swim."

"Well, goldfish swim, too, don't they?"

"Yeah, goldfish swim. But at the risk of sounding stupid, what's the connection?"

The cheerleaders exclaimed, "We think it would be neat if you guys would swallow goldfish at the pep assembly on Friday."

Yes, they were serious.

Well, a few of the more popular varsity swimmers took the suggestion seriously; they actually volunteered to do it! I didn't really want to swallow a goldfish, but as I glanced around, I saw a chance to fit in with the popular crowd. These guys were varsity; I was junior varsity. These guys were party animals who freely used alcohol and drugs; I was a nonuser — and therefore not part of the guest list for parties. In fact, because I abstained from alcohol and other drugs, the party animals perceived me as a threat; I might "tell." Although I always felt confident that my choice was right, there was still a sense of loss at being banned from the group — a very important group. To achieve their approval would mean the world to me. Thus, swallowing goldfish became a form of barter, a compromise that I could accept. I knew that I could swallow the goldfish and not sidestep any of my values. So there I was, raising my hand in an attempt to be a part of the group. Eleven volunteered; I was last.

A thousand students herded themselves into the auditorium the afternoon of the pep assembly. I peered through the curtain at all

those eyes curiously pondering the presence of a ten-gallon aquar-
ium poised on a table center stage. When I got up in front of the
assembly with the others, I felt absolutely compelled to do the
same thing that the rest of them were doing. Were *they* making
me swallow the goldfish? No. Was the *audience?* No. Who was?
Who was making me swallow that goldfish? I was! No one else!
But inside I felt as if I had to go through with it. I was putting the
pressure on myself.

Because I was last in line and didn't really want to go through
with the whole thing, I was a bit slow in my performance. All
eyes were on me. Ten guys on-stage and a thousand students in
the audience were staring at me. Were they pressuring me? No.
All pressure I experienced was self-inflicted: *If I don't go through
with this, I'll be laughed out of school. If I do go through with this, I'll
be in with the popular crowd.* In reality, the only person who was
making me eat the fish was me. I popped the fish into my mouth,
felt it flip on my tongue, and swallowed. *Never again!* I thought to
myself.

*Nobody knows how much this hurts me. No one knows how I feel
inside. No one cares how I feel inside. I tried so hard to get people to
like me and accept me. It didn't work, and now I feel like crap.*
> —ANGIE, 8th grade

Everything starts with that self-imposed, internal pressure.
From there, we create the internally based message that says, "I
am like everyone else. I won't be excluded because we've all done
the same thing." Especially during adolescence, the lure to succumb is intense. Yet equally strong is the basic core of values that
the young person has been grounded in.

Let's understand what we, as parents, can control. We can control the time we spend with our kids, and we can control the
degree of trust and mutual respect that characterize the relationships we have with our kids. We can control the love we give and
the example we set. In this way, we instill in our children the qualities they need to take a stand for and help them discover what is
just and moral.

POINT TO REMEMBER

- *Parental values that have been modeled faithfully over the years will be copied by the adolescent.*

Chapter 5

Why All the Rebellion?

THE FRUSTRATION associated with adolescence isn't really a new phenomenon. That interesting time of physiological and psychological change has been a mystery for generations over centuries of time.

William Cobbett wrote in 1829: "Every man, will recollect how many pranks he has played; how many wild and ridiculous things he has said and done between the ages of sixteen and twenty-two; how many times a kind glance has scattered all his reasoning and resolution to the winds; how many times a cool look has plunged him into the deepest misery."[1] In 1968 the British sociologist Cyril Smith observed that "youth provides a contrast to the dreariness and restriction of adult life, for it appears exciting, unrestrained, engaged in conflicts with authority, and deeply involved in meaningful relationships with the opposite sex. It is envied for this drama and preyed upon by adults who wish to prolong their own adolescence."[2]

Parents themselves quietly spend time fondly reminiscing about their own period of adolescence. Usually, what we hear in therapy is, "I was rebellious, but I was just plain lucky and everything turned out okay for me." Counselors spend considerable time trying to teach parents to "trust the process — all will be okay eventually — but until then they need your continued love and support."

Children will follow our lead! Not always on our desired time table, but the bottom line is clear: As parents, we do lead. Ironically, before our children will follow us, they must first work through the process and turmoil of adolescence and seek out their own clearly defined rites of passage, regardless of the pain.

Adolescent Rebellion: What's It All About?

Rebellion at adolescence is nothing more than a painful search for power, independence, freedom, and significance. Rebellion comes in different shapes, sizes, varieties, and time periods. Some forms of rebellion are visible, and others are masked so well as to avoid detection for years. Much of this rebellious energy is nothing more than young people's need to be different from their parents and a need to establish a separate identity.

It is usually the adolescents who initiate the change in parent-child relationships, even though they may be as baffled by it as their parents are. The fact is that the child is no longer a child — and yet in some ways is more childish than ever. Adolescent rebellion may be viewed by parents as ungrateful, callous, and senseless behavior. In one way, adolescents demand privileges and protection, as dependent members of the family, but on the other hand they object violently to the least curtailment of their activity.

To adolescents, who do not understand the unconscious reasons for revolting any more than parents do, their behavior appears somehow justified, even though they may at times regret it. The best advice that we can give is that rebellion is essential in our culture and its presence is a sign of passage, something healthy, even though uncomfortable. There are some adolescents who never succeed in emancipating themselves. Some of them remain as grown-up children in their parents' home forever; some transfer a childlike attachment to a marital partner, who may be satisfied with it; some remain forever in chronic rebellion without clearly realizing what they are rebelling against.

Responding to Universal Statements

The overt rebelliousness that parents see is a sign of health, and regardless of how uncomfortable it might be, it is okay. Much of the rebelliousness is based on the adolescents' personal perception of what is going on in the world around them. As an example, the adolescent comes to his parent and demands a later curfew time, telling the parent in a rather loud voice that "everybody has a later curfew than I do." That statement necessarily triggers the response, "Which parents? Whose parents? Give me their names and let me call every one of them. I'm not trying to punish you with an inappropriate curfew. I am only trying to watch out for you — care for you. So, if all the other parents are doing it differently than I am, then maybe I should know about their reasons so that I can change my technique if need be. Give me their names, and I will call them." This parental response is without question positive and supportive, but in its support it will almost always stop the argument and discussion, because it exposes the elements of reality. Yes, it will cause some brief embarrassment to our adolescents, but it will put an end to the "everybody else does it" defense.

> *Tell parents to trust us and tell us that they love us. Tell them that when they discipline us, we know that they love us. Tell them the reason I don't use drugs is that I know that if my parents caught me, I'd get killed. Tell parents to love each other, so we can learn to love. So we will feel secure. So we can look forward to the same kind of relationship when we grow up.*
>
> —BARB, 10th grade

Setting Limits and Boundaries Amid Teen Temper Tantrums

> *If they would just not put me down about everything, maybe I wouldn't get mad at them as much.*
>
> —KATHLEEN, 9th grade

Work to maintain a sense of humor and calmness, then sit back and watch what happens. Typically, parents get so mad because their authority has been challenged that they are unable to back up a little and play with the teenager's mind, while at the same time holding a slight semblance of a smile.

The adolescent tantrum is designed to take us down and separate us from our values and moral ethical beliefs. Within the tantrum, at the subconscious level, young people know that they want their parents to rein them in (there is not even a slim chance that our children could recognize this dynamic). I have had young adolescents tell me over and over that they don't like "no for an answer," but once the no is delivered, they are able to save face with their peers. They are able to defend themselves in their social context because, "I didn't have any choice. My mom said no, and that means no." Standing tall with our beliefs and positions is the greatest living legacy we can give to our children, and a legacy that will bless our children not only in their lifetime, but in generations to come.

As a way to avoid being perceived as dictators, let's dialogue with our kids on topical areas that will become relevant in the near future. By asking open-ended questions and tapping into the opinion and judgment of the teen, we place ourselves in a position of unrecognizable control. As the pressures develop, let's remember that adolescents thrive in a structured environment. The absence of that structure sets up a climate for insecurity and future mental illness. Let's set the parameters and hold true to our commitments, convictions, and limits.

Clarifying Expectations

Parents are wise to be compassionate and understanding. That does not mean we should endorse the adolescent regarding issues contrary to our value system.

> *It makes you feel good to know your parents care about you, but if they're really listening and they give you a straight answer it may not be what you wanted to hear. When that's the case, you either have to live with it or change what's wrong.*
> —KATHERINE, 12th grade

Dr. David Wright, from the Iowa Department of Education, has said, "Parent, you don't have a leg to stand on in disciplining your kids if you haven't discussed the consequences ahead of time." This is not to say that we use consequences as threats. Instead, we should sit down with our kids and very calmly lay out the cause-and-effect relationship that will be adhered to. In this process of effectively raising an adolescent, we must always address issues and expectations in the quiet of a calm period rather than in the hysteria of emotional moments and situations. It's very much like a job description. We need to know ahead of time what the expectations are for functioning satisfactorily. Knowing where we stand, at any given moment, creates a sense of security. Anxiousness is fostered in an environment of uncertainty.

As parents, we will be effective to the extent that we have the courage to outline our expectations ahead of time. When those expectations have been met, we will be able to compliment our children, and when violated, we will have the courage and the conviction to react exactly how we said we would.

Prom Parties

Several years ago, during a parent seminar, I was asked a specific question by a concerned mother in the audience about the upcoming prom and its implications for her daughter. The questioner sought my opinion about a common high school activity in their affluent community. Kids were pooling resources and renting hotel rooms for "after the prom parties." I could tell by the nodding of heads that this was not the first parent who had been approached with this presentation related to the "safety and welfare" of the prom participants by keeping them off the streets where careless drinking and driving occurred late into the night. This particular mother talked about the pressure being applied by her daughter as she revealed that "everyone is doing it and I would be the only one excluded if you refused to grant permission."

The parent felt intense pressure to comply, fearing her daughter's self-esteem would be forever impaired as a result of a negative response and all hopes for social expansion totally shattered if permission was not granted. There is a part of the parent in each of us that says, "Some of the argument makes sense." The thought process of the parent goes on to consider, "I don't want my child in a car where someone is drinking. All the other parents seem to be in support. It's only one night, and the prom is a special event and a lifetime memory." Nonetheless, the parent needs to understand what will serve the best interest of their young person over the long term, rather than just for the evening of the prom.

Most parents will hear the argument "You don't trust me," which is generally an accurate perception on the part of the teen. (Sometimes you don't trust them! Are kids really mature enough to make all decisions?) In considering how to defend our position, we need to continue reviewing the state statutes, understanding that alcohol is illegal for individuals under the age of twenty-one. Then, as a defense (for starters), we could contend that our family values object to all rationalized illegal activities, including underage drinking. If you happen to be one of those parents who honestly believe that the kids are going to the hotel to play Monopoly all night with friends, call us in Minneapolis for a brief presentation on some of the realities of adolescent life. Essentially, you want to say yes to the question "Do you trust me?" What you don't trust are environments that are high risk.

The purpose of the overnight experience is related to alcohol consumption. A secondary consideration is the fact that alcohol lowers inhibitions, and as a result the chances of becoming sexually active rise dramatically with the consumption of each successive drink.

> *I've never told anyone this, but I trust you. I was at a party several years ago. There were these guys who were really wasted. They raped me. That seemed to change my life forever. I then found out that I was pregnant, but I didn't tell my parents. I just went off to Texas to spend the summer with a friend. I lost the baby, and now it is really hard because I haven't told anyone about this.*
>
> —CAROLE, 12th grade

An interesting statistic is that 57 percent of all rapes happen on dates, and 84 percent of all rape victims knew the perpetrator before the rape occurred. Now the question that surfaces is, "Do I really want my daughter to be overnight in an environment that is ripe and open for problems and abuse? Second, can I handle being unpopular or hated by my teen for a short period of time? Third, am I easily affected by the opinions of other parents?"

In the hotel setting, just the close proximity of others in the area creates an opportunity to be exposed to what others are doing. If they are drinking, all people present become vulnerable. The tendency to be drawn into the group is tremendous, and keeping the pressure at bay challenges mature and capable adolescents. Even the best-intentioned and best-behaved adolescent becomes vulnerable to the pressures of the moment.

Refusal to be what the teen might refer to as a "cooperative parent" can invite unbelievable pressure from our teen. In their mind, permission must be granted or their life is over.

> *Teenagers need to have more freedom to make their own choices and decide if the consequences are really all that bad. If we don't learn to make our own decisions, then when we graduate or start living on*

our own, we will make the wrong decisions just because we've never had any freedom before.

—GEORGE, 12th grade

Let's sit down with our kids and talk philosophy. When our adolescents hear the message long enough, the message will be assimilated. Knowing and understanding fully the magnitude of our commitment to any position will motivate our teens, for survival if for no other reason, to take a firm stand themselves. In doing so, they will move their network of peers and group of social influence in the direction of some activity that they know will stand a chance of being approved within their family.

I lay awake nights crying about my pregnancy. I'm so confused about everything, I don't know if I want to live or die. I'm just so stupid for getting into this mess in the first place.

—KARA, 12th grade

In the adult world, most of us wouldn't think twice about using the services of a guide on a Canadian fishing trip. Adolescents need help in understanding that guides (parents) do, contrary to the popular belief of teens, serve a useful purpose and provide a helpful service. Remember, we are the parents, we are the guides, and because of the wisdom of age and experience, we are looking down the road and into the future for them. They will most probably not like our decisions, but then they probably wouldn't like the consequences that come with being pregnant and a mother (or father) at seventeen.

Delayed Rebellion

I personally had a delayed period of adolescent rebellion. I was for the most part a compliant teenager doing all the right things to satisfy my parents. I graduated from college and went off to the seminary to become a minister. I flunked out of the seminary after a year and a half of study. My parents were upset about the termination, and much conflict developed in the family surrounding the circumstances of this apparent disaster.

When my parents keep nagging me, I feel they don't have faith in me. What should I do?

—TAMI, 9th grade

As I look back twenty-five years, I discover that flunking and getting "thrown out" of the seminary were nothing more than an unconscious drive on my part to do the opposite of what my parents wanted.

Tell parents that they take the time to pick out our faults, but they don't take the time to stroke us.

—DONNA, 7th grade

Discovering the origin of rebellion requires that a person reveal pain. The process is very similar to that of peeling an onion. An onion has many layers of skin, just as a human being has many layers of defense mechanisms. Each layer of an onion's skin is more pungent and causes more significant tearing in the eyes; the same is true for people. By the time the onion is peeled to the core or by the time that the layers of our defense mechanisms unravel, tears almost always appear. Males in particular tend to resist talking about feelings, but the fact remains that the seeds of rebellion are planted in the hurt we experience. All of us have expectations, hopes, dreams, wishes. If life does not meet our expectations, we react with sadness. Ironically, most of us choose to hide our sadness, which then comes to the surface in lopsided and distorted ways.

In the following story of my client Craig, you will see just how difficult it can be for even the best of parents to break through the wall of defenses built by a hurting child.

The Story of Craig: Rebellion in the Context of a Case Study

I met Craig eight years ago. At that time, he was ten years old, full of energy and smart as a whip. With his engaging smile, outgoing personality, big brown eyes, and black hair, he was cute as a bug's ear. He was brought to me on referral from his school, where his behavior was beginning to cause major problems.

Craig's parents appeared to be respectful of each other and good friends. For whatever reasons, however, they were divorcing. Both had experienced tremendous stress within the relationship and had sought professional psychiatric care. At different times throughout the marriage, they had each admitted themselves into a psychiatric ward. Both parents were professional people, the father a lawyer, the mother a stockbroker.

The announcement of the divorce was a shock to both Craig and his little brother, Nathan, who was three years younger. Their parents had agreed that they would each assume the role of custodial parent for one child. Mom moved eight miles from the family homestead, taking Nathan with her; Dad stayed in the family home with Craig.

Nathan and his mom seemed to settle comfortably into their new surroundings. From the beginning, Craig's negative behavior, however, continued to escalate at home and at school. As a result, his parents decided that Craig might be better off with his mom and younger brother in an effort to head off further behavior problems that seemed to be directly related to the divorce. A change was implemented, but within a short period of time Craig's behavior in the new location with his mom and brother deteriorated further. Temper tantrums, violence, foul language, and disrespect toward his mother and brother made for a chaotic atmosphere in the house. His mother simply could not control Craig.

When Craig turned twelve, he returned to live with his father. The teaching staff at the receiving school questioned his reentry into the school system. Reluctantly, they admitted Craig, but major behavior problems surfaced shortly thereafter. At home, Craig and his father experienced mounting tension as a result of Craig's lack of respect; altercation followed altercation.

Counseling was initiated, discontinued, and then tried again. By the time Craig was fourteen, he was out of control. Both his parents helplessly struggled with their obnoxious and arrogant teenage son, who was now taking drugs, stealing, and flunking everything possible in school.

Counseling became a routine part of Craig's life. Fortunately, Craig liked me. He tolerated our counseling sessions, and on rare occasions, when I was present, he could have a good exchange with his parents. I seemed to be his friend. Looking back, I think we were friends because I never passed judgment on Craig, and I represented a philosophy of flexibility for the parents to follow.

Craig and I worked together for many years. His continuous

respect for me was amazing, especially considering his constant and blatant disrespect for his parents, particularly his father. I am convinced that Craig's respect for me was an unconscious move on his part to recruit the help of an unbiased adult who was not emotionally involved in his struggle with both parents.

Assessing the Situation

In the midst of outrageous behavior and defiance that stripped his parents of energy and dignity, Craig became a dictator within the structure of his home. He came and went as he pleased, and his abrasive personality constantly demanded things — designer jeans, designer shirts, the most expensive tennis shoes. Eventually, we learned that Craig's material demands were an effort to medicate the pain of a life that, in his words, "sucked royally," and Craig's parents responded out of guilt.

When I tried to teach Craig's parents the concept of tough love, I found myself faced with an incredible task; they each had so much unresolved baggage of their own. The immense guilt they both harbored as a result of the divorce and their subsequent ineffectiveness as parents made it difficult, if not impossible, for them to be firm with Craig. He would scoff at their attempts to set boundaries and would issue threats and obscenities at his parents when I suggested strategies that would bring some sanity into this out-of-control situation. Each time I pressed the parents to make a move on Craig, Craig reacted with verbal assaults on his parents — not me — chastising them for not having the backbone to do their own dirty work: "You wouldn't have the nerve to even suggest something like that if he wasn't sitting right here!" As parents often discover, bringing a child in for counseling will invariably introduce the parents to their own issues. This can be very threatening to parents who want us to "fix" their kid, and counseling is often terminated for that reason.

Craig never dumped his anger on me. Through the years, he never once missed one of our scheduled meetings. Occasionally, he would yell and scream about the inconvenience, but in the end, he always showed up. Why? Because he understood the relationship, and he knew — even though unconsciously — that he needed the help of a friendly adult as he pushed himself further and further into a corner.

Tough Love and Consequences

Progress was slow — incredibly slow! As the situation evolved, Craig's behavior became more and more overtly delinquent. With encouragement, the parents gradually — and courageously — moved forward with the court system, allowing Craig to get tangled into the legal arena as a result of his incorrigible behavior.

Results were sometimes less than encouraging, however. On one occasion, when Craig landed in juvenile jail, his parents really pulled together. They looked beyond their guilt and their differences and presented a united front of tough love for their son. Prior to that, when Craig ended up in trouble, one of them would eventually weaken and give in, thus enabling Craig's behavior. This time, however, they remained firm — and Craig, shocked at his situation, promised there would never be trouble again. But the keys to the jail cell were not out of the lock an hour when the routine started all over again. Although Craig eventually ended up doing a three-week stint in a short-term correctional program, his dictatorial behavior, his drug use, and his incorrigibility continued. His parents, however, were slowly learning the way of tough love.

In January of Craig's fifteenth year, a miraculous event occurred in the course of an evening counseling session. Surrounded by his entire family, Craig stood up and announced, "I'm through! I can't stand this any longer. Do something with me." It was like the rider breaking in a horse, as the horse respectfully acquiesces, letting go of control. The horse determines when the pain will cease by giving in to the rider. It's then easier on the rider, too — and in this case, on the parent.

A Passage Completed

We wasted no time in making the next move. Within five days, we had Craig admitted to a Midwestern military academy where, essentially, his life turned around. For whatever reason, Craig accepted the authority and structure of this controlled setting. Not only did he adjust and embrace the limits, but he actually thrived! At the end of the first year, this incorrigible young man who had been flunking everything in school surprised us all by turning out to be a scholar of great achievement.

The experience was an excellent source of structure for Craig. But at the end of his first year, as he packed to head home, Craig informed his parents in no uncertain terms that he would not return to the academy the following term. Relying on his old and familiar techniques, Craig leveled threats about what he would do if he were forced to return. What's more, Craig's incorrigibility and general disrespect were in full bloom before the family even arrived in the driveway of their home. This continued nonstop, throughout the summer, until Craig returned, kicking and screaming, to the military academy for the fall term.

Craig seemed to operate with two personalities. At the military academy, he was a popular kid, actively involved in everything from scholarly pursuits to athletic activities, a model of positive behavior and attitude. In the presence of his parents, however, Craig exhibited tremendous anger and disrespect.

Craig graduated with honors this past year. Craig's address to the commencement audience is an insightful study in the psychology of human behavior.

The time we thought would never arrive is finally here. Today will be a day to remember for our entire life. This is a day of transformation from a boy into a man, a day of parental pride and self-satisfaction, and a day of long sorrowful good-byes from one brother to another. We must now look towards the future, and see the challenges that lie ahead.

From the beginning, our class has been a collage of young, diversified people all sharing a common interest: the interest in completing their final year of high school and being relieved of the burden a military academy can place on someone. Our school has prepared us to be equipped academically and trained in a disciplinary and athletic aspect, but not from a practical view. Here we are sheltered from the everyday actualities of life and live within a fabricated existence. Out in the real world the struggle will be long and hard for each one of us, and we will encounter a rude awakening. At this moment we are engulfed by structure and confinement to a point where everyone feels secure. Today all that disappears. The life we are about to encounter will allow us to come and go as we please, eat whenever we want, grow our hair down to our knees if we so wish, and spend our time in any selected manner we choose.

Now is the time that we must, for our own sake, get our hands dirty and strive for our goals. If we don't, all of our class's talents and hunger for success could easily diminish.

For every varsity letter we earn, every medal we receive, or every "A" we get on our report card, we collect all of the credit. Rightfully so. But there are those silent contributors who can easily be overlooked from most of the praise and thanks: our parents. Without them, we wouldn't be sitting on this picturesque campus with all of our accomplishments. From the beginning they were the ones who paid the bills, and accepted those numerous collect calls, and provided their wholehearted love and support through all our accomplishments and tribulations. They deserve our earnest gratitude, and we are in their debt. A sufficient means of repayment would be to go out there, work hard, and make something of yourself. Stay close to them throughout the years and don't abuse them, for they're the only family you will have. Parents, on behalf of the class, I'd like to thank you and send out love to all of you.

Well, my comrades of the senior class, we will shortly be getting off our pedestals, and the title of "senior" will evaporate. The cycle will start over again, and we'll emerge as freshmen New Boys somewhere. All of our medals, ranks, and reputations from here will be inconsequential to others and of no significance. What we all shall remember out of everything about our school is the strong lifelong friendships that have flourished. We got to know each other better and became a tightly knit group of friends. We have been willing to offer that hand to help one another in time of need. Most of you have been there for me day after day to provide the answers to my problems, the motivation to cheer me up on the bad days, and the devotion to stand by my side on a certain point of view or to dream about the future while reflecting on the past. I hope I've been as good a friend to you as you have been to me. I really look to you as brothers and have cherished the moments we shared together. I wish you all the best of luck with whatever you choose to do. Don't let anyone or anything change the way you want to lead your life. Search yourself to find what you truly need and go for it. Reach for the stars and make yourself proud.

God bless this year's class and good luck to all of you.
Thank you.

How to Guide Versus Control —
Understanding the Paradox

A wonderful analogy for parenting an adolescent comes in the comparison of the art of parenting and the art of dancing. When you bring two people together to dance, it can be a wonderful and pleasurable experience. In dancing, the roles of the participants are clearly defined. One person leads, and the other follows. If that concept is followed precisely, the dance becomes a wonderful experience. Conversely, if a person has been taught to dance yet violates the steps, rules, or choreography of the dance, somebody's toes get stepped on, and the fun is gone. Continuing the metaphor a bit further, the person who experiences the bruises gets upset and will possibly consider leaving, not wanting to return for another dance and a similar experience.

Let's Dance With Our Kids

The same thing can happen to the parent-child relationship; there needs to be a clearly defined set of rules so that all parties involved can respect each other and discover that the relationship has a keen sense of synchronicity.

> *When I try out for a sport, my parents support me and build my confidence. They encourage me when I begin to think that I can't do something, and they help me make it through the disappointment if I am not selected for the team.*
>
> —Josh, 9th grade

The uniqueness of the individuals can still be celebrated, but even in their uniqueness, both parent and child need to work within a thorough understanding of roles — parents lead, children follow. The push-and-pull of adolescence takes on a predictable rhythm if we are prepared to dance to the "music" of adolescence. Understanding the adolescent rhythm makes the experience both predictable and entertaining.

> *The one thing that my parents need to understand is what it exactly is that I am going through. I wish that they'd put themselves in my shoes and see how they react. It helps a lot when they talk about what*

they would have done in the same kind of situation. It's actually kind of weird because it kind of brings us closer when they do that.
                                                              —DᴇAɴɴᴇ, 10th grade

A similar lesson can be discovered in an analogy of trapping an animal. If the animal knew that pulling on the snare trap would cause it additional pain, it would stop pulling. If the animal knew that by refusing to pull and using the strategy of relaxation, it could get out of the trap, snares wouldn't work. But the animal doesn't know that, and it doesn't think to go against its instinct.

Palm trees can withstand tremendous hurricane winds because they are created to bend rather than stand unyieldingly firm. Earthquake-proof buildings are designed to give a little and actually sway. You open the windows during a tornado to let the pressure out of the house. Houses in tornadoes don't cave in; they cave out. They explode because they didn't vent fast enough. In many similar ways, so do parents and adolescents.

Many of the martial arts use the momentum of the other person to that person's disadvantage. Martial arts experts profess that staying relaxed is the key to balance and control in any situation. Stephen Segal, Chuck Norris, and Bruce Lee have all demonstrated their incredible talents at using their opponent's force against themselves and to their advantage. In the TV series *Kung Fu*, Caradine is always so darn relaxed, even when facing what appears to be death. Nothing is life-threatening to that guy. Why? He understands his enemy, emotionally, physically, and, in an uncanny way, spiritually.

If we understand that in the course of parenting adolescents situations will change dramatically, with almost no prior warning, we will be prepared to *respond* rather than *react*. This goes against the very fiber of our being. Our instinct says fight, hold on, stand firm, don't vent. Doing so may cause a break in the relationship.

I really do believe that my parents are the best. I am the oldest of three, so they really expect me to be the leader and encourage my little brother and younger sister to stay out of trouble. Sometimes when I have done something wrong, it is tough to tell them that accidents can happen. But I really appreciate being looked up at and being trusted by them to show responsibility to others.
                                                              —Mᴀʀɪssᴀ, 11th grade

The paradox of control has been demonstrated in the previous analogies. Anything that we try to control will be lost. If we try to control our spouses, they will leave us, control our children, they will rebel, control our life, and we will become neurotic or die from stress. Counseling offices are filled with patients defending their lives rather than taking responsibility, facing and modifying the patterns of their lives. Until they are ready to let go, they are unable to heal and move on. Scripture is filled with references to losing one's life to discover life. Parents need to relax through the rebelliousness of adolescence or fill their homes with stressful trepidation.

We're not saying back down in principle. Just be aware of the dynamics of resistance, be prepared, and expect change, therefore having the flexibility to move with the flow. Step back and let natural consequences take over. If as parents we break down and lose it, let's accept that we are human. We need to regroup and remember the phrases "I'm sorry" and "Forgive me." Where pride, power, and control block growth, humility is a natural healer. Adolescents will help us practice and perfect humility.

Tough Love

In some instances, it is important for an adolescent who is out of control and incorrigible to experience a major fall without being saved in the figurative sense.

> *The police called my parents. I was scared to death when the phone was handed to me. My dad was on the other end and explained that we had talked about the use of alcohol many times before. He said that he would not bail me out of jail. I stayed in jail for two days, and I really learned a lesson. It's not going to happen again.*
>
> —LENNY, 12th grade

This is referred to as "tough love" and in effect is a loving strategy that simply says that there is nothing that I can do to help you at the present time because you are so unreasonable. In that situation, the most loving action is to let the consequences take control. This obviously can't and shouldn't be done in life-threatening situations, but in those situations where the adolescent has turned dictatorial, logical and natural consequences can do more educating than anything else.

The best lesson that can be learned by our adolescents can come from the problems that our kids face and the mistakes they make.

Going to court was unbelievable for me. My parents came along but they didn't get me a lawyer and didn't try to talk the judge out of excusing my DWI charge. I ended up getting a sentence of community service. I was glad it was finally over, but what I was really glad about was that my parents didn't put me down as a result of my drinking, but they did let me learn my lesson.

—LENNY, 12th grade

It is important to understand that we can't really prevent our adolescents from making all the mistakes that are predictable to us. It's best to explain the consequences that can result from certain behaviors, and then, if a problem develops, let's continue loving them but not shield them from their mistakes.

Whenever I need to make an important decision in my life, my parents will support whatever that decision may be. They don't care if it is a good decision or a bad decision; all they really care about is that I am happy and that decision is what I really want.

—SANDY, 9th grade

It is important that a parent not bail the child out of the difficulty. As an example, a parent who runs for an attorney the minute an adolescent gets into legal difficulty is enabling the child's deviant behavior and preventing the child from learning the real lessons of life.

I got in trouble a couple of times when I was in the tenth grade. My mom always came to school and defended me even though I was not totally innocent in some situations, and she knew it. Now that I am pregnant, I wonder what she is going to do.

—JENNIFER, 12th grade

Getting Them to Love Loving Us

Getting them to understand their love for us will come at another time, in a different period of their lives. What they may hate in us now provides for security, but after adolescence (assuming that all survive) it will be the greatest reinforcer of their love for us. Let's trust the process.

My mom took two days off from work to drive me to Kentucky for a soccer tournament. She stayed with me at the hotel. My dad flew down to see my championship game. This made me feel very special because it showed that my experiences and time were more important to them than money, or their own responsibilities. It showed me that they put their child first.

—KRISTEN, 11th grade

Love is something that is given, not taken. Anything taken or given to meet a need is founded in using another. To give, simply to give, again is pure love.

The attention of my parents makes me feel so important and loved. When someone puts themselves second and puts you first, it really feels good inside.

—CHARISSA, 11th grade

As I tell teenagers in my assemblies, you can either love someone or use someone. You are either being loved or being used. The serendipity of love is that in giving and loving, life becomes fulfilling. Waiting for love is an empty existence. In therapy sessions, one of the most effective cures for depression is helping patients to stop thinking about themselves and instead reach out and give to others around them.

Sometimes giving of your life hurts. Providing structure, discipline, guidance, and limits is done even though it is not necessarily popular. When the child comes home to an environment that is safe and consistent, that child feels a sense of peace.

Dancing to a Different Drummer

After my father's death, because I was the oldest it was natural for me to fall into a surrogate father role with my siblings. My mother reinforced this dynamic by telling me how proud she was of me. I got these messages all the time for taking care of my family. Sounds innocent enough. The most curious dynamic then occurred. I developed perfectionistic qualities that were rewarded with praise from my mother, my teachers, and society, caused friction with my siblings, and then considerable stress in my emotional life. I never rebelled, because to do so was to rebel against myself. That wasn't logical; therefore I needed to develop more perfect behavior and then deeper reasons to rationalize my convictions. (Think of the character Spock on *Star Trek*. All logic and no emotions.)

I hope that my family will remain close and love each other no matter what because tragedy can strike at any time.

—SARAH, 11th grade

I ended up in relationships that I could control in order not to risk vulnerability. Eventually, at age thirty, I wound up in a relationship sufficiently loving that I could finally rebel. At last, and somewhat emotionally exhausted, I found myself in counseling, sorting out the mess. I discovered that I was attracted to women who could fill the emotional void of my lost childhood. I was dating women whom I could parent and who needed parenting. I called this phase of my development "from parenting to partnering." I needed to mature through my emotional adolescence, thereby becoming secure enough to be vulnerable and emotionally available to someone in a healthy, equal way.

As my brothers and sister matured through adolescence, they moved into the stage of rebellion. The question obviously surfaced for them, albeit unconsciously, "Who are we going to rebel against? Well, the old saying fits: 'If it looks like a duck, walks like a duck, and quacks like a duck, it's a duck.'" I acted like a parent, talked like a parent, and, apparently, to them looked like a parent.

I fulfilled my role and became more authoritative and logical in my communication. My siblings rose to the challenge and staying true to their own roles as growing children and budding adolescents, pushed even harder. The band played on, but the dancers left the floor. I was slow to learn that convictions developed within oneself are seen as character, but when imposed on others, these same convictions are seen as judgment. Even if you're right, you're wrong when you continually share with others without their permission. One person expounding ideas in one-way communication for two hours to an audience of six hundred people leads to applause; to an audience of one over dinner, the same kind of communication of ideas can lead to no further dates. People need to first seek our advice before they will ever grant us the necessary permission to give that advice. Thinking back to my role as the surrogate father, no one was seeking my advice, but they were sure getting it!

Eventually, my brothers and sister grew up and were mature enough to simply stop pushing. They left the house and went on with their lives. My siblings would call each other for advice, but they would not call me. I was cut out of the loop and out of their lives because I was still trying to force my views onto them without their permission. Now, in our adult existence and since we've all been through counseling, my brothers and sister will be the first to admit that often my views and advice were valid, but back then they just couldn't accept the apparent righteousness of my remarks without feeling they would lose face.

My sister got pregnant, and I was the last to be told. One of my brothers took drugs for eleven years, and I didn't know until two years after he quit. My other younger brother would sneak the car out on long-distance dates, and everyone was in on it except me. What was I doing? Checking odometer readings. "Four hundred sixty-eight miles? Kind of a late night, huh?" "Why did my dad have to die and leave me with his job?" I asked myself constantly. I wanted to be a brother, but I couldn't assume the irresponsibility of that role because my agenda was different from theirs. I would have to tie half my brain behind my back, cover my eyes, and not say a word. That was a requirement very difficult for a guy who was destined to professional speaking.

After my counselor gained my confidence, he began the painfully slow process of re-parenting. He gave me the homework assignment to not offer any advice unless asked. No debates about religion. No dialogue on lifestyle choices. No commentaries on family fiscal responsibilities. Just show up at a few family events with a stupid smile on my face and a hot dish. Months went by, and like turtles slowly poking their heads out of the protection of the shell or young couples on their first date after a big fight, everyone slowly and tentatively opened up. Trust came slowly, but as I stopped stepping on their toes, they asked me to dance! The repair had taken place, but not until I stopped dancing to *my* tune and heard *theirs* instead.

Creating the Right Environment — Defining the Solution

The question and solution are one and the same. What can we do to create an environment where our adolescent feels safe and secure in seeking our advice?

If I get into trouble my mom doesn't freak out like some parents. My dad lives in Kentucky and he shows me love by calling me every night, and I talk to him for about an hour. Even though they are divorced, both of my parents treat me like I am a god.

—SEAN, 10th grade

If they do not feel secure, see that as a signal to first look at yourself, and then to them. Pull back, learn a few of their steps, and maybe they'll want to learn yours. Share in their discoveries and rekindle in yourself the feelings of your own adolescence.

I hear all kinds of stories about parents being weird, mean, and strict. I have two parents who are just the opposite. Somehow they seem to know what I am going through. When I tell my friends that I don't dislike my parents like they do theirs, my friends seem to really envy me. That's not to say that I don't have fights with them — I do, but for the most part they really try to understand what I'm all about. I guess I am lucky.

—LILIANA, 9th grade

Push your memory back to the good old days. Always remember that in working with adolescents, the "party" is "by invitation only." Dance!

POINT TO REMEMBER

- *Anything that we try to control will be lost. Tough love is a loving strategy that lets logical consequences take effect.*

Part III

BUILDING, MAINTAINING, AND NURTURING QUALITY RELATIONSHIPS

Chapter 6

Helping Our Adolescents Make Responsible Choices

MAKING CHOICES is difficult for an adolescent. The challenges occur on two levels: the parent level and the child level. Parents are the power brokers in their children's lives up to the time of adolescence, when a tug-of-war begins as adolescents jockey for control. Teenagers want more freedom; they want to assume responsibility for some of the major areas of their lives. Good-bye security and hello natural laws of physics: cause and effect.

The Pathway to Making Successful Choices

This phase of adolescence, which lasts for several years, can be the most exciting and the most intimidating time of parenting. Learning to let go and allow our children to endure the risks of life is as hard on us as it is on our adolescents. Let's try to remember their past: Falling down didn't kill them. They survived with only a small burn when they bit the electrical cord. The fall from the roof was cushioned by the bushes. They made new friends when we moved, and every time they said "I hate you," we died a little inside, only to come alive again as they fell asleep in our arms a few hours later. All things considered, no one should survive childhood. If God had crammed all the disasters of childhood into a one-hour movie and showed it to us before we conceived, we would never have given children a second thought!

People tend to forget how important their family really is, like I did. When my brother died, it made me realize that my family means the world to me. I took for granted the time I had with my brother. Now I regret it. My family is a unit that works together through the good and bad times. My family is always there for each other, to talk to, to help one another, etc. My family has taught me self-worth, how to achieve goals, and how to love. My family has been there for me and will continue to be, because they love me. I don't understand why they always love me, with some of my behavior, but they do.

—STEPHANIE, 9th grade

We have discovered that all of us, parents and children, are pretty resilient. Scrapes heal, and hearts mend. The crises of childhood appear relatively insignificant, and most are even fondly remembered, as adolescence looms on the horizon. There are so many more things to consider and frustrations to cope with as the young person continues to learn about life.

Our children are going to grow up whether they like it or not. Their future will come, and in our hearts we're hoping they'll make us proud. How are they planning and preparing for this time, and how are we helping them plan? Clearly, these years of confusion, frustration, and exploration can result in roadblocks that make the entrance into adulthood very difficult. Or we and our children can create pathways that make the journey an adventure of growth and discovery. Will our children enter adulthood with scars that will take years to heal, or will they blossom into young adults who have learned how to make choices? Through the process of thinking and planning ahead, knowing what to value and setting goals, adolescents become responsible, healthy adults. We play a major role in guiding them through that process.

Making choices with an appreciation for how that choice will influence the future — negatively and positively — is a sign of maturity. Short-term thinking can be expected in childhood, but when children enter adolescence, they need to develop a broader base. Initially, adolescents live for the moment. Rather than thinking and planning, they base their decisions on feelings. They seek approval from their peers, overlooking or rejecting the wisdom of adults.

Healthy maturation leads to individuals who are able to live confidently in the moment, understanding that each moment adds up to a lifetime. Mature adolescents decide what is important to them and then create their own pathways to achievement. The steps along the pathway are simple, and when followed, will eliminate most of the roadblocks. Personal success then just happens naturally. As speaker and author Scott McKain says, "Life isn't just about getting what you want; it's wanting what you get." It's about designing a life that considers all that is important to us and involves all that we are. That's fulfillment!

To adolescents, for example, alcohol, drugs, and multiple sex partners may appear as fulfillment, but at the end of life, few individuals look back and defend these choices. As a matter of fact, they usually wish that they had made wiser choices rather than the choices that created roadblocks. Sometimes individuals will try to rationalize their pasts by saying, "As bad at it was, I'm thankful because it helped form me into who I am today." This is accurate in many ways, and we respect the premise. But this is hardly a sufficient rationale for young people to use as they blatantly make poor choices. Let's keep in mind that it's what we learn from our bad experiences and not the bad experiences themselves that makes us into better people. The saying "If it doesn't kill you, it will make you stronger" may have some truth to it, but what if it *does* kill you? What if it kills your child?

> *With courage I can stand up to things I don't like and have the willpower to say no. You need courage to try your best and always make the right choices so that you can be happy in life. My family feels courage is important so I may face challenges and stay out of trouble. I feel I have shown this value by being independent and not following the crowd.*
>
> —JEFF, 8th grade

It becomes our responsibility as parents to dialogue with our children, constantly asking, "Are you making good choices, and will you be able to live with those choices five, ten, or fifteen years from now?"

> *Family is the most important value in my life. Everything I do, I want to succeed in for the gift of sharing it with my family. Whenever I have to make a choice, I try to think of what my older brothers and sister would say. I discuss everything openly with my parents. I*

love being close to them, and I respect them very much. Families are very important in a person's life, and I'm glad mine is great.
　　　　　　　　　　　　　　　　　　　　—KELLY, 10th grade

Let's help our adolescents define excellence and identify the process that will allow them to accomplish their goals. Believe it or not, they do not "naturally" know how to do this; they do not "naturally" know how to plan for the future they want. The following suggestions can guide us in our attempts to guide our children:

Encouraging Our Children to Dream

Motivation, in its true sense, is powerful and energy-laden. "If I really want something bad enough, I will find a way to get it." Dreams fuel desire.

Dreams are an exciting source of conversation for parents and adolescents. It is not unusual, however, to see young people who are devastated because they find some career choice to be incompatible with their likes and desires. Because they declared their intentions earlier in their lives, a change of course seems like failure to them. With the experience of years and the wisdom of age, parents have the opportunity to help their children discover that it is okay to change directions.

So often we have seen family communication break down because parents have tried to dictate hopes, desires, and aspirations on behalf of their adolescent children. That doesn't work now and never has. It sets up a dynamic for rebellion.

Dreaming hurts when young people take on the dreams of their parents. They will not understand the psychological dynamics surrounding their lack of achievement. It is almost impossible to fail at something that is really and truly desired. On the other hand, it is relatively easy to fail when an individual is working on someone else's goals. A common example involves a shift in majors at the college level. Too often, young people feel that they are letting Mom or Dad down because they are unable to follow in a parentally predetermined manner a set of footsteps that isn't really their own. As a result, they feel much anger and disappointment, not to mention guilt.

One of the biggest obstacles to developing a healthy self-esteem is the inability to dream. Because of an internally driven fear of failure, people often discard their dreams if something appears too difficult or too time-consuming. Such premature conclusions suffocate dreams, and young people are left wondering "what if?" The inability to dream and reach for dreams depresses one's self-esteem.

Individuals differ greatly in their willingness to take risks. Those who harbor attitudes of apprehension and fear are the ones who believe that failure will be humiliating and will affect the remainder of their lives. The reality, however, is that all decisions affect the rest of our lives. Only through dreaming will young people be given permission to consider risks — risks that can lead to either opportunity or failure. And neither opportunity nor failure determines personal worth.

One of the greatest and most important goals of the functional family (as compared to the dysfunctional) is the support that family provides to its offspring when risks are taken and failure is encountered.

> *To me family is love, family is caring, family is helpful, and family is all good things. You can spill your guts out, and they will care about what happens to you. You can cry with them and not be embarrassed. You can laugh, and they will laugh with you. They will always love you no matter what happens.*
>
> —CHRISTINA, 9th grade

We love to tell stories about the failures of Walt Disney, Helen Keller, Dr. Martin Luther King, Abraham Lincoln, and Babe Ruth. These people all experienced failures, but their definition of failure did not translate into poor personal evaluations of self-worth. Instead, these very successful people used the knowledge gained from their failures to move ahead. They relied on the wisdom gleaned from their failures to teach them how to avoid making the same mistakes again.

Properly functioning families do not curtail the dreams of their children. Instead, they provide the support and encouragement that nourish the foundation of a strong self-esteem.

> *Education is important to me because if I don't get good grades, I won't get a good job. Good education is important to my parents*

because they want my brother and me to support ourselves, so they won't have to.

—Ross, 7th grade

Parents who encourage their children to dream and to risk equip their children with a personal sense of confidence that helps inform their choices. Parents who fear their children's dreams about the future, who dictate and attempt to control the future of their children, rob their children of a vital tool. Messages like "It just won't work," "You can't do that," and "You'll never amount to anything at that rate" strip young people of their natural desire to embrace the world of adulthood they are just beginning to explore.

Let us encourage our adolescents to think about all areas of life including the intellectual, physical, emotional, spiritual, as well as social (family and friends) and personal (abilities, personal appearance, health, and professional growth). What would they like their life to include? Not include? Let's dream! Let's challenge! Let's invite our adolescents to think about what they would do or be if they knew they couldn't fail. What about the qualities, characteristics, and values of the person they would like to date? What about the high grades they could get in high school or college? What about their level of involvement in school organizations, sports, and activities that prepare them for a specific career? Discuss and dream!

I am eighteen years old, and I am a virgin, and I am planning to stay that way until I get married. Sometimes I wonder if it's worth it since everybody else seems to be doing it (having sex). Where am I going to find a guy like myself? It seems like an impossible probability. Who are they? Where are they? Do they even exist? I can't tell you how confused I am right now. My parents have their problems, so I can't talk to them. My friends at school don't believe in what I believe in. What do you think?

—Kristi, 12th grade

Kristi has a dream of remaining a virgin. Somehow this dream of hers needs to be processed with her parents because it is just begging for reinforcement. Ideally, that reinforcement will come from her parents: "Wait, Kristi, you're worth it!" This message of reinforcement can have a profound and meaningful impact on the choices this young woman will face.

All of us at one time or another tend to make personal perceptions into universal beliefs. Unfortunately, Kristi's situation is limited to the guys she knows, and they are demanding sex. She hasn't yet experienced the part of the male population that shares her vision — and that population does exist. In fact, every point of view is represented by some portion of the population. When dreams are not reinforced by parents or significant adults, adolescents second-guess themselves: "Am I weird? Am I the only one who feels this way, thinks this way, behaves like this?" Kristi needs to have her hope rekindled. She needs to hear that her dream is realistic and worthwhile, that one day she will meet someone who admires, cherishes, and values her character and who, too, has waited to enjoy that mutual dream.

Adolescents have a difficult time seeing past the moment. Like a bird learning to fly, teens are clumsy in their negotiation of day-to-day life. Their world is filled with extremes that appear to be matters of life and death. Dreams are the means by which young people expand their visions, gain perspective, experience balance. Let's think about it! There first must be a dream in order to have a dream come true. As parents, we have an exciting opportunity to be part of that dream process.

Helping Our Adolescents Define Goals

Dreams are fantastic, but they are nothing more than fantasy without goals and the motivation and maturity to work on those goals. It is one thing to dream about being a professional baseball pitcher in the final game of the World Series. It's something else to appreciate what it takes to experience the reality of achieving that dream.

So often we hear people talk about how "lucky" others are. These people are quick to dismiss tremendous accomplishments as luck. This is jealousy — and jealousy significantly reduces the success quotient. In reality, successful people are individuals motivated to work out a plan for their dreams by turning them into goals and then following through, expecting achievement.

Today's young people have a hard time defining goals. Because they are surrounded by a culture that values instant gratification, working toward an end simply has no meaning. Everything they need or want is, in some way, available immediately.

Moreover, a good many of our young people have been raised by parents who proclaim, "I want my child to have it easier than I had it. My child will never want for anything." There is merit to this value, certainly, but the degree to which it has been applied to many of our young people has netted a generation that does not know how to dream, how to set goals, and how to work toward those goals.

As parents, the best thing we can do is encourage all the ideas that our adolescents express. If our children have clearly defined dreams but are not motivated to work on the goals necessary for the accomplishment of those dreams, let us explore whose dream it is. Adolescents can get bogged down in externally implanted dreams that come from a parent, a teacher, or some other adult.

For a long time now I have wanted to die. I often think up ways to kill myself, but then I think of how much is going for me. The only thing that matters to me is music and my voice. I sing real good, but then there's that conflict. I'm a guy, and guys aren't supposed to be in choir and stuff like that.

—NEAL, 10th grade

As our adolescents prioritize their dreams, let us encourage them to consider what is most and least important. Their list of dreams will initially include those that we, their teachers, their coaches, their religious leaders, and other adults who have their best interest in mind, may have for them. Let's invite them to explore these dreams realistically: "What will it take to accomplish this?" As we participate in this process, let us use the opportunity to uphold the family values we want to pass on to our children. Resorting to criticism or name-calling, to cut our youngsters' dreaming short, only leads to rebellion.

There will come a time when our adolescents seek our advice. When the time does come, let's help our adolescents understand that through examining the experience of others, many of life's obstacles and unnecessary mistakes can be avoided. That means fewer roadblocks and a straighter path. Let's use this opportunity to help our children think of their dreams within a time frame. After all, a goal is simply a dream with a corresponding date. For a dream to become a reality, it must have a time frame assigned to it.

Preach as we may, if our children are not willing to hear about the experiences of others, it becomes our role to simply back away and look for opportunities to be helpful if and when they hit an obstacle. Many adolescents are not yet ready to heed their parents' advice, so try as we may, we may discover that it is impossible to help our children avoid the pain of their mistakes the first and second time through. Our job is to help them focus and reflect on their strategies and the outcomes they have experienced. There are very few people who enjoy being told what to do or how to do it. Let's discuss and reflect, and the answer will come from within. Let's offer encouragement so that, in time, no matter how far they drift, they will come back. Let's emphasize the values that we personally espouse, and our children will eventually espouse these values, too.

Extracurricular activities are excellent training grounds for goal-setting. Normally, young people will freely participate and will realize that their success is determined by their dedication to the goal-setting and fulfillment process. Self-discipline is crucial, and the rewards are tremendous. Many of us learned this ourselves during our own adolescence; some of our most exciting memories are of accomplishments in activities while we were teens. Some of the most important lessons of life are likewise discovered there.

One of the added benefits of extracurricular activities comes in the presence of an adult leader other than the parent. Adolescents will mysteriously take advice and stern direction from a respected teacher or coach who, in effect, is saying the same thing their parents are saying. When a coach says something, it is immediately assimilated as important and totally logical. When the parent says the same thing, using identical words, the message is often discounted and downplayed. Let's take advantage of this wonderful opportunity. Let's quietly encourage our children's active participation in extracurricular activities.

Participating in Our Adolescents' Decision-Making

This is a critical step in determining adolescents' pathway in life. Making decisions is a difficult proposition for all of us, regardless of our dream or goals. The journey toward the realization of a dream can be taken only on the schedule of the dreamer, not anyone else. As coaches, we have the right to offer suggestions, but the pace is set by the dreamer alone. Some of us are late bloomers, which essentially demonstrates that everything in life is done on a schedule that cannot be completely dictated by external sources. Our children were toilet-trained on their own schedule and learned to walk when they decided they were ready. Unfortunately, many parents build their own self-esteem on the accomplishments of their children. As a result, the realization of those dreams never materializes and undue pressure is projected onto children to perform. Again, the temptation is then to label because the child's time frame doesn't match that of the parents.

As parents we need to encourage our children to make their own decisions and, within limits, support the decisions they embrace. Every decision an adolescent makes now affects his or her future. My mother often said, "Just because something looks good to you doesn't mean it is good for you." Let's suggest to our children that they honestly consider each of their goals from a position of personal responsibility and self-control. Our biggest responsibility as the parent, coach, and confidant is to encourage and help our children process what is happening. Our job is to consult and offer honest commentary based on the wisdom of experience. The self-discipline and responsibility that is thereafter required is not our obligation; it is the obligation of the adolescent.

> *You gave me a sense that I was strong and able to make my own decisions. Many of my friends and classmates are really into getting high whenever possible. Last year I joined them many times. Dope just seemed like the right choice at the time. Lately I would smoke the stuff just to fit in. Tonight all of us were going to do the dope thing again, but after your message today, the guy who had the stuff threw it down the toilet. I smiled, and we all talked after school and agreed your message hit home. We have a pact to steer clear of it.*
> —NICOLE, 12th grade

Life is a journey, and the quality of the life that is created and lived along the way is more important and fulfilling than the destination. Peace, joy, and fulfillment are found in wanting to do what we need to do. The best decisions are made through consulting with others and by reflecting on one's character. Let's gently direct our children to build on who they are (their character) and what they want to become (their goals) rather than on what they want right now (instant gratification). Let's encourage them to trust the process. Let's help them to look ahead first and then work backward to plan and decide on their pathway. This will determine what they need to do today to get where they want to be tomorrow.

Education is what you need to get someplace in this world. It is the key to the future and opens doors to many opportunities. It's yours forever and cannot be taken away. An education is available to all of us. What we do about it is our choice.

—SALLY, 6th grade

When we talk to our children about their friends, let's avoid judgmental labeling and discuss only the behavior. As we suggested earlier, it's best if we try to love our kids' friends. Let's bring them into our home, participate in their lives, and love them. If we avoid the issue of personalities, we will avoid our own embarrassment and help our kids in the process. Let's talk issues and behaviors and not personalities. When we speak openly about our kids' friends, in a nonconfrontational way, our kids will receive an ongoing commentary on their peers. This will have an impact on our adolescents' peer selection and will place them in a position of support because they will be inclined to choose friends who share similar base values. If our children don't have foundation friends, they are at higher risk and are vulnerable to succumb to the whims of the group.

Although I'm a senior and my friends drink, I think I would feel very guilty if I ever drank, mainly because I would be afraid of what my parents would think of me. I know they would lose all their trust if I ever came home drunk. I'd have all my privileges taken away. But because my parents can trust me, and I'm a good student and don't get into lots of trouble, I have very few restrictions.

—DAN, 12th grade

At the core of all decisions are values. Values represent what is believed and what is really important in life. When decisions are based solely on a desired outcome, values are redefined, even disregarded, to justify the end results. As an example, the arguments for safe sex and responsible use of alcohol are based on the end result. Young people want to "do it," so they say, "Let's redefine what is acceptable to remove shame." This approach simply enables the behavior while disregarding any values or consequences. The following letter from Dave is a classic example:

I am writing you this letter because my teacher is making me. I think your values are messed up. Don't get me wrong. You have some good ideas, but you contradict yourself. You tell us not to use condoms, just not to have sex, but if you happen to get pregnant don't have an abortion. Drugs destroy lives, but if you are a fourteen-year-old girl and pregnant, what are you supposed to do? Keep the kid and destroy your life in a different way? Kids are going to have sex because they are curious, no matter what you say, so you might as well tell them to have it safe.

—Dave, 11th grade

Dave wants to have it both ways. He wants to justify sex without the inconvenience of pregnancy and children, but pregnancy is a natural outcome of sex. Abortion is not a natural outcome of pregnancy. Abstinence eliminates the risk of both. No other method is guaranteed. Nothing protects the emotional, psychological, spiritual, or physical well-being of these youngsters better than behavior that reflects values; condoms don't provide that kind of protection; birth control pills don't provide that kind of protection.

Young people can give back the class ring, return the letter jacket, tear up the letters, and burn the pictures, but they will never be able to give back the memories. Dave is arguing for redefining values to maximize pleasure and diminish pain. His socially relative plea is to legitimize all choices, rationalize all outcomes, and make them equal. Dave is reasoning that kids are going to have sex, so teach them that having sex is okay provided they exercise precautions. But such teaching is unethical. Pregnancy and sexually transmitted diseases are not always avoided by using condoms. To say that having sex is okay is to teach a value of permissiveness; to say that safe sex is possible is to lie — and our young people become victims.

We have to challenge adolescents to become their best! Let's teach them that saying no will not harm them, that saying yes, even with protection, will leave them without any guarantees. They are not going to know what to do until they know what to believe. As parents, let's lovingly guide, teach, and model for our children what we believe, and, interestingly, they will then know what to believe. Dave continues:

You tell us not to take away from a woman's future spouse by having sex with her, but what if you are planning to be her future spouse?

Plus, you will probably never meet her future spouse anyway, so why would you care what he thinks?

—DAVE, 11th grade

Dave is rationalizing for purposes of satisfying his own need for instant gratification. "One for all and all for me. I want what I want when I want it." This is the absence of self-discipline and justifies, for the person involved, a lack of self-control. Dave's motives are purely self-centered. It is a style of narcissism that permeates our society today.

Dave shares one last thought:

Write me back if you think my values are messed up, and I'm sure you do. I have studied some psychology also, and I knew everything that you were talking about, such as depression and everything like that. As I said, I thought you had some good ideas, but some are out of whack.

—DAVE, 11th grade

Dave is insisting that his views be treated as the standard. And certainly all of us are entitled to our own opinions, but we are not entitled to our own facts. What's obscene is that a desensitized nation of teens doesn't even know what is obscene anymore. When students are asked, "How do you make decisions?" the most common responses are "It depends on how I feel," and "I see what my friends think." This is dangerous and ultimately leads to a confused population of teens.

Sound, responsible decision-making always looks to core values before a choice is made and action is taken. The values chosen will therefore reflect, reinforce, and drive all decisions. Therefore, as they evaluate their goals and determine their decisions, young people need to ask themselves three key questions:

- "What is important for me to value?"
- "What do I really value?"
- "Do I have the capacity to act on my values?"

Important Value Considerations

Let's look at the question "What is important for me to value?" Thomas Paine said, "The long habit of not thinking a thing wrong gives us the superficial reality of thinking that it's right." Whom do adolescents look to and what are they taking in?

Let's encourage our teens to look to us and to extended family, teachers, advisers, religious leaders, and public figures whose lives have withstood the test of time. Let's search out the virtues and qualities at the core of greatness and challenge our adolescents to make those qualities their own. Let's help them with their heroes; many of today's heroes are people who are popular, not people of character. Many are "vogue" on the outside and "vague" on the inside. Let's encourage brutal honesty, self-discipline, and responsibility from our teens as they select the adults they respectfully wish to emulate.

> *I think honesty is very important because Jesus taught us to be truthful. If you are not honest, it hurts the relationship with God and you are cheating yourself. Honesty strengthens your relationships with your peers and with God.*
>
> —NICK, 7th grade

Late in 1993 I noticed an article in the *Pioneer Press* (St. Paul, Minnesota) about teaching values. "Across the country, school districts are starting programs specifically aimed at teaching values to their students. There has been a resurgence of interest nationwide in the whole issue of the degree to which our kids are picking up the cultural values in the United States. In public schools for ten or twenty years, the whole idea of even discussing values has faded away."[1] In response to parents' demands for values to be reinforced and taught in schools, a "Respect and Responsibility Program" was developed in two school districts in suburban Minneapolis. This initiative called for a program of nine monthly themes, which included understanding the school and community environment (including courtesy, kindness, and manners), understanding and appreciating others, understanding and appreciating self, communication, conflict resolution, character development (including honesty, fairness, and empathy), making responsible choices, citizenship, and respect.

In 1993, the Prior Lake–Savage community, located just south of Minneapolis, established a goal for the year: developing values as a way to promote a higher quality of life in the community. The seven values that this community highlighted are worth repeating here, as an example or framework for instilling values in our families, particularly our adolescents. Let's consider the following values: (1) Courage, (2) Education, (3) Family, (4) Honesty, (5) Human Worth and Dignity, (6) Respect, and (7) Responsibility.

COURAGE: finding the wisdom to abstain from making harmful decisions for ourselves and others regarding sexuality, chemical use, and other issues; standing up for our own convictions and the rights of others; daring to attempt difficult things that are good; showing the strength not to follow the crowd; saying no and meaning it and influencing others by it.

Courage is not when you slay a dragon and rescue a beautiful princess. It is standing up for yourself and not taking drugs.
—KEELAN, 7th grade

EDUCATION: a willingness to strive to learn more and increase personal levels of fulfillment and competence throughout life; to use reason and respect to resolve differences; to improve solutions to existing and emerging problems for the betterment of self and society.

Education is very important. My mom showed me that you should never stop learning. She desired to work on her master's degree. It took a lot of hard work, but she got it. It did pay off. She made her goal.
—LUKE, 7th grade

FAMILY: where we can learn and experience security and belonging; where human worth and dignity are nurtured; where we can come to know the warmth of positive and loving commitment and where our positive values and goals are developed.

Family is important because they make you what you are today. Your family makes you feel secure and also gives you a sense of belonging. When you're around family they make you feel more confident in yourself. They also teach you their values and other important things. Families also help set goals for each other.
—LATISHA, 8th grade

HONESTY: dealing fairly and truthfully with others in all circumstances; creating a personal integrity that fosters trust.

Honesty is what makes the world a good place. Honesty is the best policy to go by. Some people don't tell the truth, and I would guess

that these people don't get trusted too much. I think the good people
really stand out.

—JOE, 7th grade

HUMAN WORTH AND DIGNITY: celebrating the diversity and creativity of all people; recognizing our sameness in spite of our differences; holding dear the life each of us has been given; viewing others with tolerance, kindness, and compassion.

I think all people are important and worthwhile, no matter what their
race, nationality, religion, gender, abilities, or whether they are rich
or poor. If people would think about what it's like to be someone who
they look down on and put themselves in that person's place, perhaps
they would be more understanding.

—DEREK, 9th grade

RESPECT: high regard for self and other people, for life, for the law, for the environment, for property, and for the rights of others.

The value I hold dearest is respect. It is important to me because I
really enjoy the environment. We should have respect for everything
that God has put on this world. A police officer helped me to respect
the law. I drove around with him for a day, and he showed me what
it was like to be a police officer and to respect the law. Respect for life
is also very important. I believe God has a certain purpose for all of
the people he has created.

—MARCUS, 11th grade

RESPONSIBILITY: a quality in which individuals are held accountable and accept the impact their actions have upon themselves, their relationships, the community, and the environment; self-control, dependability, and commitment displayed in good citizenship, patriotism, and community service.

Being responsible makes me feel grown-up and wholesome. I have
shown my responsibility by being in school every day and giving
one hundred percent to everything I do. I have been there for my
family and friends when they needed me. I know I'm responsible for
my actions so I try to stay away from bad situations, but when I do
something wrong I take full responsibility.

—TRAVIS, 8th grade

Next, we consider the question "What do I really value?" Teens need to know what to believe before they'll know what to do. Do they know what to value? Do they know how to build their life on what is proven and question what is not? Do they know how to recognize a lie?

> *When I was a junior I went out with this girl for about a month and a half. She wanted to have sex, and I wasn't sure whether I should have it or not, but I did. The next day I received a phone call from this girl, and she said that she never wanted to see me again. I later heard of her reputation. I was so hurt that I cried for one whole day. I was so hurt and felt so guilty that I just didn't know what to do. I told my mother and she cried with me. My mom was so nice, and I told my mom how much I love her and how much I needed her. Now I just wish I would have gone by what I knew was right.*
>
> —NATHAN, 12th grade

Helping Them Consider Their Personal Capacity to Act

Finally, consider the question "Do I have the capacity to act on my true values?" Let's help our children determine if their actions honestly line up with and are founded in their true values. Difficult decisions become very simple (not easy, just simple) to make and act on when young people discover what ethics, values, and virtues are ultimately important. Following their core values faithfully will ultimately lead to personal freedom.

> *I wish to thank you for making me believe that being a virgin isn't something that I should be ashamed of. My friends, well, only some of them, tell me that I am sixteen, and I should be very sexually active. Yesterday you made me realize that by being a virgin, I'm what I want to be, not what they want me to be. I'd rather be a sixteen-year-old virgin than a sixteen-year-old unwed mother.*
>
> —SHAWNA, 10th grade

Good Decisions as a Stable Foundation

Good decisions, even when the consequences are less than satisfying, give young people the base on which to stand with confidence and pride. A trail of good decisions gives young people the freedom to make honest mistakes, to rethink, and to try again. Adolescents learn to blaze pathways for themselves instead of erecting roadblocks. Choices that could lead to possible roadblocks are seen as risky, unavailable, or unacceptable options. Though everyone can choose again, choices that will always place us in a position to freely choose again are pathway choices. Good decisions always align with values. Let's appeal to our teens to consider whether their decisions will take them where they want to go for the long term.

> *Our daughter is twenty years old. From birth she has been pro-foundly retarded. Her entire life she had to be diapered and totally cared for. She still eats pureed food. Her ability is totally limited. It breaks my heart to see kids ruin their lives with alcohol and other drugs. Our daughter never had a chance. The kids I teach have so much to offer the world. I pray they don't waste it!*
>
> —SANDY, teacher and parent

Holding Our Adolescents to Commitments

Commitments are promises made to self and/or others. They are the whys behind the whats of life. When people make commitments that are not in line with their values, they end up feeling uneasy, depressed, and often physically ill. Without commitment, all actions are empty promises that will lead to a process of just going through the motions. Whether in school, work, or relationships, the level of success is founded in the degree of commitment.

> *Responsibility is important to me because it helps me lead a good life and have self-control. I have shown responsibility by getting good grades, saving money, and cleaning my house. My parents have shown responsibility by being able to take care of my family and pay bills.*
>
> —SHANDA, 7th grade

Strong commitments naturally lead to right actions or a worthwhile path. Just as that which is entered into without commitment will eventually fall apart, almost anything undertaken with commitment will eventually succeed. With true commitment the pathway and resources to get there will naturally develop as a reality. Commitment puts the influence of peer pressure into perspective; committed young people do not need the acceptance or approval of others to complete their identity. Commitments give young people control over their future. When they know the whys, the whats will make sense.

Helping Our Adolescents Align Commitments, Choices, and Action

When all the preceding steps are followed faithfully, the toughest step becomes the easiest. It's called action. As we work with our adolescents, let's have them look at their commitments, choices, and performance. Let's ask, "Do they match?"

> *I made the biggest mistake of my life about five months ago with my boyfriend. We did have sex, but as soon as I got my act together and told him I couldn't do it anymore, he broke up. I thought he "loved" me. I learned my lesson.*
>
> —DENISE, 11th grade

Denise made a choice that went against her original commitment to herself, and then she realized her mistake. When she realigned her behaviors with her values, her boyfriend's true colors came to light, and they broke up. It's unfortunate that this lesson had to be learned in this manner, but Denise learned nonetheless.

Acting on dreams or feelings without going through the process leads to wishy-washiness and frustration. For example, we can ask our kids to reflect on the classes they like and are committed to. These classes are usually the easiest to find the time for, and studying is more meaningful and enjoyable. How about the classes or activities they're not committed to? Most will find them tough, perhaps boring.

Popular radio personality and host of "Casey's Top 40" Casey Kasem has touched several generations of listeners with stories of compassion, dedication, and loving sentiment. Each week he shares commentary that has a significant impact on his listeners' lives.

Casey once shared with me that he carried in his wallet a saying that changed his life. From Friday, December 30, 1955, until sometime in 1963, when he had it framed, Casey gingerly toted and reflected upon "The road to success is dotted with many tempting parking places." For eight years, a simple "thought for the day," a tattered, crumpled teletyped clipping off the UPI/API wire service, had the greatest impact on Casey's success. It reminded him to keep moving: to act.

Most people try to compromise on the price of success. They look for "parking places" and hope that success will find them.

High achievers, however, are willing to do what others aren't willing to do; high achievers find motivation in their vision as they dream about who they want to become and what they will be doing. They have the ability to envision the future, and this vision ensures their success. As Casey Kasem has said at the conclusion of his radio broadcasts for almost thirty years, "Keep your feet on the ground and keep reaching for the stars."

Pathways and Roadblocks

Review the following lists. With your adolescents, compare and contrast pathways and roadblocks.

It's a Pathway When...

- You can look at yourself in the mirror after the choice and like who you see.
- It gets you closer to becoming the person you want to be.
- Deep down inside you are proud of your thoughts, feelings, and actions.
- Your actions fit perfectly with your values and morals.
- You encourage others to do the same.
- It shows love and compassion for others and at the same time demonstrates respect for yourself.
- It helps you academically.
- It strengthens you emotionally and builds your character.
- Your actions match your commitments.
- Your action builds you up and builds up others.
- All long-term consequences and benefits are considered first.
- You take a stand for what's right even if it's not popular.
- You associate with a friend you'd like everyone to meet.
- You try something new and challenging that causes you to grow.
- You take responsibility rather than blame.
- You focus on *who* you are rather than *what* you are not.

It's a Roadblock When...

- You wouldn't want the world to know what you've done.
- You're unable to discuss your choice with others, even God.
- You are embarrassed by the action you took.
- It's just flat-out wrong or illegal.
- It hurts other people or yourself.
- It uses or violates yourself or others.
- It involves compromising your values.
- You have considered only the possible short-term outcomes of the choice.
- It's founded in an "I don't care" attitude.
- You do something just to be popular.
- You date someone you don't respect.
- You compare yourself to others.
- You let the group determine what you believe is important.
- It involves using alcohol, cigarettes, or other drugs.

POINT TO REMEMBER

- *A sign of maturity is when choices are made based upon first considering the future consequences.*

Chapter 7

The Biggest Concerns of Parents

To CHALLENGE AN AUDIENCE in motivational-speaking circles to reflect on their current attitudes and behaviors, I often ask, "How do you cook a frog?" Once everyone is convinced that I'm not crazy, that I'm actually serious, they generally get those puzzled, pondering looks on their faces.

"Okay, how?" their blank stares seem to say.

"Well, if you put a frog in a pot of boiling water, it will immediately jump out." Gradually, the audience's expression changes to, "Okay, I'll buy that, but so what?"

"But," I go on saying slowly, "if you put a frog in a pot of cool water, water that it is already accustomed to, it will swim around contentedly in these familiar surroundings. Then, if you slowly turn up the temperature, the frog, being a cold-blooded creature, will adjust its body temperature to its surroundings — and eventually it will cook itself."

With that, the audience's expression seems to say, "Okay, that makes sense. We get it. So what's the point? How does this relate to my life?"

"Well, how do you cook a society? How does someone become an alcoholic or reach a point where suicide is an option? Why do nudity and sex on TV become acceptable and how does an entire culture become desensitized to vulgarity? How does what once was considered obscene become art and how does what once was considered a religious or moral fabric of society become passé? What causes divorce to become so prevalent and differences to be-

138

come so irreconcilable? How does life become a matter of choice and the value of life doesn't seem to matter at all? How? Through slow, subtle, seemingly logical adjustments — just like increasing the temperature of the water to cook the frog. Why? Because it seems to make sense! Compared to what? If we forget history, we are prone to repeat it."

We've Got Change

In America over the last three decades, there has been more than a 500 percent increase in violent crime and more than a 400 percent increase in illegitimate births. The percentage of children in single-parent homes has tripled; the teen suicide rate has tripled, the divorce rate has doubled, and the average SAT score has dropped nearly seventy-five points. Gangs are replacing families, and (for the sake of seeking power) guns and knives are brought to school.

Discovering what these statistics mean requires some time and objective assessment that is often difficult because of our own subjectivity. We automatically become biased because of the baggage we carry and because we filter all information through the lens of our own personal life experiences. It's not just how the information comes to us; it's how we come to the information that determines its meaning.

Our country has allowed itself to disregard the importance of the family and those social institutions that once supported families and family values. The move toward a more sophisticated environment without the influence of the family, church, school, and community is a mistake. The strategies that we as a society have developed are like putting Band-Aids on massive wounds rather than dealing directly with the injury. We develop educational programs for sexuality, drugs, low self-esteem, violence, and AIDS, yet these are mere symptoms of a greater problem rooted in the dislocation of the family and those social institutions that support it. In the past, it was the strength of the family and the backup the family received from social institutions that developed healthy young people ready to live in a world that was relatively safe and friendly.

This shift, indeed this social decomposition, brings an unbelievable and unprecedented challenge to the present American family.

According to Harvard psychiatrist Armand Nicholi, "only Great Britain rivals the U.S. in parental absence," a fact that he believes Americans should find troubling. Nicholi goes on to say, "If one factor influences the character development and emotional stability of a person, it is the quality of the relationship he experiences with both of his parents. Conversely, if people suffering from severe nonorganic emotional illness have one experience in common, it is the absence of a parent through death, divorce, time-demanding job, or absence for other reasons."[1] The evidence seems to consistently demonstrate that not all family structures are equal in their ability to shepherd children through adolescence so that they can arrive safely and securely at adulthood.

Families are there to help you when you are in need. They help you get a good education. When you are hurt they help you to get better. They help you with your schoolwork. They are kind to you. Moms help you to learn good manners and how to take care of yourself. Dads help you learn how to stand up for yourself. Brothers help you to learn how to play games and teach you how to ride a bike. Sisters help you learn how to be a person. They can be your best friend forever. Grandparents love you and take care of you and your family and they never let you get hurt. As you get older, your family will always love you, take care of you, and should never hurt you. And no matter how you are, or who you are, they will always love you the way you are.

—KATIE, 6th grade

Virtues like respect for authority, self-control, honor, fidelity to commitments, and civic-mindedness have become almost extinct. In addition to the loss of "old-fashioned virtues" and traditional priorities, there exist today certain environmental factors that didn't exist before: economic and social deprivation, low neighborhood attachment, transition and mobility, and community and individual norms that are favorable to alcohol and drug use as well as premarital sex. As the foundations of society continue to crumble and in many cases are formally attacked, discredited, and destroyed, the values that were inherently taught, modeled, and reinforced in the past are no longer introduced to the child. If these trends are not compensated for in some way, however, the child being raised in this environment has a set of very difficult circumstances to cope with.

The Impact of Media

Music and Music Video

Without a doubt, music and music videos can have a tremendous impact on the development of a teenager. Susan Baker, speaking on behalf of the Parents' Music Resource Center, says:

> It's no secret that today's rock music is a very important part of adolescents' and teenagers' lives. They use it to identify and give expression to their feelings and emotions. Studies indicate that adolescents listen to rock music from four to six hours daily. Common sense dictates that anything we are exposed to that much has some influence on us, therefore we believe that the music industry has a special responsibility as the messages of songs go from the suggestive to the blatantly explicit. There are certainly many causes for the explosion in teen pregnancy, suicide, and drug abuse, as well as the growing number of violent crimes and bias crimes committed by kids under eighteen in our society. However, it is our contention that pervasive messages aimed at children which promote and glorify casual sex, drugs, bigotry, suicide, rape, and sadomachism have to be numbered among the contributing factors.[2]

The addition of a video component to the music intensifies the impact. Together, in a subliminal way, music and media can exert a tremendous influence on young minds. The behavior that is eventually demonstrated when the pressure is on and the desire to get something (sex, drugs, relationships, etc.) is intensified can be irrational, illegal, immoral, and dangerous. The struggle to distinguish reality from illusion is made considerably more complicated. Once the subconscious mind hears something thirty to fifty times, it begins to believe the message even if it's not true. Then, when alcohol or drugs are added to the equation, the conscious mind is disconnected and removed altogether from a sound decision-making process. All that remains are thousands of unedited suggestive images locked into the subconscious waiting to drive, guide, and seemingly legitimize behavior.

I just can't talk to my parents. To them, everything is a joke. Until I find someone to talk to I'm afraid that I'll do the same thing that I did a year ago. I started to listen to Black Sabbath. I got really depressed, and I became anorexic and wouldn't eat anything. I started to break away from my family. Three or four times I had serious thoughts about suicide. I don't want that to happen again. I'm scared.

—JENNA, 9th grade

It is not our intention to generalize and put down all music. As the Parents' Music Resource Center says in their booklet *Let's Talk Rock,*

Many musicians act responsibly, which results in a great deal of good music available to the public....Musicians rallied worldwide to raise money for the poor, underprivileged: USA for Africa, Farm Aid, Hear 'N Aid, Live Aid, Hands across America, Amnesty International and Band Aid. Rock music can be a force for social good as is evidenced here.[3]

In *Let's Talk Rock,* Jennifer Norwood puts music into perspective in the context of communication:

With this in mind, parents can understand that a solution should not focus on the music as the main cause of a child's problem. Music, however, is a clue to help parents understand what fears and anxieties their children have. For instance, a child who is extremely depressed and suicidal will most likely listen to music that reflects that state of mind. Becoming aware of the content of your child's musical favorites can help you to detect depression and perhaps prevent a possible suicide. Discussions about what your child's favorite songs mean to him/her will help you to understand how your child views life and build better communication and more openness between the two of you. Don't let that conversation polarize along generational lines. Keep your discussion focused on the content. Explain firmly but nonjudgmentally why you disagree with a particular song's point of view. Challenge your child to think about what the song means in the context of his/her life.[4]

Television

Television was developed back in the late 1940s, and since then has evolved into the most powerful influence on our young people today. Parents and children alike have literally put one another on pause until the conclusion of a television program.

Television has the capability of creating images on the screen that are often sustained in the human mind for a lifetime. Back in the days of its conception, television programming represented wholesome entertainment that taught and reinforced moral and ethical messages congruent with messages advocated by the family, schools, and churches. Over the years, however, these images and messages have changed tremendously.

Remember the old saying, "Garbage in, garbage out"? That's the process that today's television audience is exposed to. Not only is the quality of that message questionable, but that message is constantly repeated — and eventually, repetition makes imagined things seem real.

In 1960 the average daily television viewing per household was 5:06 hours. By 1992, it had increased to 7:04.[5]

The average teenager spends 1.8 hours per week reading, 5.6 hours per week doing homework, and an average of 21 hours per week watching television, or about three hours per day. In contrast to the three hours per day they spend watching TV, teenagers spend an average of five minutes per day alone with their fathers, and twenty minutes with their mothers. These figures include time together at meals.[6]

The average child watches up to eight thousand made-for-TV murders and over a hundred thousand acts of violence by the end of grade school. Today's young people are digesting and recording into their brain "undeletable" messages of violence, as portrayed in shows like *Rescue 911, NYPD Blue,* and *America's Most Wanted.* This kind of show, along with the evening news, music videos, and talk shows, are inundating our young people with messages of violence, sex, vulgarity, insensitivity, and self-centeredness.

The media industry, of course, claims that their work is an entertainment contribution that *reflects* the essence of society, rather than *directs* it. But is this true? Why do companies spend millions of dollars to advertise on the same media if their commercials only *reflect* what people are doing with their products and don't *invite* (sell to) new consumers? How can a movie *reflect* society when it's shown on television, but be used as "today's lesson" when it's shown in the classroom?

> *I think that a lot of teens think that it is okay to drink because they see the beer commercials where all they are doing is having fun. What makes me mad is they never show the side-effects of drinking and what it really does to your body. I also think teens think that it is fine to drink because they see their parents drink.*
>
> —RYAN, 10th grade

The media has promoted the likes of Michael Jackson, Madonna, O. J. Simpson, River Phoenix, Kurt Cobain, and many others — all heroes who have fallen or demonstrated a dark side. The indictment of O. J. Simpson, the death of River Phoenix, and the suicide of Kurt Cobain represent symbols of an American tragedy. Yet the message remains that there is glamour, money, and excitement involved in the process. Further, sex, alcohol, and drugs are portrayed as vehicles to happiness; even Joe Camel permeates the minds of the young by glamorizing the benefits of smoking (and research indicates that, in the past few years, smoking is on the increase among seventh to twelfth graders and college students).

Why are we so surprised, then, when we see youth buying the message?

Are we willing to commit to making the necessary changes to offer them more, to show them what they can become? That may involve monitoring television viewing or simply turning it off. If children are to become lovable and capable, they need to experience dialogue and collaboration within their family. Yet television destroys the family's ability to dialogue. When the television set becomes a member of the family, it competes for — and often claims — more than its fair share of attention.

Adolescent Alcohol and Other Drug Use and Abuse

Young people who get involved with mood-altering chemicals are looking for a change of feeling. It starts as an exercise of curiosity, an experiment. Using and experimenting with mood-altering chemicals — including alcohol — comes at a time when the adolescent feels like life is forever; warnings from parents, schoolteachers, or clergy are discounted because teens don't believe negative side-effects could ever happen to *them*. As our young people begin the passage through the adolescent years, they are exposed to the opportunity for involvement with mood-altering chemicals daily. Those of us who have been around adolescents know that mood swings are frequent and often severe. Adolescents often believe that:

1. Harm or addiction will never happen to them.

2. They can quit any time they wish.

3. Information presented to them to discourage use of mood-altering chemicals is not true.

4. They themselves have no value — so who cares?

According to the Center for Substance Abuse Prevention, most young people begin experimenting with alcohol between the ages of eleven and fifteen. That's sixth to tenth grade. Young people make a decision as to whether they are going to drink (or not) long before they take their first drink. Very often this choice is based upon the use by other family members that they see at home.

Even if they get the alcohol at home, one out of seven teens who begin to drink will eventually go to addiction. Five out of seven will become abusers, with symptoms that include physical and/or emotional pain. For the adult population it is about one out of ten whose alcohol use will progress to addiction. It takes two months to two years for a child under the age of twenty-two to become addicted to alcohol. The average time is eighteen months. It takes four years to fifteen years for an adult to become addicted to alcohol. For an adult, the average is about eight to nine years.

The reason for the age disparity between adult and adolescent addiction is related to maturation and the physical development of the person. The intellectual, cognitive, and emotional development of the adolescent is not complete until the twenty-first or twenty-second year of life. The ingestion of mood-altering chemicals can potentially damage the brain at this early age and create permanent problems. It is therefore of utmost importance for us to do what we can to delay the beginning age of alcohol consumption or drug use in kids. There exists a possibility of being a full-blown alcoholic or drug addict before high school if kids begin usage at younger ages.

Consider the following analogy simply called "The Cake Story." I'm baking a cake. In the process of baking the cake, I substitute a cup of salt for a cup of sugar. I mix the ingredients and blend everything together, and then I bake the cake. When that cake comes out of the oven, it is wrecked. There is nothing that I can do to separate the salt from the cake at that point. But if I mixed the ingredients properly and then, after the cake was fully baked, poured a cup of salt on the cake, it could be brushed off without harming the cake. This can be compared to the entry of poisons (alcohol/drugs) into children who are still in the process of developing. The cooking process of their life is at its peak in adolescence. It is at this time that they are developing emotionally, psychologically, spiritually, and intellectually as well as physically. Fully matured adults respond differently to the introduction of alcohol to their system and have a greater, though not guaranteed, opportunity to consume it safely. Unfortunately, we have a tendency to measure our adolescents based on external signs of physical maturation. Consequently, we believe that our children are far more capable of handling things than they really are.

Kids are going into puberty two or three years earlier than just a couple decades ago. They are therefore looking and acting like adults earlier. We respond by giving them adult privileges because of the way they look, but ironically they are not there yet. Biologically and developmentally, their brains will not fully mature until sometime in their twenty-first or twenty-second year of life. The poisons like alcohol and other kinds of drugs admitted into the system early on will be locked into the mind and body. Like with the cake filled with salt, it will be impossible to separate them. The decision to drink also acts as a watershed crossed, tempering values and granting the person permission to try other substances.

The average alcoholic is asked as many as forty or fifty times to seek treatment before he or she goes to treatment. The average person will live with an alcoholic for six and a half years before they "blow up" and confront the alcoholic. By this time they (the co-dependent persons) are mostly angry at themselves for stuffing their resentment for all those years. The anger is then projected and taken out on the other person. So if you have someone you're concerned about — a mom, a dad, a spouse, an uncle, a grandparent, yourself — don't give up on them. Seek support (Al-Anon) for yourself if you're in a family situation that is influenced by an alcoholic (father, mother, spouse, grandparent, son, or daughter). Alcoholism is a primary disease. It is a progressive disease. It's a fatal disease. It continues to progress, so even with treatment, there may be a shortened life expectancy.

If one parent is an alcoholic, the child has four times greater a chance of being an alcoholic than does the normal population. With two parents, it's a 50–50 chance. With an alcoholic grandparent the child has a one in eight chance. That means that if we have alcoholism in our family, we need to educate our children that we don't want them to play Russian roulette with their lives. Therefore, none of us will consume alcohol. Because once the addiction starts, it goes on for a lifetime.

For the adult, a fully developed cognitive structure provides the ability to assess objectively the impact of chemical use. A developing adolescent does not have the ability to make such an assessment.

I very frequently abuse alcohol and other drugs, and I smoke cigarettes, but until now I never wanted to admit that I had a problem. All my life I never experienced the love and affection my friends got, and still I'm so hungry for it I'd do anything to make people realize that I want to be loved, too. I've had so much pain in my life that it would be impossible to write it all down in one sitting. I want to change, but I don't know where to begin.

—KATIE, 10th grade

Campus Data About Alcohol

- At both two- and four-year institutions, the heaviest drinkers obtain the lowest grades.
- Almost one-third of the students at four-year institutions report missing class due to alcohol or other drug use.
- Nearly one-quarter of students report performing poorly on a test or project due to alcohol or other drug use.
- Almost half of college students who were the victims of crime admit using alcohol or other drugs before they were victimized.
- A survey of students at a southwestern university showed that 55 percent of sexual assault perpetrators and 53 percent of

sexual assault victims said they were under the influence of alcohol at the time of the assault.[7]

In the seventh grade I had an alcohol problem. See, the only thing I ever wanted to be was popular in school. I had only a few friends because I had just moved here and didn't know anyone. I found this "friend" who rode the same bus with me. She drank, used drugs, and had sex. I knew that she was not my type of friend, but I thought that I would get popular by hanging out with her. One day my friend brought some vodka on the bus. I drank it, and then at school I was stumbling around, and then I passed out in the middle of the floor. I did this often, and I was always sick to my stomach, and I was flunking out of school. I hated every minute of it. I thought I was really popular and all. I discovered that I was more unpopular than I was before I started drinking.

—MARIA, 9th grade

Drugs: Facts for Parents

Handling and coping with drug use, especially when it directly involves our children, can be one of the most stressful and volatile activities of family existence. Adolescents reach for drugs in an effort to be included, to medicate pain, to escape, to offset boredom, to challenge authority, and just to step out to the very edge of danger. We have seen families literally torn apart by simply bringing up the subject in family discussions.

Parents must show their children tough love. On the Bill Cosby show, Bill Cosby says this to his son, Theo: "You won't use drugs in this house. When you're eighteen and out on your own you won't use drugs. When you're seventy-five and I'm dead, you still won't use drugs." That parent is talking about a partnership for life.[8]

In therapy the biggest catalytic force for change is pain. The prospect of incurring pain can therefore be a wonderful motivator for the adolescent if the parents have the confidence and the courage to make a move when their expectations have been violated. Peter Benson, president of the Minneapolis-based Search Institute, said in a recent speech, "The families of the 80's and the 90's have loved their children to death, but they have forgotten to set boundaries and articulate specific expectations." In the event that the parent chooses not to assign a consequence to drug-related behavior, I as a counselor would have to ask, "Why? What's the rationale for not making a responsive move?" A lack of response is essentially a message of endorsement: "It's okay to drink; it's okay to use."

There is a definite "gateway" present in drug use. Research shows that the use of one drug leads to the use of another. As an example, according to Dr. Gold at the Cocaine Hotline, "Almost everyone who has tried cocaine has first tried marijuana." The gateway concept alone should serve as an urgent message to the parents of the world: We must assign immediate consequences for drug use.

What Should a Parent Do?

The first and most important rule of thumb in dealing effectively with our adolescents is to understand that the person discovering or dealing with a problem of adolescent usage (or any problem, for that matter) will need help also — a support system. Dealing with the chemical usage of a child is traumatic and emotionally exhausting for parents. Many parents have joined Twelve Step groups like Nar-Anon and Al-Anon for the loved ones of the chemically dependent and have found new hope and healing in these groups.

Staying calm, rational, and flexible, yet consistently firm, is the answer to fixing the problem and moving forward without additional problems, or at least minimizing additional problems. Trying to stay calm and rational is extremely difficult. A support system helps us vent our frustrations and our fears.

It is important to understand that all families have problems, so let's not be afraid to talk about our concerns with others — not just to ourselves (which we already do too often). If we try to maintain a position of secrecy, we will aggravate the problem and we will make ourselves crazy in the process. "Crazy" symptoms include feeling extremely stressed, having inflamed ulcers, or being on the brink of a stroke.

Developing a strategy of effective intervention cannot be accomplished during a war of emotions. Let's talk through our concerns with a friend, a counselor, or a Twelve Step sponsor, and then present our adolescent with a plan of action, also known as the consequences. Our credibility as parents, for the present as well as the future, is based on our ability to present an effective consequence and follow through with that consequence regardless of the circumstance. For example, my son was out last night and got drunk. I would usually consider grounding and loss of the car keys for a period of time, but tonight is the junior prom, or it's homecoming, or it's a special concert with nonrefundable tickets. What a parent does in those circumstances is the information that will be internally processed by the adolescent and seriously considered prior to the next infraction of household rules. Do we have credibility? Only we (and our children) know our prior track record.

The best of all plans are developed before any problem hits home. If we have the luxury available, let's call a meeting by appointment with our adolescent. Let's take him or her out to lunch; we might ask our child to choose the restaurant. Let's talk about alcohol, other drugs, and sexuality, and in this time of unemotional conversation, let's ask for suggestions from our children. "What would you do if you were me?" We may be amazed at what they have to offer and what they suggest. At the same time, we can talk about what our actions and personal response might be if a crisis situation arises.

As we just said, it is absolutely impossible for a parent to devise a plan of action, without extreme emotional volatility, when the crisis is immediately at hand. For example, how do we deal with our seventeen-year-old who has been in a car accident? Nobody is hurt, but the car is totaled (he took our company-issued Mercedes without permission) and he is now being bailed out of jail by us at two o'clock in the morning. We're upset, and he's upset as well as defensive. Our best and most effective strategy is to put our kid to bed and call our support system for consultation. By doing this, we avoid the immediate anger and irrational outbursts of poorly phrased words and the consequences of the "I'm going to kill him" attitude. Conversely, we also avoid the possibility of doing too little. Logical consequences are our best possible resource. Consequences without the emotional put-downs can be powerful and effective, but they must be planned. Remember: Parents who yell the loudest and elevate their blood pressure the highest create children with selective hearing; some are even deaf to the auditory tones of a parent.

Consequences might also include some sort of professional help — for example, treatment for drugs and alcohol as well as hospitalization or outpatient therapy. Since these alternatives are extreme, it makes sense to process our thoughts with a person who is not emotionally involved in the specific problems. The best way to find help is to ask what other people did with their adolescents and inquire about the name of a highly respected counselor to help when the time comes.

Over the years, I have had dozens of parents who tried to simply dump their adolescents on my doorstep with the mandate to "fix" him or her and do it quick. Responding appropriately to the struggles of adolescence will almost always have to include the entire family in the process. Counseling has the capability to bring happiness and tranquillity to a family, but it requires the efforts of everyone living within the household.

Sexuality and the Adolescent

To begin with, it is important for parents to understand that in the early teen years the closest friendships will usually occur with the same sex. In the mental health field, this is referred to as the "homosexual phase," and it is important for parents to understand that this is normal and a reflection of a transient adolescent stage — so let's not panic. We have found that both parents and their adolescent need assurances that this is a normal and transient process.

Adolescents do begin their sexual lives by having friendships with members of the opposite sex. This will usually occur sometime during the thirteenth or fourteenth year. These relationships are almost always superficial. Same-sex friends during this same period spend a lot of time comparing notes and talking about the opposite sex. Girls are usually ready to start dating at about fourteen or fifteen; boys seem to lag behind a bit and start their dating around the fifteenth to sixteenth year. As the sexuality of our child begins to surface, it is important we parents remember to trust our children to be responsible. Let's deal with the problem of trust violation when it occurs, but at the beginning, let's learn to trust them and let them know very clearly what our expectations are so that they can understand where their limits have to be.

Let's make sure that they are well informed about the issues that are involved and our expectations, but most important, let's not be intrusive and overwhelm them.

Sexual behavior and adolescents' response to their rapidly developing sexuality are different for boys and girls. In boys the sex drive is intense. At first the drive may be satisfied by masturbation. Virtually all boys masturbate, and at first it is done without fantasies, sometimes even in the presence of other boys of the same age. Girls tend to be preoccupied with sex, but on a more romantic level, where feeling is a priority and action is a secondary consideration.

Most everyone I know drinks, does drugs, and sleeps around. I have decided not to get involved and especially with the sex thing. I want to wait for my wedding night.

—ANGIE, 11th grade

Dating is an adolescent rite, and it is dating that begins the preparation for understanding the dynamics of human interaction that will occur later in life with a spouse. Successfully relating to other people is a sophisticated activity that requires the ability to be empathetically "other-centered" rather than "self-centered."

Adolescents often see their feeling for early dating partners as true love. Part of adolescent turbulence lies in the frustration and sadness that come with the realization that there is no permanence to these early loves. For adolescents, the purpose of dating, in reality, isn't to find a person to love as much as it is to discover who they are and what is important for them.

It was just like you said. The first time we met we talked, the next time we talked a little and kissed a little, the next time we talked a little, kissed a little, and petted a little. . . . Then we started having sex. After a while we didn't talk quite as much and all that was left was sex. After seven months we broke up.

—AMY, 12th grade

Does carrying negative emotional, spiritual, and psychological baggage from previous multiple sexual encounters make a person more or less desirable as a future spouse? The presence of children, or the status of already being a mother or a father, or even worse, the presence of a permanent sexually transmitted disease (STD) like herpes, impairs the quality of life and limits substantially the desirability of an individual. As a result, an individual is set for a rude wake-up call (after the fact) as the question surfaces daily, "Does anyone love me? Does anyone want to be with me? Does anyone care?"

Adolescents are not good at long-term future planning, but in the crucial circumstances that have lifelong implications, it is important that parents hammer home the message of urgency: Instant gratification is not "free," and regardless of how good it feels, irresponsibility has ultimate costs that are unfathomable at adolescence.

On the average, by the age of seventeen, half of all boys and well over one-third of girls will have experienced sexual intercourse; by the age of eighteen around three-quarters of all boys and about half of all girls will have had intercourse.

Almost five months ago I could have had sex, but I said no. But right after that night I wished that I had said yes. Even now I wish I had agreed to have it, yet I don't understand why. My friends tell me that it was right to say no, but I get so confused. Could you help me?

— STACEY, 11th grade

Sexuality is a very private area, and it is extremely difficult for vulnerable adolescents to cope adequately with the pressures that surround this activity. Most often it is their insecurities that open up the opportunities for sexual contact.

I have an eighteen-year-old boyfriend. We are having sex. We got confused by the emotions we were feeling. Both of us are very insecure. He has been through a lot in his life, and now he has to watch as I go through a lot. Sometimes I am just so overwhelmed that I feel like killing myself.

— LEAH, 12th grade

Studies suggest that there is a direct association between alcohol and other drug use and unsafe sexual behavior. And this poses significant threats to the adolescent community. "The use of mood-altering chemicals impairs adolescents' ability to make judgments about sex and contraception, placing them at increased risk for unplanned pregnancy, sexual assault, or becoming infected with a sexually transmitted disease, including HIV/AIDS."[9]

I always thought that sex was supposed to be one of the most beautiful things that a man and woman could share. Boy, was I wrong.

He apologized that night and said that if I wanted to I could hate him and he'd understand. I wish that I would never have done any of these things. It's like you said, once you have given your virginity away, you can never have it back.

—ALISON, 11th grade

Ways to Empower Teens to Postpone Sexual Activity

Teens don't come home after their first sexual encounter of heavy petting or intercourse and say, "Mom, Dad...Guess what I did!" Communication with your teen needs to take place in the form of an ongoing dialogue, beginning prior to puberty and continuing throughout adolescence. There are no quick fixes, and waiting to have "The Talk" normally involves waiting until "after the fact," and then it's too late.

Parents are the best teachers of their kids on almost every issue, especially relating to those most intimate areas involving character development and values-based choices. When surveyed, "95 percent of teens wanted sex education from their parents, 44 percent indicated that they received some education, and only 10 percent said that they had good communication on these and other sensitive areas of their development."[10]

It is a parental privilege to share our ideologies and values with our children and to be involved with their character development. Discussions such as these are exciting and insightful. They will introduce us to our deepest self and force us to move beyond our personal inhibitions as we openly share about the most intimate areas of our past and current relationships. In the context of an open dialogue, we can explain the characteristics that make up of successful relationships and the proper place and purpose of sexual intimacy.

1. MAINTAIN OPEN COMMUNICATION AND ALLOW FOR TWO-WAY DISCUSSIONS. This is not the time for "The Talk" and a memo with a list of our expectations. Waiting for the school to cover sex in biology class is not communication.

- Let's begin by listening more and talking less. The more that our kids say and the less that we say the better.
- Create an environment where our teens feel invited to ask questions.

2. SHARE YOUR HOPES, THOUGHTS, BELIEFS (WHICH MAKE UP YOUR VALUES), AND EXPECTATIONS. Teens naively believe that any activity that leads to a positive feeling must enhance their relationships and that all euphoric pieces of relationships are signs of "love." They often believe that sexual intimacy is a natural part of their reality in relationships. Teens haven't yet experienced how, in reality, sex before marriage leads to confusion. Feelings of lust will inevitably become confused with love and blur the decision-making process.

- Let's begin by writing down our own values and views on sexuality. This includes the meaning behind sexual intercourse — physical, emotional, spiritual, and social. Let's share our views and let our children know the reasons behind our feelings and values.

- Ask your teen what qualities are important to them in the individuals they choose to date.

- Let's invite our teens to explore "our" past dating experience, including what we did, how far we went, what we felt, our mistakes and successes, and what we discovered. How did we meet our spouse? What feelings were present on our first dates, break-ups, and everything in between? How did it feel to be used or to use someone else?

- If we could date all over again, what would our adolescent years be like?

3. LET YOUR CHILD KNOW THAT YOU WANT SUCCESS FOR HIM OR HER. Success is not just the absence of pain but complete, lifelong fulfillment. Every choice they make now is part of their journey, and these choices create pathways or roadblocks. We want our children to live a life free from distractions so they can become fruitful, independent, fulfilled women and men.

- Let our teens know how they benefit from following the guidelines set before them.

- Express how their sexuality is a gift.

- Explain how sex is good in the context of an appropriate relationship and at the right time.

- Help your teen understand that saying no to sex doesn't mean saying no forever, but just "not now."

- Explore with them the realities of desire in the context of short-term dating relationships. If our kids are unable to still be friends after breaking up, they went too far.

4. SHARE HOW SEXUAL INTIMACY IS MUCH MORE THAN A PHYSICAL ACT. Research demonstrates that in dating relationships, the physical tends to confuse and damage good relationships while extending bad ones. Physical intimacy doesn't create love; it is an expression of love.

- Share what sexual intimacy does to us and how it creates bonding in a loving relationship.

- Talk about how difficult it is to break a physical bond once it's established. It is hard to go back to holding hands after becoming physical.

- Relate how having a physical relationship can tend to cause a breakdown in communication outside a committed, lifelong relationship.

5. EMPHASIZE THAT NOT EVERYONE IS HAVING SEX, AND THE MOST EMOTIONALLY SECURE TEENS ARE CHOOSING TO SAY NO. At adolescence the "need to be" physical in a relationship is normally founded in feelings of inferiority and insecurity. It's much easier to go against the flow and overcome peer pressure when adolescents feel good about their individual characteristics and understand that it's okay to be different.

- Help them understand that self-discipline and self-control are possible and lead to personal freedom.

- Share how in any relationship, including marriage, exclusive use of physical contact as an expression of love is a sign of a very shallow relationship.

6. EXPLAIN THAT TEENS ARE READY TO DATE WHEN THEY ARE ABLE TO SAY NO. Adolescents need to understand that they are ultimately responsible for themselves and their bodies. Dating will eventually lead to some level of intimacy, whether desired or convenient.

- Ask them what this means to them.

- Let's share with our adolescents information about how to date. Discuss every facet of dating, including how far to go physically and why.

- Let's empower our teens to believe that it is okay to say no and help them feel they have permission to decline physical activity — at any level.

- When dating, our teens need to be able to:

  - Know their standards.

  - Live these standards.

  - Communicate these standards, even if it means facing rejection.

7. **EXPLAIN CLEARLY WHAT DATING IS ABOUT.** Discuss how dating is designed to help teens discover and develop who they are. Dating is more about *becoming* than *finding*; it's about *becoming* a person that someone else would wish to *find*. Dating is about:

- Socialization.

- Personality development.

- Emotional and spiritual development.

- Having fun.

- Discovering the qualities for future mate selection.

8. **IF IN OUR DISCUSSION WITH OUR TEENS WE DISCOVER THEY ARE SEXUALLY ACTIVE, THEN:**

- We need to calmly ask them what it means to them to have become sexually active with someone they haven't made a lifelong commitment to.

- Have them own up to their behaviors and look at their values.

- Let them know how we feel.

- Explain confidently and gently what we think, and why.

- It's okay to say that we are disappointed, discouraged, and sad. It's okay to tell them that we are confused and then ask our teens to help us understand.

- Keep in mind that in all communication, our discussion, empathy, and understanding do not mean we are granting our teens permission to be physical.

9. BE PATIENT.

- If we're angry and judgmental — we lose.

- If we're looking for quick fixes — our children lose.

- Look to resources with values-based programs because these programs educate the whole person with a commitment to the long-term benefits and consequences.

- Reinforce discussions with materials such as books, pamphlets, and videos from local health facilities, crisis pregnancy centers, libraries and churches supporting our values. These will also include facts on sexuality as well as the realities of STDs.

10. DEAL WITH BIRTH CONTROL AND ITS IMPLICATIONS. Contraception deals only with the physical aspect of a relationship. For a healthy understanding, it is necessary to talk about the holistic aspect of sexuality as it relates to the entire person and his or her lifelong best interests. Contraception is not 100 percent effective as a physical means of birth control. Condoms fail 5–15 percent of the time for pregnancy and 2–20 percent of the time for sexually transmitted diseases. "Kelly and her son's father — the only sex partner she has ever had — were using condoms, and Kelly was also taking the pill, but she became pregnant anyway."[11] If we mislead our teens into believing that "safe sex" is possible, we set them up for even greater risks. All forms of birth control fail to protect our teen emotionally, psychologically, intellectually, and socially. Additionally, birth control will not protect our teens from feelings of being used, taken advantage of, violated, and cheaply valued, which eventually will lead to resentment.

- Saying that we don't want our child to be at risk but then saying go ahead and accept sex puts our child at risk with or without birth control.

- Believing they are going to have sex anyway and suggesting birth control moves our communication directly to intervention and skips prevention. This is founded in an assumption that our kids are not teachable.

Pregnancy Termination or Adoption?

These are possibly the five most sensitive paragraphs in the entire text. Just thinking about the word "abortion" touches the core of everyone's being in some way. As you reflect on the next few words, please understand that our objective is not to impose a belief or to moralize about "who" gets to make "what" choice. Rather we respectfully ask you to consider what the choice signifies and, ultimately, what are the feelings, needs, beliefs, and values that may be guiding this choice — either way. Beliefs don't just happen. They are formed by coupling information and life experiences with feelings.

Abortions in the United States have steadily increased from a little over half a million in 1972 to well over a million and a half in 1991. Sixty-three percent of these abortions are performed on women never married.[12] "Abortion terminates 30 percent of all pregnancies. Twenty-five percent of the abortions are for teenagers, and nearly forty percent are for women who have had at least one abortion in the past."[13] Every year over two million requests for adoption go unsatisfied. Would adoption even be an option?

As we discussed in Chapter 5, there are pathway and roadblock choices in life, and no decision is consequence-free. What will our adolescents choose to do should a pregnancy occur? Do they know? Do they know why? We also suggested that the best time to assess a situation, reflect on core values, and make a choice is ahead of time. Our kids will then already know what to do when a situation arises and will be able to ward off potentially painful outcomes. Internal pressures will also be eliminated, while at the same time external pressures are diffused.

> *About six months ago I found out that I was pregnant. I tried to get some of my friends to help me, but no one would. So, I went to a party about two weeks later and tried to get this guy mad enough to hit me. My plan worked! I don't know what I was thinking when I did that. I feel so ashamed of myself, and I've been trying to forget it. I just wished that I had gone to my parents.*
>
> —CHAR, 11th grade

In Chapter 2, we said that pure love is selfless and always focuses on giving the gifts of one's life to others. In pure, genuine, and compassionate concern, could having an abortion — or not having an abortion — possibly lead to gnawing emotional or spiritual questions for our sons or daughters or their future children as they mature into adulthood? Psychologist Vincent Rue, Ph.D., states, "Abortion has a painful aftermath, regardless of the woman's religious beliefs, or how positive she may have felt beforehand about her decision to abort."

> *I was eighteen years old when I got pregnant. I wasn't serious about my boyfriend. It was a casual relationship. I thought I had to have an abortion in order to make something of my life. I now talk to youth groups and students about abstinence and I share my story. To them I plead, "Please don't make the same mistakes I did."*
>
> —MICHELLE, young adult

Let's explore this topic delicately with our teens. This discussion is highly emotional and off-limits almost everywhere else in society. Every week in school gyms, auditoriums, and hallways, teenagers fall into my arms, sobbing about the choices they've made or feel pressured to make. Who else is going to confer with our children on this issue? The family is possibly the only forum left to help our teens make these critical discoveries and decisions regarding premarital sex, pregnancy, and the value of life — one way or another.

Depression and the Adolescent

As already noted, one of the biggest sources of depression for the adolescent is the separation of parents by divorce or death. Kids will forever spend their energy wishing and hoping that Mom and Dad could have stayed together or might get back together. No matter how good or how bad a marriage might have been, the child will almost always love both parents. Even parents who have been abusive discover that there is a sense of forgiveness on the part of children and a fantasy that "we can begin again and this time be free of problems."

> *Have you ever felt like sometimes the world would be better off if you weren't even born? I feel worthless. Like I can't do anything right to please anyone. Especially my mom, she's always coming down really hard on me for no reason. Right now I enjoy going to school or any other place just so that I can be away from the house and my mother.*

*I am also considering running away from home. I'm really sick of life
at home, and I get confused about what I should do now.*

            —JACKIE, 9th grade

For Jackie her perception is 100 percent real. If we talked to her
mother, we would probably discover another story that doesn't at
all resemble this one and find that her interpretation is also 100
percent accurate. As we have all heard, "Reality is in the eyes of the
beholder." Jackie is no doubt having the mood swings that all adolescents have. Parents in situations like this need to patiently sit
down with their children and talk through frustrations and help
them to clarify in their minds over and over again that they are
loved, but love means providing structure. Structure is often irri-
tating for the adolescent, who feels a need to run away. Again, for
all of us, the grass is always greener on the other side of the fence.

*I'm the guy who wrote to you a couple of months ago concerning my
life. I wanted to die. I recently joined a musical at school, and as a
result I became friends with these two other guys. They really helped
me raise my self-esteem. They couldn't have cared less how I dressed
or the way I looked, but they always found good things to say about
me. There are many other kids who tease me (I'm overweight). In the
past I kept thinking that if I didn't look the way I did, I'd get more
friends. Strange, but that's what I always thought until I met these
new friends in the musical.*

            —TRENT, 10th grade

Trent doesn't tell us how he arrived at the decision to join the
school musical, but it is clear that it changed the course of his life
in a dramatic way. Such situations can come to every one of our
adolescents if, first, they can be patient and, second, look for alternatives that create the needed solutions. Adolescents (and the rest
of us for that matter) are always looking for the easiest way out
of painful situations. Somehow today's adolescent has been taught
that suicide is quick and easy and takes away all the pain.

*I'm scared to talk to my parents because sometimes I get emotional
and cry and that's not acceptable behavior, at least not at my house.*

            —CATHERINE, 8th grade

The American Medical Association has told us that 75–85 percent of all physician office calls for medical reasons are due to

stress. What a statistic! If we, as the adult role models, could only demonstrate for the young people of the world how to talk about feelings and deal openly with the secrets within our families, we would contribute toward making America a healthy nation, and one free of stress-induced psychopathology.

Suicide and the Adolescent

Since 1960, the rate at which teenagers take their own lives has more than tripled. Hopelessness, helplessness, depression, and not having the appropriate controls available to cope with their excruciating pain plague many adolescents. They want the pain to go away. They want to be in control, and they want to be loved.

Finally, I got sick of everything. I tried to take all my problems away by hanging myself. Luckily the rope wasn't tied right, so I fell to the ground. I decided to just quit drinking all together. It wasn't easy, but I did it. Now I'm an honor student and a freshman in high school. I've never told anyone this until now. Thanks for sharing your letters and experiences. I now know that I am not the only one.

—FELICIA, 10th grade

Suicide is a cry for help. It's a sign that screams "I am losing control, and I want the control back." We have had teens tell us that they sleep with razor blades under their pillows or bring pills to school in their purse or pocket. Why? It's not that they plan to kill themselves, but just in case they want to, they can. Again, we witness a need for control at a time when the loss of control and fragmenting foundations are the key characteristics in a whirlwind of life changes commonly called adolescence.

I want desperately to feel special. I hate when I compare myself to other people. How do I stop?

—DODI, 9th grade

From an adult perspective, the problems that plague the adolescent might seem to be minor, but from the adolescent perspective they are monumental. An example might be failing an exam or breaking up with an important friend. Potential suicide victims almost always feel isolated and unable to talk to parents and then often feel that there is no close friend or confidant with whom they can share their distress and who will understand. The problem is therefore analyzed (in the presence of emotional swings) by a person who has concluded that there are no other alternatives.

If we as parents even begin to suspect our teen has suicidal thoughts, it is important that we seek immediate help with a professional counselor. Recall that one of the major characteristics of adolescents is that they choose to distance themselves from their parents, often for no apparent reason. Even the adolescent doesn't fully understand it. Therefore, the parent cannot work through the intensity of this kind of problem alone.

About seven or eight years ago, I was working with an adolescent boy named Ted. Ted had been a real problem for his parents behaviorally, and he had been referred to my office by the school. We had developed a good relationship over a period of weeks, but the parents really disliked the intrusion of a counselor into the privacy of their lives. I knew that Ted was suicidal, and so I developed an agreement with Ted that he would call me if he ever got so depressed that he felt suicide was the only way out.

I got a call at my home one Saturday night. Ted told me that he had just overdosed and was ready to die. I immediately called his parents, who were upstairs in the living room of their home. Both parents disregarded my call as "just talk" on Ted's part — "he's always saying stuff like that." I was quite frustrated and scared for Ted, so I drove directly to his house and without even ringing the doorbell entered the home and went to his room. By that time he appeared to be sick, and so I alerted the parents that I was taking Ted to the hospital. The parents arrived at the hospital about an hour later and heard the doctor explain that Ted's stomach had been pumped, and he would survive. They were also told that without medical attention at that time, Ted would have died.

Not all teens who talk about suicide try to commit it, but if we even suspect that our young person is down and dejected — let's make a move.

It's been so long since I heard "I love you" from any relative that I wonder if I exist to them. Last year a friend of mine shot himself. I had attempted suicide a year before that and I was close to being the same way. I needed to unload after Dave's death. My parents just said, I'm sorry. If my own parents didn't care, who would? I let that anger and frustration and hurt build up inside of me. Again, I tried suicide. Slit my wrists. Well, my counselor called my parents and all they said was, "You know better, you're smarter than that." End of conversation. I am sixteen, work three jobs, baby-sit weekends, I'm in band (vice-pres.), choir (treasurer), swimming (captain), several clubs, why? To get a little recognition. I try so damn hard to get just one, "I'm proud of you." I'm an honor student, don't drink alcohol or do other drugs. What do my parents want? Last year they did not attend one of my concerts. I am slowly dying inside. HELP!!!

—HESPER, 12th grade

I don't know if Hesper's parents do or don't really care. That isn't the issue. The issue is that Hesper's perception is that they don't care, and she is shouting out for someone, in particular her parents, to notice. Children's perception of the world around them and their life is their reality. The only way for the reality to change is for the perception to change.

Hesper needs validation. Her parents have a tremendous opportunity, but for whatever reason they are electing not to fill the need. The only way for Hesper to get through her pain is, to paraphrase her words, "to listen, be present, grant validity and significance to my feelings, take me seriously, cheer for me, show up, grieve Dave's death with me at my pace, take the time to communicate, and please say I love you." The solution is in the letter. It almost always is.

Suicidal Warning Signs to Look For in Your Child:

- Sees life as very difficult and impossible to master.
- Seems to be sad a lot and cries frequently.
- Doesn't sleep well and has changed eating patterns.
- Becomes isolated and has lost friends.
- Is unable to talk about feelings and explain the periods of dejection.
- Shows self-destructive behaviors (driving recklessly, drinking heavily, taking drugs).
- Sometimes says things like: "I wish I was dead"; "What's the use in living anymore?"
- Inquires about techniques of successful suicides.

The last few months have been terrible! Life is not fair! Two months ago a classmate was killed in a car wreck due to alcohol. Two weeks later my uncle was killed. That was bad enough, but then my grandpa dies. Why? Is this some kind of punishment from God or something? These people meant everything to me, and now I'm supposed to say good-bye to the people who have always had a major role in my life. I can't and I won't do that! Why couldn't he have taken my life, too?

—BRENDA, 8th grade

Young people want their pain to go away, yet they don't seem to have the resources available to work toward a solution and develop a support system. In the past, family and extended family networks were in place to lend support. Today, children are just too isolated.

Chapter Commentary

The content of this chapter could be read as a message of gloom, but the material is presented for purposes of encouragement. The family and the adolescent of today need to know where they are and where they have come from if they are to move forward with clear direction for the future.

The family is the most important influence in the life of an adolescent. In order to maintain that position, the family needs to attack whatever tends to move its adolescents away from the family unit. Teaching values is an indispensable resource for generations to come, so let's not take the responsibility lightly. Let's consider how we and our family can offset societal trends and voids.

The world of today is definitely interesting for average teenagers and their families, but the bottom line comes down to ethics and values. Who are our models? Who are our heroes? Who are our rock stars?

Young people operate in a world governed by popularity; they will sell out their ethics and values to "be popular." Girls will "give" sex to be popular; boys will take steroids. Whatever it takes to fill the void of friendship and loneliness is directly related to what teenagers will do to capture a bit of the limelight and the attention they want.

The family as we have known it is at great risk unless the pendulum begins to swing in the opposite direction in favor of family and family values.

POINT TO REMEMBER

- *Establish standards of behavior concerning drugs, drinking, dating, curfews, and unsupervised activities, and enforce them consistently and fairly.*

Chapter 8

Rites of Passage and Assets That Create Identity

$\mathbf{I}$T WAS MANY YEARS AGO NOW that I was thrust into a coaching situation. Two of my early adolescent sons wanted to play Little League baseball. At the time of registration, a plea was sounded for coaches, who apparently were in short supply. I didn't know anything about coaching baseball, so I did what so many of the other fathers were doing — I just ignored the call for help. Eventually, a representative of the league called me directly. I told him about my lack of experience, not only as a coach but as a player. He told me that the process was simple and involved nothing more than letting fourteen kids have a good time. I was further coaxed with the pitch that there were three fathers who would work as assistant coaches, but nobody had the time to commit himself as head coach.

A sense of responsibility welled up within me, and I suddenly found myself accepting a position for which I had never been trained and had absolutely no experience. Baseball was a game I occasionally watched on television or infrequently at the baseball stadium. Suddenly, with no experience, I was about to become a teacher of baseball skills. Now that I look back, I see it as a situation very similar to that of being a parent. There I was — no experience but carrying the title of head coach.

I did what any honorable person would do in that circumstance. I began to research the process and see if I could quietly discover how baseball coaching was done without divulging too extensively my ignorance about the specific details related to techniques and especially team development. My initial trip to the local bookstore brought to my attention a text called *The Psychology of Baseball*. It seemed to contain all the information that I would need, so I bought it. I carried the book home in a brown paper bag in an attempt to enter my home without the embarrassment of my children knowing what I had in my possession. I didn't have the book a day before it was discovered, and I was exposed as a true rookie.

I could tell that my kids were proud to have me as the "head coach," but nevertheless they ridiculed me ad nauseam about my need to keep referring to what they called *The How to Play Baseball Book*. To this day, my kids still make fun of my coaching experience, ball in one hand and book in the other.

The irony was that it actually worked. Three fathers came forward as my assistant coaches and — probably out of fear of being elevated themselves to the "head coach" position — never said a word about what I was doing and how I was doing it. I became a sponsor for the team, and we were called the ESA Counselors.

The kids and all the coaches wore hats and shirts broadcasting the ESA emblem, making all of us look as if we knew what we were doing. I felt like a fraud, yet I parroted the concepts that I acquired in the book, and I actually sounded as if I knew what I was talking about. I would call out some of the familiar sayings: "Choke up on the bat," "Give the ball a ride," "Everybody down, get those gloves ready."

I came to my coaching experience with a bias. I had always been offended by the seemingly abusive yelling of other coaches and the dictatorial pressure they placed on young impressionable kids. I told myself that I would be a different kind of coach. I would treat everyone with dignity and patience, I wouldn't yell at anyone regardless of what errors were committed, and, contrary to other teams, I was going to let every team member play any position that he wanted to play. I would not favor the alleged superstars, and instead I would give equal playing time to all players.

Human worth and dignity is important to me. I like seeing all people treated equally and with respect. This is important to my family, so we treat others with respect, honor, and equality.

—JEFF, 7th grade

I called an organizational "beginning of the year team meeting" at my home, and I was rather startled to find that everyone on the team showed up, excitedly enthusiastic and with a parent in tow. My book said that the design of this initial meeting was simply for purposes of having the team get acquainted and hear about the coach's philosophy of baseball. Since I honestly had no philosophy of baseball, I pretended that I was confident and somehow demonstrated that I knew what I was talking about. It seemed to work. People left the meeting smiling, enthusiastic about my comments and believing my statement that "more than anything else we will be having fun together." I also said that "winning wasn't nearly as important as enjoying what we were doing," to which the audience responded with a hearty applause, indicating their approval.

> *I can show my courage by not doing anything against my beliefs. I've been doing that all my life. I've seen other people use courage by standing up for what they believe in by going on strike. It has been shown to me that I can do it, too.*
>
> —ANDREA, 7th grade

I did exactly what I had promised. Every two innings I rotated every team member into a new position. Everyone got to bat, and as a team we participated in a special out-of-baseball activity every week. After practices, especially the hot practices, I would invite the boys over to our home to cool off with a swim in our pool before heading home. We bonded well, and everyone seemed to like each other and enjoy their time together.

One problem I never anticipated was resistance from parents. People would come up to me and tell me that I was short-changing their youngster by not letting him always play the same position — third base, or short stop, or whatever. One of the comments I still remember was, "You're making them jacks of all trades and masters of none. Can't you just help them to specialize?" Interestingly, the kids never complained, but the parents did. The ones who wanted their kids to be superstars wanted their kids to play and others to be benched. In spite of everyone's misgivings, we won very frequently. We even made it all the way to the league championship that year.

One of the more exciting events in my short coaching career came the final week of the baseball season. Winning the upcoming game would make us the league champions. A boy named David approached me after practice one day and asked, "Coach, I have always wanted to pitch, but nobody has ever let me because I don't have very good control of the ball. I know that next week is our final championship game, but do you think that I could pitch in that game?" He reveled in my positive response when I told him that he could work with me all week in practice as preparation. I know it was one of life's thrills for the young kid, David, as well as for his parents, as they watched their son pitch the final three innings of the year-ending championship game. What an experience for myself, David, his parents, and the team. We won and were the league champs, but most of all, everyone played and had fun.

Parents as Coaches

This baseball vignette is very similar to the experiences of parents as we move toward the development of families. As parents, we all come to the experience as rookies, and we do the best job that we can possibly do. Much of our work is based on intuition and the modeling that our own parents demonstrated for us. We make mistakes, and we work to correct those mistakes, but all in all, we love our kids and want nothing but the best for them.

As in the baseball experience, sometimes it is important for us as parents to pick up the "how to do it book" and with that reading stimulate within us some ideas that might successfully bring our parenting style into sync with what we intuitively believe and want for our children. Parenting is a difficult job and is the only profession that doesn't come with an owner's manual. Baseball is a mental game, just as survival as a parent is a mental game. All of us from time to time wonder if we are being effective and doing the best job that we can.

Parenting Tips for Developing Happy and Successful Families

As a single-parented family:

- Let's keep our spirits up by developing a support network. Let's accept that our job is more than twice as hard as a dual-parented family, but we will survive.

- Let's not tell our children about problems we are having with the other parent, or problems we are having with life. Let's save that for our adult network. Let's allow our child to be the child and not fill our needs for a best friend.

- Even if we are totally broke, let's look for ways to develop excitement and have fun with our kids. They will remember the fun times, not the tough times.

As a dual-parented family:

- Let's lead by example. The respect and helpfulness that we display with our spouse will be emulated by our children.

- Let's share the responsibilities of parenting.

- Let's work to insure that both parents deal with discipline in equal proportions — that is, let's not threaten the kids with the arrival of the other parent.

- Let's look for ways to have fun together. Let's set up weekly "specials" as an opportunity to get away from the general routine. One week Mom leads, the next week Dad leads. As our children get older, let them lead or pick the family activity. Let's create memories related to fun activities and the presence of the total family.

Rites of Passage

Over the generations society has seen what we now refer to as a "rite of passage" as a declaration that "I have finally made it." Bud Grant, the former coach of the Minnesota Vikings, tearfully declared in his Hall of Fame induction speech, "If my father were here today, he would yell out with pride from the audience, 'Ya finally made it, kid!'"

All of us want to feel important, and we all want applause to ring in our ears. Ironically, applause can be heard differently by all of us, and therefore it often has to be interpreted by individuals themselves.

Examples of rite of passage experiences in the past were clearly found in the message that was sent with the arrival of special opportunities. Back on the family farm of decades past a youngster knew for sure that he was growing up when he got his chance to go out alone and retrieve eggs from the chicken nests, eggs freshly laid that day. A youngster also received a clear message that he was growing up when he got to drive the farm tractor. Right around the age of ten or eleven years, when the feet were barely able to touch the tractor peddles, there existed a sense of pride when the child had control of the tremendous power of a machine that was previously controlled only by adults, or at least those older than he.

Along with those rite of passage activities came clear definitions that stated that a person was now old enough and mature enough to make a contribution to the welfare of the family. All human beings desire the importance that comes with making a contribution. When and how that contribution is delivered is individual to every human being, but there has always existed a clear message that "you can only do certain things." Doing those certain things therefore meant that growth was occurring.

Farm families exhibit an innately healthy tendency that we all could find a lesson in. The need to shape the work and chores of the farm naturally bred values and messages of significance that came from one's ability to contribute. For the most part, society has made it more and more difficult for young people to grow and discover that same growth experience based on their contribution.

Back in what we call the old days, a contribution might be made by helping with the dishes. While the children were doing the dishes, or at least helping with the dishes, a parent might find significant opportunity to teach and pass on value-laden messages as well as validate contributions made by their children. In today's world, the opportunity for dish-time teaching has been deferred to a process of loading one machine as quickly as possible so that we can run off to watch another machine.

Rites of passage in our society today don't reflect opportunities to help as much as they reflect on the aging process and what "I am entitled to do" as a result of age. Healthy, positive examples might include: driving a car, dating, lettering in a sport, getting a spot in the band, a role in the school play, or a job, staying up later, graduating from high school, graduating from college, going into the service, getting married. Outside of these activities, it is perceived that there aren't a lot of opportunities to validate the significant opportunity of contribution and the internal message that contribution can bring to an individual. As a result, adolescents reach for their own rites of passage that foster personal messages of significant value. They may find that value in a rather perverse way through activities like use of alcohol or other drugs, sexual involvement, smoking, peer and gang affiliations. A powerful and painfully real "rite of passage" can be found in the increase in teenage pregnancies.

More than one child in eight is now being raised on government welfare through Aid to Families with Dependent Children (AFDC). Social spending by the federal government (in constant 1990 dollars) has increased from $144 billion in 1960 to $787 billion in 1990.[1] That is a fivefold increase in only thirty years.

Contributing to these statistics is the underlying belief that I can count on a guaranteed amount from the government for each child I have. In some ways, the current policy actually encourages illegitimacy and rewards a lack of responsibility. Welfare does not economically penalize people for having children, which would be a natural deterrent. What's more, the stigma of having children as a teenager has been removed, or at least neutralized. Today, the teenage mother is found in the hallway of the school showing off her "cute little one." We actually see and counsel children who have chosen to have babies so that they have somebody to love or to be loved by.

These strategies discourage commitment and marriage as a prerequisite to having children by not providing consequences, clear expectations, and limits. There is no need for the father to stay in the home or participate in the responsibility of raising children, yet for the young man, having sex is often a rite of passage within his peer group.

If adolescents feel very strongly that something is important to validate their growth, some sort of behavior will probably move them in that direction no matter what: for example, alcohol is adult, sex is love, a baby will fill my need for love, speed is power.

I am still a virgin and I want to save that for my husband, but I'm so screwed up that I use the very thing that I cherish (my virginity) to get attention.

—CINDY, 12th grade

Families can create their own rites of passage for family members, but at the same time we need to understand that implementing these rites of passage is extraordinarily more difficult today than in decades past because of the decomposition of the family structure and the alluring societal pressures of the environment in which adolescents live.

Families could certainly move forward with the message of growth for members with activities as simple as putting the star on the Christmas tree, mowing the lawn, washing the car, shoveling the driveway, cutting the turkey at Thanksgiving, cleaning the bathroom, and taking out the garbage. These are in fact activities that represent a message of growth and contribution. Sometimes for a parent it just seems so much easier to let high-tech inventions take over for us and eliminate the activity. By doing this, we avoid the conflict and arguments from the adolescent, who is, for the most part, self-centered and not generally ready for "other-oriented" activities that represent contribution.

Other positive activities that promote growth are Scouting, youth clubs, church groups, extracurricular programs, and volunteer activities, as well as anything that involves a meaningful contribution to the welfare of the family. Rites of passage are important and necessary to validate identities. They help young people determine where their existence actually lies in terms of "my place in the family." When I can understand my place within my family of origin, I will then find myself, the validation of existence, and my place in this world.

Organizations like the Scouts provide healthy guidelines for rites of passage. Achievement in the Boy Scouts and a person's rite of passage are determined very specifically by the accomplishment of certain activities. Mastering a task brings the award of rank advancement. You know exactly where you stand from minute to minute. In the family of today, young people seem to have a good deal of difficulty understanding where they stand and how they fit in.

Creating Opportunities for Positive Growth Through Asset Development

Recently, Dr. Peter Benson and the Search Institute have developed some interesting research on the profile of American youth.[2] In the course of his research, Benson found that there is a direct relationship between the prevalence of trouble at adolescence and the lack of something that he refers to as assets. In *The Troubled Journey*, Benson defines assets as "factors promoting positive teenage development. These assets may result from 'external' factors such as positive relationships in families, friendship groups, schools and the community, or they may result from 'internal' factors reflecting the teenager's personal convictions, values and attitudes."[3] Assets have the capability of equipping adolescents with the ability to make wise choices. Benson found that the average young person has only 50 percent of the external assets and 60 percent of the internal assets.

Search Institute also explored what it referred to as "deficits," which it defined as any factor inhibiting healthy adolescent development. These deficits include influences that limit access to external assets, which then block development of internal assets. Deficits are the liabilities that make harm more probable.

Adolescent Deficits

We will list the deficits first, as a way to help us see which factors influence our adolescents, and then look at strategies for building good and positive behaviors. As you reflect on this list, think about the needs of your adolescents, and how you may compensate for, offset, or eliminate the following deficits. We have also indicated the frequency that the deficit applies to the 47,000 students surveyed in grades six to twelve in 111 communities spanning twenty-five states.

LIST OF DEFICITS
(percentage of all surveyed who could identify with this deficit)[4]

1. **Home Alone.** Student spends two hours or more per day at home without an adult.   58%

2. **Hedonistic Values.** Student places high importance on self-serving values.   48%

3. **TV Overexposure.** Student watches TV three hours or more per day.   40%

4. **Drinking Parties.** Student frequently attends parties where peers drink.   31%

5. **Stress.** Student feels under stress or pressure most or all of the time.   21%

6. **Physical Abuse.** Student reports at least one incident of physical abuse by an adult.   17%

7. **Sexual Abuse.** Student reports at least one incident of sexual abuse.   10%

8. **Parental Addiction.** Student reports a parent "has a serious problem with alcohol or drugs."   7%

9. **Social Isolation.** Student feels a consistent lack of care, support, and understanding.   6%

10. **Negative Peer Pressure.** Most close friends are involved in chemical use and/or are in frequent trouble at school.   2%

Adolescent Assets

This research is particularly relevant for parents because it demonstrates, quite impressively, the correlation between positive adolescent behaviors and asset possession. The greater the number of assets an adolescent has, the more success that adolescent has in avoiding problems, especially some of the major problems associated with adolescent development.

> *The first time I was ever drunk was when I was fourteen. My friends didn't ever ask me to smoke or drink. I did it because I wanted to try something different. My life was getting bad. I hardly ever see my father. It hurts me that I can never have those father-daughter talks about boys and stuff.*
>
> —JENNIE, 10th grade

Examine the following list of thirty assets while reflecting on your own family environment. We can use it as a checklist for both ourselves and our teens. Let's develop a strategy to incorporate and reinforce as many asset opportunities as possible and to eliminate or compensate for deficits. Strive to create an environment that fosters and models as many of these assets as possible; we can also edify others in our adolescent's circle of influence who are doing the same.

Consider how we as parents are working in an effort to encourage our adolescents to incorporate these assets in their personal lives. It's a great place to start effective communication. Let's let our teens know the significance of these assets and why we are striving to help them incorporate these qualities into their life. We might just discover that they want to be cooperative.

THIRTY ASSETS

I. Asset Type: Support

Teen   Parent

— —   1. **Family support.** Family life provides high levels of love and support.

— —   2. **Parent(s) as social resources.** Adolescent views parent(s) as accessible resources for advice and support.

— —   3. **Parent communication.** Adolescent has frequent, in-depth conversations with parent(s).

— —   4. **Other adult resources.** Student has access to nonparent adults for advice and support.

— —   5. **Other adult communication.** Adolescent has frequent, in-depth conversations with nonparent adults.

— —   6. **Parent involvement in schooling.** Parent(s) are involved in helping the adolescent succeed in school.

— —   7. **Positive school climate.** School provides a caring, encouraging environment.

II. Asset Type: Control

— —   8. **Parental standards.** Parent(s) have standards for appropriate conduct.

— —   9. **Parental discipline.** Parent(s) discipline adolescent when a rule is violated.

__ __ 10. **Parental monitoring.** Parent(s) monitor "where I am going and with whom I will be."

__ __ 11. **Time at home.** Adolescent goes out for "fun and recreation" three or fewer nights per week.

__ __ 12. **Positive peer influence.** Adolescent's best friends model responsible behavior.

III. *Asset Type: Structured Time Use*

__ __ 13. **Involved in music.** Adolescent spends one hour or more per week in music training or practice.

__ __ 14. **Involved in extracurricular activities.** Adolescent spends one hour or more per week in school sports, clubs, or organizations.

__ __ 15. **Involved in community organizations or activities.** Adolescent spends one hour or more per week in organizations or clubs outside of school.

__ __ 16. **Involved in church or synagogue.** Adolescent spends one hour or more per week attending programs or services.

IV. *Asset Type: Educational Commitment*

__ __ 17. **Achievement motivation.** Adolescent is motivated to do well in school.

__ __ 18. **Educational aspiration.** Adolescent aspires to pursue post–high school education (e.g., trade school, college).

__ __ 19. **School performance.** Adolescent reports school performance is above average.

__ __ 20. **Homework.** Adolescent reports six hours or more of homework per week.

V. *Asset Type: Positive Values*

__ __ 21. **Values helping people.** Adolescent places high personal value on helping other people.

__ __ 22. **Is concerned about world hunger.** Adolescent reports interest in helping to reduce world hunger.

__ __ 23. **Cares about people's feelings.** Adolescent cares about other people's feelings.

__ __ 24. **Values sexual restraint.** Student values postponing sexual activity.

VI. Asset Type: Social Competence

__ __ 25. **Assertiveness skills.** Adolescent reports ability to "stand up for what I believe."

__ __ 26. **Decision-making skills.** Adolescent reports "I am good at making decisions."

__ __ 27. **Friendship-making skills.** Adolescent reports "I am good at making friends."

__ __ 28. **Planning skills.** Adolescent reports "I am good at planning ahead."

__ __ 29. **Self-esteem.** Adolescent reports high self-esteem.

__ __ 30. **Positive view of personal future.** Adolescent is optimistic about his/her personal future.

This list of assets and their definitions is a great road map for creating a strategy and a sense of direction as we work toward becoming the best parents possible. The following "Dear Mom and Dad" letter tells us, in a wonderfully concise fashion, how to most effectively parent our children. The author is anonymous.

Dear Mom and Dad:

Don't spoil me. I know quite well that I shouldn't have all that I ever ask for. I'm only testing you.

Don't be afraid to be firm with me. I prefer it. It makes me feel you care about me and are protecting me.

Don't let me form bad habits. I have to rely on you to detect their presence in me during the early years.

Don't make me feel smaller than I am. It only makes me behave stupidly "big."

Don't punish me in front of people if you can help it. I'll take much more notice if you talk quietly with me in private.

Don't protect me from the result of my actions. I need to learn the painful way, sometimes.

Don't be too upset when I say "I hate you." It isn't you I hate but your power to control me.

Don't take too much notice of my small ailments. Sometimes they get me the attention that I need.

Don't nag. If you do, I'll have to protect myself by appearing deaf.

Don't forget that I cannot explain myself as well as I would like. This is why I'm not always very accurate.

Don't make rash promises. Remember that I feel badly let down when promises are broken.

Don't tax my honesty too much. I am easily frightened into telling lies.

Don't be inconsistent. That confuses me and makes me lose faith in you.

Don't tell me my fears are silly. They are terribly real, and you can make me feel better if you try to understand.

Don't put me off when I ask a question. If you do, you will find that I stop asking and look for information elsewhere.

Don't ever suggest that you are perfect or never wrong. It gives me too great a shock when I discover that you are neither.

Don't ever think it is beneath your dignity to apologize to me. An honest apology makes me feel surprisingly warm toward you.

Don't forget how quickly I am growing up. It must be very hard to keep up with how I am changing. But please do try.

Don't forget I love experimenting, trying different things. I couldn't grow without it, so please put up with it.

Don't forget that I can't grow up healthy without lots of love and understanding. But I don't need to tell you that, do I???

With Love,
Your Child

POINT TO REMEMBER

- *Let's lead by example, not by dictatorial edict.*

Chapter 9

Enhancing Self-Esteem Through Communication

$\mathbf{I}$N OUR WORK WITH FAMILIES, we see that parents are clearly regarded as more influential by their children when they show affection and are uplifting and supportive (even in the tough times). Parents regarded highly also express appreciation to their children freely and are available to talk with their children in an environment free of judgment.

> *My parents give me good advice but most importantly they listen to me and they don't make a joke out of my problems and stuff. It makes me feel better about myself when I know they are listening and interested in helping me.*
>
> *—*ANDY, 9th grade

The primary factor in the success or failure of a relationship, both within and outside of the family, is communication.

> *My dad tells me he loves me, he always hugs me, and he makes me feel that my time with him is valuable. He talks to me about sex, girls, guys, religion, and study habits. He talks with me in a way where I feel I can be open because he treats me more like a friend. My mom encourages my self-esteem.*
>
> *—*TRAVIS, 10th grade

Effective communication and rapport-building begin with two or more people asking themselves several questions: "Can I trust you?" "Will you be honest with me?" "Are you sending consistent or mixed messages?" "Will you be open with me?"

If my parents could understand more about a teenager's life today and the difference in how it was for them, they would probably be able to understand me more. They would have a better idea about what's going on in my life and they might be a little easier on me.

           —STERLING, 12th grade

The best and most effective time to establish and build rapport is in situations where no problems exist. During these times everyone is in a good mood. Connecting in conversation is greatly improved, for all of us, when we are alert and calm.

As we encourage you to communicate in your family, we would like to share with you twenty-three positive self-esteem-enhancing areas to consider as you reflect on how you interact with your children, spouse, and family.

1. Let's Develop Trust

What is the greatest cause of problems in communication? Jerry Johnston, author of *Why Suicide?*, believes that it is a breakdown in trust. "Whenever trust is lessened or lost in a relationship, communication suffers severely. Teenagers and their parents can relate in a wholesome, positive way only if they trust each other. And this means that there is room for failure and forgiveness."[1] Trust is developed in a relationship that involves consistency, knowing that something or someone will be there.

How can I talk to my mom about my drug problem? How can I ask for help?

           —DEAN, 9th grade

Individuals who grow up in the absence of a trusting relationship become self-contained, independent, and unwilling or unable to interact and be vulnerable in the world around them. Violation of trust creates a natural survival reaction, leading to the building of walls to prevent further pain. If this is part of our children's past, whether through mistakes of their own or as a result of being victimized, they need time to heal.

A couple of years ago I started having flashbacks about being sexually abused. I see my brother in my old house. He starts to do something, and then I don't remember the rest but it scares me. I'm scared to tell my parents or anyone in my family because I know they won't believe me.

—TAMMY, 12th grade

It's not that Tammy's parents won't believe her, but her perception that they won't is causing her to freeze up and leads to her lack of trust. Trust violations are painful and create deep memory anchors that are difficult to dislodge. Professional counseling may be necessary to help a person fully grieve and be released from the grasp of painful memories and patterns.

The best way to set up a safe environment is to start early with our kids, to demonstrate that they can always sit down with us and talk over what's happening in their lives. The conditioning that occurs with the little crises when they are younger helps our adolescents learn how to risk and then confidently invite us to share in the intimacies of their ever-expanding concerns.

If the only time that we sit down with our children is in the midst of a major crisis, then the foundation for trust and sharing is not established, and we set them up to expect ineffective communication.

You need honesty to build relationships and trust. If you don't have trust, you don't have friends or any relationships. Therefore, you are all alone.

—LEVI, 7th grade

One of the best things that we can do as parents to foster trusting communication is to take the time to be personally vulnerable and open with our adolescents. We can make an effort to reach out and talk about our own teenage experiences and then let our children talk with us and ask us questions. As they mature into young adults, we can experience teachable moments with them by talking about our own past mistakes (as they apply to their lives) and what we learned from those mistakes. If we put aside our need to be in control, to correct, to criticize, to complain, and to teach, as well as our alleged perfection, we will create a trusting environment where our adolescents feel safe to risk expressing themselves openly.

I try to talk about the guy who broke up with me with my friends and they tell me that I am stupid and that I shouldn't think about him because he hurt me so bad. So I never get to talk about it, but I can't help thinking about him.

—MELISSA, 10th grade

Let's not be preachy, and let's refrain from telling them the old story about walking to school seven miles, without shoes, uphill — both ways. If we give them the real stuff, we will lovingly overwhelm them with our sincerity, vulnerability, and honesty, all the while creating respect. This sharing can be a catalyst to facilitate deeper and more meaningful communication.

When our kids see us reflecting on our past mistakes, this grants them permission to make mistakes and reinforces the trust necessary to have the courage to share, forgive, let go, and then move forward. Through embracing our past mistakes, we set aside all blame and model responsibility. Parents who defend their pasts inadvertently set their kids up to be defensive, untrusting, and irresponsible. Defensiveness almost always tends to reflect issues that have not yet been dealt with. One of the wonderful gifts of adolescents is that they introduce parents to realities of our own pasts that have not yet been openly addressed. Together we can share the moment, make new discoveries, and create deeper, more trusting relationships.

2. Let's Be Models

Our actions speak so loudly that our kids can hardly hear our words — much of the time. Research consistently demonstrates that non-drug-using and nonsmoking adolescents are least likely to have fathers and mothers who smoke or drink. Even elementary school children will tend to unconsciously select their friends based upon the perception of their own parents' values. Remember that you set the example. Your kids know what you're doing.

My real mother does drugs and I could have done them also. But, instead I'm now living with my dad and stepmom. Life is worth more than pot and speed. I didn't know then if I did the right thing, and now I don't even speak to her. I've lost respect for her. Is that okay?

—JEN, 8th grade

We teach children how to blow up balloons by showing them how. We teach driving skills by showing them how to drive. We

teach them how to drink and smoke by showing them how...
modeling. But then we expect to teach them how not to drink
or smoke by telling them, "Don't do it!" — all the while showing them how. That doesn't work. Teach them safe drinking by
modeling safe drinking. Teach them safe sex by modeling a loving
relationship for them and speaking openly about what constitutes
a loving relationship.

Back in college, a buddy of mine by the name of Dave invited me
over to his place for dinner. What did that mean? We were going
to have something out of the microwave oven, right? We actually
had a two-course dessert: milk and Oreo cookies. Dave grabbed a
handful of Oreo cookies, and he set them on the table on top of a
napkin. Then Dave started spinning the tops off the Oreo cookies. He then ate one of the little cookie parts while putting the
other part of the cookie down; little white faces were shining up
at him. Well, because I was in his home, it felt right to do the same
thing. I didn't want to mess up, or feel out of place. So there I was,
spinning the tops off my Oreo cookies, too. This is the power of
modeling at work.

Dave is spinning the tops off his Oreo cookies, so I'm doing the
same thing. He sets three rows of three on a napkin; I've got seven
cookies lined up. While waiting, so as to not get ahead of him and
mess up, I'm thinking, What's he going to do next? Make double
thicks? Take all the cream and scrape it into a ball and eat that sep-
arately? Possibly just eat the cookies? What's he going to do next?
So I waited.

One by one, he ate the Oreo cookies. I did the same thing. Well,
months later, long after that incident, Dave invited me home for
a weekend to get away from college and hang out on the farm.
That evening we sat down to enjoy dinner with his family. After
dinner we were sitting on the couch, and his mom was sitting
beside Dave. Dave's brother, father, and I were also sitting there.
Dave's mom said, "Hey, would you like to have some dessert?"
I responded that I would. Dave's mother went off to the kitchen,
and after a few moments she came out with a bag of Oreos. Dave
grabbed a handful of Oreo cookies, I grabbed a handful of Oreo
cookies, Dave's brother, mother, and father each grabbed a handful
of Oreo cookies. Wouldn't you know it, Dave's dad started spinning the tops off the Oreo cookies. As I looked around the living
room, everyone was spinning the tops off the Oreo cookies.

Thomas Jefferson said, "When it is a matter of taste, go with the flow. If it's a matter of principle, stand like a rock." Morals are built on values. Values are built on principles. Eating Oreo cookies is a matter of taste. Underage use of alcohol or other drugs and premarital sex are matters of principle. As parents, we need to help our children stand like rocks.

I was out with my friend and speaking colleague Bill Sanders, in Kalamazoo, Michigan. We were sitting at a Hardee's, and after I had eaten, I took my straw from my drink to make a whistle. Bill's four-year-old twins and seven-year-old daughter were sitting there. I demonstrated how, after you pinch the bottom of the straw and slide your fingers up to the top of the straw, you can make a little whistle out of it that goes *shweee*. It's a shrill sound, and it just gets higher and higher as you go *shweee*. So I was doing this *shweee*, and the kids were trying to duplicate it, and they were going *pbrisst* and spitting in their drinks. Well, Bill and I thought it was cute and were splitting our sides laughing. After blowing and whistling for about two minutes, we noticed that all the children in Hardee's were trying to whistle with their straws, just as we were doing. Two tables over, a mother was getting frustrated with her three small children. She and her friend were watching their three kids trying to mimic me. She turned to her friend and said, "See how those kids will copy anything?" Then she turned and continued to smoke her cigarette. Who is going to teach her children not to smoke? Will this parent be threatened by the school teaching her children to live out a value different from her own — though healthier?

3. Let's Support Family Values

Family values and expectations give children the foundation for making the difficult choices they must face day in and day out. The clear transfer of values is important to help them establish their identity and withstand or neutralize peer pressure. Roy Disney, brother of the gifted illustrator and visionary Walt Disney, said, "When values and standards are clear, decision-making is easy." People don't cave in from what is on the outside; they cave in from a lack of what is on the inside. What's on the inside with your kids? When young people know what they believe, they not only know what to do but know who they are.

In our families, what values are we striving to model for our children? Values are not transferred to children. Information is shared. How parents live their lives gives information to their children. The children then establish their own values. Children learn from what we say and from what we don't say, from what we do and from what we don't do.

According to some studies, 7 percent of our communications are in our words, and our words are almost always in line with the values we would like to teach. But 93 percent of what we communicate is transferred through our tone of voice, voice inflections, and body language — in other words, how our life is lived. This, of course, reflects our true values and determines what we are actually teaching. What we live is what we learn, what we learn is what we practice, and what we practice is what we become. Are we living our expectations *for* and *with* our children, or are we teaching one thing and living something else?

My dad showed me that you should be honest. Once he was buying something at Target and got back $100, which he should have not received. He gave it back, and that is a time my dad showed me to be honest.

—DAN, 7th grade

If we are not living in line with our stated values, we will experience an incredible sense of internal conflict. Emotional pain and depression begin to develop at the moment we compromise on and begin living outside of our value system. At that point, we often want to blame the world and its pressures for the pain we're in, when the real issue is related to something lacking in our lives or is rooted in something that we haven't adequately dealt with. When we line our behaviors up with our values, we are able to achieve peace. It's also easier then to communicate to our kids a consistent message of what we are expecting and hoping about how they will live their life.

We had a panel of men with AIDS come and speak at our school. It was pathetic! Even with AIDS they said that they were still sexually active, but they did tell the men that they slept with that they were infected. They said that it's all right to be sexually active because we are young and it's impossible to control our hormones. I'm still upset because the school didn't research and find out what these men believed in.

—Sarah, 11th grade

What are our personal values and standards? What are our family values and standards? Do our children know what our standards are?

4. Let's Instill Compassion Instead of Tolerance

While the pressing goal in our society seems to be tolerance for everything, the outcome is complacency. Tolerance sounds like a fair and desirable objective, but as I tell parents, the most unloving thing we can do to our kids is to tolerate them. Tolerance does not guide, direct, or discipline. Tolerance does not teach. Nature abhors a vacuum, and tolerance creates a vacuum that simply will be filled with someone else's values.

Compassion, on the other hand, is what is really desired. We hope that our society will be compassionate, that our friends will be compassionate, that as parents we will be compassionate. Compassion involves lovingly presenting a truth or standard. With compassion, the truth is not changed, watered down, or discarded; standards are not relativized. Rather, compassion simply shares truth and standards with care.

When I was a child, my mom locked the cupboards where the liquid cleaners were kept. My father put the gasoline for the lawn mower out of my reach. In both cases, they said that these chemicals were poisonous and off limits. They did not concern themselves with the fear of imposing their values on me or infringing on my civil rights. Freedom of choice was not granted or tolerated. To tolerate and empower all my desires would have been unloving and would have taught me that life is consequence-free. They could have said, "Here's the information on the liquid Drano and gasoline. If you drink them, you will die. Now, knowing that, make your own choice. We don't want to impose our values on you." As ridiculous as this sounds, how different is that from the current family, school, and societal discussions surrounding alcohol, other drugs, condoms, and sex? It's an intriguing state of affairs when a child needs a permission slip from home to get an aspirin from the school nurse but not to get a condom or an abortion.

The world is right when it cries, "Do not judge me, love me!" We have misinterpreted judging *people* with judging *behaviors, attitudes,* and *thoughts.* I'm glad my teachers graded my work in the classroom and that my coaches responded to my performances on the field. I need my parents to be involved in my development in the home. Through their delinquency, incorrigibility, and rebelliousness, the kids are shouting, "Teach me, guide me, form me!" They are not crying, "Ignore me, enable me, tolerate me!"

5. Let's Strive for Consistency of Discipline

Children remember the consistency in our discipline, and they also remember the inconsistency in our discipline. Discipline means to educate toward changing behavior and developing self-control and character. Punishment is to inflict pain or to impose a penalty. To punish is to hurt; to discipline is to guide.

Our child comes home, we smell alcohol on his breath, and we say, "Have you been drinking?" What is he going to say, "No, I was next to somebody who was"? Okay, so then we say, "How many have you had to drink?" What number does the child give the parent? Either one or two. Where does the child get that number? From his parents. It's a number he believes his parents will accept. From there he might offer a smokescreen of sorts. He'll say something like, "Well, there were other people there smoking marijuana, and somebody else was doing coke and crack and speed." "Well, you didn't do any of that?" "No, Dad, Mom. I only had two drinks." "Oh, thank God, you only had two drinks. Now go to bed; we'll talk about it in the morning."

This is an example of situational ethics. What was bad is now not as bad as something else, so therefore it's okay. It's also called value clarification, line-continuum, or sliding-scale values. And we just made right something that we know and believe to be wrong. Let's take a stand and not be afraid to be consistent. The primary teacher of children is the parent. We need to know what we're going to stand for. We need to know what we believe in and what we would like our children to believe in. Then let's consistently reinforce and discipline with those standards in mind.

There are very few families who haven't discovered that a five-year-old child can easily wear down an adult with persistence. Can you imagine then the capability of an adolescent? In the end, when all the discussion is concluded and the facts are in, it is in the best interest of the child — the adolescent — to comprehend this very important message related to security and stability:

> *I have parents who love me, and care about me. They have expectations and I know what those expectations are. I know that what they say, they mean! If I violate those expectations, I know that I can expect consistent consequences, no deals, just the consequences.*

Adolescents test the limits, and from time to time they will move toward the edge of trouble, but in the back of their minds they are glad for their parents' loving guidance. Limits, consequences that are embraced as fair, and consistent discipline lead to assurance and peace of mind. The lack of consistency leads to anxiousness on the part of our children and an environment that doesn't foster self-control.

6. Let's Be Available

Who is the number-one source of help? Who do kids want to go to before anybody else? They want to go to parents, but by the time high school arrives, peers become number one. Parents are then number two, and out of nine choices, teachers are seventh. Why? The Search Institute in Minneapolis has discovered that 75 percent of children *wish* they could go to their mothers for help. Sixty-three percent of the children do go to their mothers for help. Fifty percent of the children wish they could go to their fathers for help, while 31.7 percent of the children do go to their fathers for help. And 7.7 percent of the children wish they could go to their teachers for help; 12.7 percent actually do. As helping resources, teachers are the only group where more people go than actually want to go.

So often we say it's the counselor's responsibility. Fix my kids. After all, I'm just the parent, what do I know? You're the counselor; you understand kids. Well, 2.8 percent of the children wish they could go to their counselors for help on the most sensitive of issues, and only 1.8 percent do.

My assistant, Jane, has four boys. A few years ago they had 126 home basketball games between them. She and her husband were playing tag team trying to get to most of these games. One night one of her sons came home and announced that he hated math. Not only did he hate math, but he hated the math teacher, and he hated school. Why? The answer was clearly in the fact he couldn't do the math, and his dignity was on the line. So he said, "I hate it!"

The solution was a parental response of involvement. Jane sat down her son for several hours and worked through each of the math problems with him until he felt comfortable and confident that he could do the problems himself. He then liked math again. Education in the early years has to be a partnership between us and our children. They need our support and, as parents, our greatest investment in our children can be an investment of our time.

Another great time to communicate with our kids is in the car. What's on a child's mind? To find out, join a car pool. Kids are convinced that nobody is driving that car. They will share secrets in the back seat; they will sing dumb little songs; they will talk about anything. So we might try saying to our son or daughter, "Tell you what. Let's go out for an ice cream cone and bring some of your friends." Then drive them to a town two hours away for an ice cream cone and then drive them back. Take some time in the car to discover that young people will share and open up — and that we will, too.

7. Let's Strive for Quantity Time That's of Quality

Kids need their parents' time — and the more, the better. Although research affirms this, we certainly don't need proof. As life gets busier, however, "quality time" is being substituted for "any time."

Our children spell love "T-I-M-E." Time. Our being available to our children teaches them that they are valuable and important and nurtures the natural needs of our children.

Parents spend only minutes per day with their children in comparison to past generations, who spent hours with their children. According to Stephen Glenn in *Developing Capable Young People*, "Parents today are spending only 14.5 minutes per day in meaningful dialogue with their children and 12.5 minutes of that is what is called bulletin board work. Have you cleaned your room? Have you done your homework?" That suggests that there are only two minutes of love and affirmation left for one-on-one contact with each child. Two minutes a day, fifteen minutes a week, talking to the child about what is important to the child. Generations past used to spend two to three hours a day interacting with meaningful dialogue with their children.

One of the primary reasons that peers have such power in our adolescents' lives is that they spend more time together. It's not peer pressure. It's peer influence. What can we do to increase the time we spend with our kids above the national average? Let's ask ourselves, "What can I do to increase the time?"

The family is the only core unit left in our society for supporting and nurturing the moral development of the child. Still, we've come up with the notion of "quality time" to justify our changing priorities.

When I was a swimmer at Ames High School in Iowa, Coach Whitmer expected the whole team to stay after school for about two hours. In response I said, "That's ridiculous, coach. I think if you could give us a thousand-yard quality-time workout, we could be out of here in fifteen minutes." The coach insisted that we would stay for the full two hours.

My teachers expected me to attend eight classes a day, fifty minutes each. Can you imagine that? What would have happened if I had gone to each of my instructors in high school and said, "The only reason I have to be here so long is because of your own inadequacy and inefficiency. If you could just come up with a fifteen-minute quality-time lesson plan — eight lessons, two hours — I'd be out of here by ten in the morning." They would have thrown me out of their office, perhaps with a polite comment: "I'm sorry, some things just take time." Sounds a lot like raising children, doesn't it?

8. Let's Talk to Them About What Is Important to Them

A couple of years ago I presented the keynote address to the Future Homemakers of America State Conference for the state of Iowa. It was an upbeat, loving presentation. Afterward I sat down with five girls, juniors and seniors in high school, and three adult leaders at a table where we shared a pizza. Turning to the girl sitting next to me, a junior in high school, I looked over and said, "Did you enjoy my speech?"

She said, "Yeah, and my grandfather, he died three months ago."

I didn't give a speech on death and dying, I thought to myself. Why did she bring up her grandfather? What did she want to talk about? Her grandfather! What did I want to talk about? Me! My speech! My favorite topic.

How often do we strive to meet children on their agendas, rather than fit them into our agendas? Children sense love the most not when we talk about what's important to us: "Have you cleaned your room? Have you done your homework? Have you done your chores?" Children sense love the most when we talk to them about what's important to them.

So I responded to the young lady sitting next to me and said, "What about your grandfather?"

"Well," she said, "you know, he had cancer, and he was really sick. And I knew he was going to die. I went over to his house, and I got a lot of those grandfather hugs. And I said to him that I loved him and he said that he loved me. And then he died. And he was gone. And I didn't cry. What's wrong with me? I didn't cry."

I again turned to her and asked her to tell me about her grandfather. About five seconds later she burst into tears, and the grieving process began. I immediately gave her a hug, and we talked for quite some time — about her agenda.

Another girl sitting directly across from us spoke up and asked, "Would you be my daddy?" At first I was startled by the question, especially since this girl had a daddy already. What I discovered was that a human being, while watching an expression of love, in her hunger for some of that love was asking for the same kind of attention I was giving to the girl with the deceased grandfather.

Parents, there is so much to be hopeful for because our children want to receive our love and our messages of love. Are we prepared to meet our children on their agenda?

I really need some human love. My life feels unbalanced in every way. During Christmas and Valentine's Day, boyfriends and girlfriends are all huggy-huggy. Watching this depresses me, and I feel very empty. I need someone to love me.

—TERI, 10th grade

Many adults have a hard time getting close to other people. As fathers, especially with our daughters, we have a hard time when they turn twelve, thirteen, and fourteen and start going through the changes of puberty. "I wonder if I'm going to touch them in the right way. I don't want to come across as abusive. Those are girl/woman-type problems. Talk to your mother." But what often happens is the daughters interpret this response as, "Dad doesn't love me as much anymore." And they search for a boyfriend to give them what they really want from their father. Often the first sexual experience of young adolescent girls is in search of their father's love. In *People* magazine, a teenage mom's mother said, "My girls never had a decent male figure in their lives. I know from my own experiences. They were seeking that ultimate love, to feel special. You're blinded by your needs — and you end up wrecking your life."[2]

A nineteen-year-old girl called me up once and said,

> *You know, the day that I had my first period, my mom told my dad. My dad took me out for a drive. And he said, "Dear, your mother shared with me this great miracle of life that has just begun with you. I want you to know how proud I am of you, and that now you can create birth, the miracle of life. I want you to know how special and precious that is. The gift that you now have to give to someone is worth preserving." I'm nineteen years old, and I'm still a virgin. My dad knows that I have urges for guys. I figured if he could talk to me about my period, he could talk to me about those urges, too. We share everything. And I feel closer than I've ever felt before.*

I happen to know that five years later she is still a virgin and often reflects on the conversations she's had with her mother and father.

It is really important to understand that things don't have to be just Mom's stuff or just Dad's stuff. If there are two parents in the family, God put them both there for a reason, so let's use them both. And if there is one parent in your family, do what you can to reach out to significant other adults of the opposite sex to help reinforce and contribute to the development of your child. And if you can, always try your best to utilize the other parent, if that relationship with that child is still available and sound. Regardless of circumstances, children will love both.

9. Let's See Life Through Their Eyes

Work hard, really hard, to forget that you're an adult, and remember what it was like to be an adolescent. Try processing life through their eyes.

I hope we're all still there for each other when we get older. I've made so many mistakes already, I'm surprised that my parents haven't thrown me out of the house.

—JASON, 11th grade

The parent has been a teenager. The teen has never been a parent. Empathy and simply striving to see life through the eyes of the teen are at the foundation of bridging the gap.

It's like when our seventh-grade daughter comes home and tells us she's in love. We know that it's a crush, the simplest of early loves. We know that it's only puppy love and the beginning of a long line of many relationships. And so, out of our wisdom and insight we say something like, "That's nothing — you'll get over it."

And our child, inside, is saying, "But this is everything to me." Then she comes home a week later and they've broken up and she's crushed and feels rejected.

We say something helpful like, "Well, there's lots of other fish in the sea."

"Thanks, Mom, I'm glad we had this little talk. I feel better now. And besides, I don't like fish, anyway."

"Well, you'll get over it."

"I don't know if I will. I've never been through this before. I don't know if I'll get over this."

"Well, it's silly for you to feel like that."

"Well, if my feelings are wrong, Mom, then I must be wrong, too!"

Let's strive to see life though our children's eyes, celebrating their world, thereby validating their existence and their being.

10. Let's Acknowledge Our Children's Feelings

The first step toward emotional disturbance is keeping feelings to oneself. Acceptance of feelings leads to a sense of security for all of us. If my feelings are wrong, then I must be wrong, too. Treating our kids with respect is teaching them self-respect. Who they are is fine. What they are doing may not be right. Life is an echo, and how we are treated teaches us who we are. Respecting our children teaches them self-respect.

When I was in the sixth grade, I was seriously thinking of taking an overdose so that I wouldn't have to worry about anything anymore. I wanted to take the easy way out. I never did have the courage to go through with it. I was very upset because I told my uncle that I wished he was dead. Well, that was the first time I ever had a wish come true. I'm sure that he knew that I didn't mean it, but I never got a chance to take it back either. He was killed in a car accident that night. I still haven't forgiven myself.

—LORI, 10th grade

Feelings aren't right or wrong; they're just simply real. It's what we do with those feelings that can be right or wrong. Giving dignity to their feelings is a way of honoring our children so that they can acquire a true sense of personal worth.

11. Let's Avoid Adultisms

Author, speaker, and trainer Stephen Glenn calls it an "adultism" when we forget what it was like to be a child, expect our children to share our insight, and then judge them accordingly. "I am ashamed of you" judges the person. "Surely you know that..." causes them to believe that they are stupid and incapable. "Why don't you think for once?" What if they are thinking? Our children could interpret our comment to mean that their minds are in fact incomplete. "It's not the end of the world." Relative to their life experience, it may very well be.

We say to our child, "Why don't you just grow up?" "Psst, Dad. That's what I'm trying to do. Help me." "Well, you're acting so childish." "Guess what — I am a child!" These kind of statements are bound to come out from time to time. Other comments come from the kids themselves: "I'm confused. I mean, I walk into the locker room at school, I look down, and I've only got seven hairs on my chest. My buddy over there looks like a carpet sample." In my mind, I'm going, "What's wrong with me? I'm falling behind, and I'm just getting started." Nothing is wrong with them. Nothing. They need us as parents to let them know that they are okay and that we care about them in every way.

If we compare our child to another child, we belittle the existence of the first child. By saying, "Why can't you be more like Jimmy? Like your older brother?" we discount our child's very existence. When we compare our children to each other, we deny them the right of being who they are as individuals.

12. Let's Ask "What" Instead of "Why" Questions When Possible

Have we ever asked a child the "why" question? "Why did you do that?" "I don't know. It seemed like the thing to do at the time." If we ask a child, sitting in the center of broken dishes, on the kitchen floor, "Why did you do that?" do we expect an answer like: "I don't know, I guess I just didn't want to watch T.V. for the next three weeks?"

When possible let's ask "what" questions. "What happened?" "What do you feel?" "What do you think?" "Well, I was reaching for the dishes and I slipped and fell and they all came down on top of me." Okay, I can deal with the "what" question.

Our son wrecks the car. We ask, "Why did you do that?"

"Well, things were going pretty smooth in the family. I just thought I'd rough 'em up a little bit."

Or we ask, "What happened?"

"Well, Dad. I was out with Sheri, and you know how I like Sheri. And I was looking into Sheri's eyes, and gosh, Dad, she's got pretty eyes. And I was looking into her eyes instead of the taillights of the car ahead of me. You know how the ones on the outside, they get bright red sometimes? You know, they just light up, and that means there is a deceleration happening in front of you. I didn't notice that they were getting bright and everything, and, well, Dad...Do you know how much plastic is at the front end of a vehicle? They're just like hanging there. I mean, the bumper is on, but just, like, hanging. These cars are not what they used to be."

Our child can deal with a "what" question. "What" questions lead to responsibility, but "why" questions invite rationalization. "What" questions are nonjudgmental: "Why" questions carry an air of judgment, making them threatening. "Why did you put this answer on the test?" causes the child to feel stupid. "What were you thinking when you answered it this way?" This is an open-ended question, which invites discussion. "Oh, this is what you were thinking. Let's talk about what you were thinking." Talk about the behavior, discipline the behavior, but love the child. Let's help the child to feel that love unconditionally.

Our son comes home — four "F's" and a "D" on his report card. "Why did you do that?"

"I don't know."

Or, "What happened?"

"Well, Dad, apparently I was spending entirely too much time in one subject."

"Tell me one positive thing about this report card."

"Well, at least I'm not cheating."

Our adolescents can deal with "what" questions. "What do you feel? What do you think? What do you sense? What's going on?" And let's listen.

13. Let's Listen to Our Children

The missing link in communication with kids seems to be listening. Our best response is always to listen and listen attentively without interruption. So often we ask children what they think, then we tell them what they think, then we tell them what they need to think, and then we say, "I'm glad we had this little talk." As one little boy said, "Daddy, I don't think you can hear me if you're always talking when I'm talking."

You know your parents are really listening to you when they respond with real answers. They aren't just telling you what you want to hear or what they always say. You can tell when the answer is an answer for you and not one that's been used on an older brother or sister.

—KATHERINE, 12th grade

If we listen to what's on their lips, we know what's in their heart. Listening involves the exchange of information and understanding. The key word here is "exchange." What that means, parents, is that we have permission to ask questions, and then we should refrain from interrupting. Even if we really don't know where to start, let's begin by listening.

I can tell they are listening when they make a comment about what I said. It makes me feel very good to know that they are listening to me because they expect me to listen to them, so I expect the same back.

—TYLER, 12th grade

If we want to be strong communicators and good listeners, we need to pay attention to all forms of body language — touches, signs, periods of silence, eye contact, full presence. Let's listen with our entire being. Let's give them our undivided attention and open body language. Let's use strong eye contact. This shows that we value them. Empathic listening means being totally present.

I know that my parents are really listening to me when they don't joke around while I'm talking to them and do things like nod and say, "Uh-huh, I understand." It makes me feel like what I have to say is important.

—MIKE, 11th grade

To validate our children, when we get into a listening mode, let's explore our kids' perceptions about their reality. Let's not tell them how to feel or how things ought to be...let's just listen. Listening and healing go hand in hand. Let's really listen. People who feel listened to will feel significant, which leads to a feeling that they are being taken seriously and sincerely loved. Once that happens, they believe "I have self-worth." A parent's way of thinking, seeing, and feeling is not the only way. Understanding doesn't mean agreeing, and acceptance is not necessarily approval, but both agreeing and acceptance will lead to a sense of rapport, intimacy, and love.

One thing that I would want to get across to my parents is that I want to have a say in conversations we have. To have them hear my side of the story, my point of view on a subject. They have to understand that saying no before I can have a say is not right, and if we talk about the situation, it would be better.

—LYNN, 11th grade

A wonderful approach by parents is to say, "I can't stop you from hating me, but you can't stop me from loving you." Loving techniques that we can incorporate into our relationship with an adolescent are to smile, be low-key, talk less, and listen more.

14. Let's Understand Our Child's Learning Style

All human beings learn in one of three ways, or in a combination of these three. They are auditory learning, visual learning, and kinesthetic learning. If we really want to reach people, we must reach them in the way that they process life, not the way we process life, in the way they learn, not in the way that we learn.

> *I am heavily into drugs. I smoke about every night with my best friend. I decided to do this because I cannot talk to my parents about anything. When we have a discussion, they do all the yelling and screaming, and I do all the listening and crying.*
>
> —JERI, 12th grade

It is our natural tendency to believe that everyone understands life the same way that we do. But it is not so much how we show love, as it is how others perceive it. Successfully reaching out to our children involves being able to see, feel, and hear life through their reality. Let's listen to everything our children are saying and how they are saying it. Let's even listen to what our children are "not" saying. Many people will tell us more through what they don't say.

Auditory people have keen hearing capabilities and can retain vast quantities of information that has been transmitted to them via the spoken word. These are people who do well in high school and college lectures and then neglect reading the book because they got so much out of the lectures. When communicating, they will say things like, "I *hear* what you are saying."

> *I don't have anyone to **talk** to. The friends I have now, I don't know if they are real friends. So I don't know if they would understand what I want to **talk** about. I don't want to go to the guidance office to **talk** to a counselor, because there are more important people that need to **talk** to them.*
>
> —JENNY, 12th grade

Visual people can see things that most of us can't, and their ability to remember or comprehend things that they have seen is superior to their ability to learn in other styles. This is the person who can read a book and digest significantly more information than others who might have to read and reread for even minimal comprehension. They respond in conversation with, "I *see* what you mean." They respond when we show them love.

> *I wish you could have **squeezed** me in to talk to me after your speech. It really bothers me when people can't **squeeze** me in. See, my parents are divorced and my father **never has time for me**. At first, I*

blamed the divorce on myself. I figured [it wouldn't have happened]
if I hadn't always gotten in the way. I was only nine.

— STEPHANIE, 9th grade

Kinesthetic people are the feeling people. They have an intuitive sense that successfully guides them through their daily activities. These are the people who will learn and understand far better in situations where they have what we call hands-on experience. They can *sense* or have a *feeling* for what is communicated. "Gosh, I'm *feeling* for you."

*I just wanted you to know that I have **learned** a lot from my **mis-***
takes that I made during my freshman and sophomore years in high
*school. I also **keep learning from the ones** that I have made this*
*year, and I also **learn from the mistakes** that my friends make and*
*I **try not to do** the same things.*

— ANDY, 11th grade

The most effective way to lead our kids is along the path on which they learn the best and most efficiently. If we try to push our learning style onto them and it's different from theirs, we will encounter frustration as well as significant resistance.

15. Let's Communicate "I Love You Unconditionally"

In Elkhorn, Nebraska, a fourteen-year-old girl was sitting at an evening community program where I was giving a presentation. She stood up, came forward, took the microphone, and said, "You know, this guy spoke of unconditional love tonight. Unconditional love. Not I love if . . . , or I love you because . . . , but I love you no matter what." "You know it's so hard. You know why? Because I haven't heard 'I love you' from my parents for three years. For three years. If just somebody would say, 'I love you.' I just wish you would, please, somebody, say you love me. Please." I remember the mothers in the first five rows leaning forward instinctively to give love to that girl — the love they'd give to their own child. One mother went so far as to write me: "Can I write her? Can I call her? Is that invading the family's privacy and territory?"

Have you heard of "I love you if . . . " relationships? I love you *if* you clean your room. Does that mean you hate me *if* I don't clean the room? I love you *if* you do your homework. Does that mean you hate me *if* I don't? Of course, you don't. But, remember, their perception is their reality. What is their perception, parents?

"I love you because you scored that touchdown, Son." The child may think, What if I dropped the ball? Will you not love me? If a son drops the ball, where does he look first? The stands for his parents. Where does he look second? Coach on the sidelines. What a tremendous opportunity to applaud and cheer and say, "Next time." Or you can look down in disgust and send the message, "You blew it!"

I love you *if* and I love you *because of* are part of approval-oriented relationships. Our children, or anyone for that matter, will feel insecure when they are involved in a relationship where love is awarded based on performance. Approval relationships base love on behavior rather than on "I love you no matter what."

How will our children respond when offered a beer if they're accustomed to an approval-oriented relationship? "You love me *if* I take the beer? You hate me if I don't?" Such messages lead to an internal sense of pressure.

I just wish someone would have told me more about drugs. I think that would have prevented me from doing drugs. I've been real depressed and I don't know what to do anymore. I don't believe in myself anymore. I think about death every day, but I can't do it because I don't want to hurt my parents. Doing drugs has certainly messed my life up.

—SCOTT, 11th grade

How are our children going to act in the back seat of a Chevrolet if they are conditioned by approval-oriented (*if* and *because*) relationships at home? "You mean you love me *if* we have sex and you don't love me *if* we don't?" Wouldn't we rather have our kids say, "I understand what love is, and love is not physical, and the physical is not intimacy, because I have love at home with my parents, and they don't have to touch me to show me."

True love seeks to give; lust seeks to get. Love is the giving of; lust is the striving for. Are you giving a hug or taking a hug? Giving a kiss or taking a kiss? Love is selfless; lust is selfish. Love seeks first the happiness of the other person; lust seeks first our own happiness. The physical is the expression of love, not the cause of love, and it can actually stand in the way of love if we're not in love. Wouldn't it be beautiful if our children could say they learned that from their parents?

In Atlantic, Iowa, a young women, twenty years old, stood up in front of the entire audience and said, "You know, I'm a virgin." She had everyone's attention and then said: "Have you ever noticed how we brag about things that we're proud of and play down the things that we're not?" It was okay for her to share that she was a virgin because it affirmed a value that she deemed important and was proud of. She said, "You know why? Because I want to have what my parents have in their relationship. It looks so special to me. I believe it's worth waiting for." What a testimony to what's happening in their family! Not, I love you *if* or I love you *because*, but *I love you no matter what.*

In Richfield, Minnesota, a 260-pound senior walked up after the parent program. He was huge, with big ears, chubby cheeks, and droopy eyes. He was bawling his eyes out. He walked up to me, gave me a hug, and picked me up, all the while mumbling, "It's so hard, it's so hard." He said:

It's so hard 'cause I haven't heard "I love you" from my mom since I was seven years old.

A big guy like that doesn't need to hear those three short words — at least that's what we might think. Apparently, he does. What's on his lips is what's in his heart. Let's listen and respond.

There are many ways to demonstrate our love. The more the better. One mother shared this with me:

You know, my son carried a little lunch bag to school every day. A little brown lunch bag. And so he could tell his little brown lunch bag from everyone else's little brown lunch bag, I would draw a little bunny face with rabbit ears on it. Well, my son got to be around fifteen years old. I thought maybe he was a little bit embarrassed that he has a bunny face with rabbit ears on his lunch bag. So I stopped drawing the bunny face with rabbit ears, and he started drawing the bunny face with rabbit ears on his own lunch bag.

The littlest things that we do are not substitutions for but an affirmation of the love we have for our child.

A mother came up to me in Michigan and said:

What I do in our family is, when I make sandwiches for all my kids and pack their lunches, before I put the sandwich in the baggy, I take a little bite off of a corner, and in our family we call them love bites.

Imagine a peanut butter and jelly sandwich, little corners bitten off. You can see how big the space is between the front teeth. Little love bites.

Self-esteem speaker and author Jack Canfield shares a story about how a parent had gotten in the habit of writing "Post-its Love Notes" for an adolescent son. One evening this mother ventured into her adolescent son's bedroom. She closed the bedroom door, and on the back of the door were 133 Post-its, soon to be 134. A wall of affirmation. Just a reminder. Not a substitute for, but an affirmation of, the love. This adolescent son, with a body full of ego, who couldn't, maybe, reach out, could retreat to his bedroom and be reminded that he was always loved.

I think being recognized for something I have done right is important, because usually when I do things to help, my parents only notice the things I didn't do. It made me feel happy that they finally showed me that they do notice when I help out even if it's not all the time.

—ERIN, 11th grade

In Elk River, Minnesota, a senior boy came up to me, boss haircut — two stripes on either side — cranial sculpturing, gel in his hair, a letter jacket on. He was a real jock. I said, "What's on your mind?" He sighed:

It's hard being a leader. I was captain of the football team. We lost the homecoming game and I was down and everybody else was down. I had to be up for them. Who am I supposed to go to when I'm down? It's hard being a leader.

The same kid continued:

I'm going to be captain of the wrestling team. They are expecting me to change my haircut for wrestling. I think I'll put arrows on the ends of the stripes. It's hard being a leader.

Then he opened up his jacket, pulled out a piece of paper, unfolded it, slid it across the table to me, and said, "You know, I've never shared this letter with anybody. But six weeks ago, I received it in my letter jacket the night of the last game of the football season. What I've been doing is, I go down to the park, I put the speakers up on the hood of the car, and I look at the moon and the stars, and every night I read this letter over and over again." The letter went like this:

Dear Son,

No matter what happens tonight, the night of the last game of the football season, we want you to know that we love you. We care about you. Whether you win or lose, we're proud of you 'cause you're our son and nothing will ever change that.

Love,
Mom and Dad

He folded it up, put it back in his letter jacket, and said, "They probably don't even know that I saved it." There's so much to be hopeful for because we could be the parent who writes the letter, who writes the note, who puts up the Post-it, who builds the relationship, who gives our presence.

Someone wrote this about parenting:

Someday when my children are old enough to understand the logic that will motivate a parent, I will tell them:

I loved you enough to ask you where you were going, with whom, and at what time you would be home.

I loved you enough to be silent and let you discover that your new best friend was a creep.

I loved you enough to stand over you for two hours while you cleaned your room — a job that would have taken me fifteen minutes.

I loved you enough to hold you responsible for your actions, even when the penalties were so harsh they almost broke my heart.

But most of all I loved you enough to say "No" when I knew you would hate me for it. Those are the most difficult times of all. I'm glad I won them, because in the end, you won something, too.

— ANONYMOUS

16. *Let's Teach Responsibility by Holding Our Children Accountable and by Role-Modeling Integrity*

The only way children can become responsible is if we first hold them accountable. When parents become inconsistent in their discipline, their children lose respect for them. Parents teach their kids about integrity and responsibility and then put fuzz-busters in their cars. The message is sent, "If I speed and I don't get caught, I'm being responsible. If I speed and I do get caught, I'm being irresponsible." The child interprets the message, "Okay, if I drink and I don't get caught, I'm responsible. If I drink and I do get caught, I'm irresponsible." This becomes confusing by reinforcing the rationalization of self-defined values.

Many communities have a discipline policy in the school that states: If you choose to drink, you choose to eliminate yourself from sports and activities for a period of time. Do our adolescents understand what that means? Let's allow logical consequences to teach the lessons. Accountability leads to responsibility, as loving authority leads to respect.

The consequences need to be predictable and agreed on in advance as logical and fair. The privileges of life are based on demonstrating responsibility. By giving up responsibility, by choosing not to follow previously agreed upon and clearly understood expectations, adolescents forgo those privileges.

A student came up to me in a school complaining that the coach had kicked him off the team. I asked him what for, and he answered, "Well, I got caught drinking alcohol."

"Wait a minute," I said. "The coach didn't kick you off the team. You kicked yourself off the team. The coach was just the bearer of the bad news." Sometimes even after the parents read and sign discipline policies, they still allow parties in their home where alcohol is served, and then they have the audacity to express anger when their kids are suspended from activities. Instead, if we parents discover our children drinking, let's call the school personally and volunteer that information. Let's say, "Please eliminate my child from athletics for a period of time. We need to educate and support and help my child." Can we parents make that phone call? I've been in communities where if they suspend a child for drinking in the home, the parent sues the school. What are those parents modeling for their teens? Are they teaching responsibility? As parents we need to love our kids enough to hold them accountable.

A student will say, "The teacher gave me an 'F.' " No, the teacher didn't. The student gave it to himself or herself. The teacher was just the bearer of the bad news. To help our teens mature, let's hold them accountable and allow for natural consequences.

17. Let's Establish a Loving Environment With High Expectations

Loving environments with high expectations foster feelings of belonging, identification, and acceptance.

> When adolescents and their parents hold values that stress responsibility, the adolescents' chances of experiencing an out-of-wedlock childbirth are significantly reduced. Responsible adolescents (and their parents as well as peers) will tend to have long-term goals that stress the importance of work and education. In addition, they will have a set of attitudes and values that will help them resist the immediate pressures on adolescents to become involved sexually. Some of these attitudes and values examined here include: religiosity, adherence to norms about childbearing within marriage, and a strong sense of control over one's life.[3]

Rules and expectations, even though perceived by the child as restrictive and "mean," provide structure and protection for adolescents. With more maturity, they will understand the process. Consider the chaos on our highways if we didn't have rules and speed limits. Or what happens to the car whose owner doesn't really feel like refilling the oil: Eventually, the car won't run; it's just a matter of time. The same analogy can be made with adolescent drug use: Whether they believe it is an issue or not, it is just a matter of time before major trouble surfaces, and like the car engine, their body or mind will be destroyed and stop functioning.

> *I would also tell them to sit me down and talk to me about drugs and other things. I would also tell them to talk to me about sex, and what to do so that I can be safe if I do have it.*
>
> —TREVOR, 10th grade

When communicating our expectations with our adolescents regarding alcohol or other drugs, let's speak from a position of fact. Where do we get facts? We have resources, beginning with our school, church, and community, mental-health organizations, and state and national agencies. (Some resources are listed in the Appendix of this book.) If we contact these sources and, every time, ask for three additional resources, in two months we'll have cases of material sent to our homes for free, more than we'll ever be interested in reading. The answers are out there tenfold — a hundredfold. Yet we're still not acting on all the information.

When my parents get upset with me, the first thing they do is accuse me of doing drugs and alcohol.

—TIM, 10th grade

Parents who fear the worst, anticipating use at every possible juncture, become paranoid. They begin to question the activities of their adolescent and the adolescent's truthfulness. This questioning and confrontation make young people feel threatened, as if their judgment and integrity were being challenged.

When a kid takes alcohol or other drugs, why don't adults try to understand instead of automatically assuming that we are losers? Could parents show they care more?

—ROCHELLE, 9th grade

Emotionalization tends to lead to exaggeration and lost credibility. Let's speak about how drugs harm people, young people especially. Let's talk about physical harm such as slowed growth, impaired coordination, heart, liver, and lung diseases, irreversible brain damage. Let's share in terms of social harm and becoming disconnected from society, loss of friendships, apathy and attitude problems, loss of motivation, intellectual harm, diminished attention levels, and reduced motivation as well as impaired memory.

Let's tell our teens that we don't find alcohol or drug use acceptable. It is surprising how many children say that their parents never stated this basic principle: that drugs are against the law.

Let's discuss the fact that there are many positive drug-free alternatives and explore with our teens what they are. The key word here is "explore." Wherever I go, to communities all over this country, kids come up and say, "There's nothing to do here in our community." It's a cop-out! You see, if there is *nothing* to do here and I drink, I've got an excuse. But if there is *something* to do here and I drink, I have a drinking problem. So they're always going to say there's nothing to do here if they want to drink. Let's not buy the excuse.

High school students will say that life is either awesome or it's boring. If it's in between, the students say, "It sucks." It's our role as adults to help convince kids that "It sucks" is really "That's life." What does that mean? Marriage from time to time is awesome. From time to time it's boring. Most of the time it's lived in between. It doesn't suck. It's beautiful, it's wonderful, and that's life. Our job from time to time is awesome. Our job from time to time is boring, but most of the time it's lived in between. That's life and that's okay. School, going out on a date, or going to a party from time to time is awesome; from time to time it's boring; most of the time it's lived in between.

TIPS FOR TRANSMITTING OUR EXPECTATIONS:

LET'S BE CALM AND BE OPEN. It is always easier to remain calm before problems arise. Let's communicate our expectations ahead of time.

LET'S BE INVOLVED IN ONGOING DIALOGUE. Bringing up topics of alcohol, other drugs, and sex all at once won't be as effective as if we trickle in our concerns over and over again. Rather than reacting, let's respond.

I would talk so much more if my parents would let me speak my mind. I feel that they don't give me enough respect in not letting me do so, so I'm not going to give them enough respect to trust them with what I am feeling.

—MOLLY, 10th grade

Let's discuss issues and behavior in a manner that separates behavior from the person. Let's find out the context of our kids' thinking before responding.

Let's be certain to encourage two-way conversation and invite differences of thought so ideals can be refined and not stifled. "A person convinced against his will, is of the same opinion still."

LET'S TAKE ADVANTAGE OF TEACHABLE MOMENTS. In contrast to relying on formal, sit-down lectures, let's watch for opportunities to plant insights and discover our children's beliefs. Let's use a variety of situations such as television news, shows, and commercials, dramas, books, local events and tragedies, newspaper articles.

In response to TV beer commercials, for example, let's ask our children what style of music the advertisers are using and why. What is the age group of the actors? Why are they doing this? Is that for real? Are they promoting a product or a lifestyle? Methodically, let's capitalize on one point at a time. Role playing is a way to practice and reinforce decision-making skills.

18. Let's Come to Our Children with a United Front

As parents, do we show up together? Do we really know one another? Let's build our relationship and communicate with one another the foundations through which we'll be directing our children on critical issues. Credibility is lost when parents contradict each other or even go so far as to put down the other parent. Children quickly will see through this and will play one parent against the other. The inconsistency also increases their sense of insecurity in the stability of the family unit.

Something we can do with our spouse is find an intimate time and place where we can be alone — together. Sit and face one another. Decide on one topic for discussion and then decide who is going to begin. Say the husband goes first: We tell our wives what we believe that they believe on that topic. And then, wives, lovingly bring your husbands into alignment with what you really believe. Then reverse it. We will become closer, because this kind of openness leads to trust, intimacy, and therefore growth in our relationship. It will also create a platform to stand on as we share what we believe in with our children.

19. Let's Create Neutral Zones

We encourage having neutral zones in the home where discipline and reprimands don't normally take place. Two natural areas are the bedroom and the kitchen. These tend to be fairly safe places that can afford some privacy so that secrets can be shared.

Parents, let's challenge ourselves to make dinnertime a positive time. Let's strive to give zero discipline to our kids at dinner and at least three affirmations to each child. We will still discipline our kids as necessary, but we'll do it somewhere else.

Often, dinnertime becomes housekeeping duties time. We talk about report cards, grades, and all the things they didn't do — chores and activities. Dinnertime becomes a negative experience, and our teens don't want to show up or consistently make conflicting plans. Let's make meals a positive experience and, especially as our children go into adolescence, they will look forward to eating with the family.

Let's keep those rituals alive in our families. We can't make all the dinners and suppers together, but maybe we can make a couple each week. Maybe we can make Saturday brunch, Sunday breakfast. Let's create an opportunity to always be there so we have that time to share. Let's condition ourselves and our children to know that this is a positive family time.

Also, if we're watching TV while eating dinner, let's turn it off. One mother wrote me:

We turned off our TV set. We had nothing to say to one another for three weeks. We'd forgotten how.

Let's really turn it off. And then we're going to find that maybe it's quiet at dinner and that we need to stimulate some conversation. That may mean that we're a little bit uncomfortable, which introduces us to our insecurities and weaknesses. That means we may need to take a Dale Carnegie class or an interpersonal communication class or talk to a pastor, priest, rabbi, or counselor. Or let's go out and talk to ourselves. Maybe even visit with our wife or husband and . . . visit, and practice, and open up.

Bedtime needs to be a positive time. Children remember the love that's given to them the most just as they're falling asleep. And we do, too. The last forty-five minutes of our day is processed about sixteen times as we sleep. Is the last forty-five minutes of our child's day positive or is it negative? If it's negative and filled with nagging, what can we do to reroute the evening so that it is more often positive? Children are born with the ability to love, but they're taught how to love two ways. The first is by how their parents treat each other in front of their kids. The second is the love they receive from their parents. What are they seeing modeled, and what do they see in us and feel from us?

Let's refrain from disciplining our children in the bedroom. If children are disciplined often in the bedroom, they tend to grow up to be a spouse or parent who may likewise discipline in the bedroom. How we treat our future spouse is determined a lot by what we see modeled for us and also how we're treated. We may send our children to the bedroom for discipline, but when we go into the bedroom, let's make it for forgiveness. Let your kids always understand that "I'm always safe in the bedroom." The resulting dynamics can be wonderful and uplifting. Our daughter comes home and says, "Mom, I need to talk to you about something." "Okay, dear, let's go sit on the edge of the bed." In the past it's always been positive in the bedroom. She feels she can open up with us.

Our son comes home and exclaims, "Dad, I need to talk to you about something."

"Okay, Son, let's go sit on the edge of the bed." We're visiting for a while, and after a moment, we say, "Wait a minute, Son, I think we need to move to the den on this one."

Another treasured neutral zone is in the car on the way home from events. These become conditioned "Lifesaver candy" moments where vulnerability is shared and not challenged, promoting openness and positive anticipation on the part of our teens. If teens fear the possibility of a shame-filled fight, they will look for ways to avoid the entrapment of a car ride.

Again, in no way are we suggesting that parents shouldn't ever discipline. Discipline is like the stake that holds up a plant and guides its growth upward, or the pruning shears that help shape its future. But also in the family garden, safety, affirmation, unconditional love, and rapport are the soil, fertilizer, water, and sunlight. They are all necessary to provide the nutrients so the fragile child can sprout, flourish, mature, and bear fruit. All the neutral-zone nutrients (rather than the discipline) are the prerequisites to forgiveness, trust, intimacy, and the growth of any relationship, including a relationship with a spouse.

20. Let's Give Hugs Every Day

Teens not involved in substance abuse are most likely to experience affection shared between themselves and their parents. It takes four hugs a day to survive, eight a day to maintain, and twelve a day to get ahead. Have you hugged your child lately? Author Virginia Satir said that seven out of ten of us are starving from skin hunger. Seven out of ten of us are not being touched enough. To give those hugs is important, and, especially as fathers, we often have a hard time giving embraces. We tend to not be very physical with our kids because someone may not have been physical with us as we were growing up. Our kids need the hugs, even if we're uncomfortable giving them. The great thing about giving affection is that we receive it at the same time.

> *All the time they compliment what I do. They tell me what I did right. I think that is important because I always know they will support me and back me up no matter what.*
>
> —JUSTIN, 9th grade

A wife said to her husband, "I can't tell if you love me anymore. I don't know if you love me."

The husband said, "Look, I told you I loved you when I married you, and if it ever changes, I'll let you know." Apparently, she needed to hear it more often than that, and your kids do, too.

21. Let's Celebrate Our Children's Accomplishments

Let's catch them doing something right or good. Let's acknowledge our child's specific accomplishments rather than sharing broad-brush acknowledgments. Recognizing and showing appreciation of specific accomplishments direct our comments by responding to what the child did. We love him or her no matter what, but significance is discovered in what we appreciate in our child.

Let's celebrate and compliment rather than praise. Praise comes out as, "You're so wonderful." Praise is a target that our children are unable to see. A compliment tells them the behavior is good *because*... (a target they can see). When our children know what they did, they are able to become confident in their ability to duplicate that behavior in the future.

22. Let's Encourage Thank-Yous

There is so much in life to be thankful for. Let's let our kids know what we are thankful for personally and that we are thankful for them. Let's ask our children to explore what they are thankful for. Let's be open about our faith and share our understandings and origins of our own personal spirituality (what's really important for us). Being loved is the greatest gift to be thankful for. Knowing that we are always loved by others inspires a spirit of thankfulness and humility.

Maybe if we all remembered to value life as a gift, we would be more careful with it and treasure every moment. Maybe if we realize all people are special, we wouldn't hurt each other in the many ways we seem to. Everyone should be loved, liked, and cared for. It doesn't matter what the color of their skin, or if they are female or male, young, unborn, or old. Value and preserve human life, and maybe we can co-exist in peace and harmony.

—STEPHANIE, 11th grade

23. Let's Develop Ourselves First

We are only able to give away what we have. We teach from our weaknesses as well as our strengths. The caboose in a train will never pass the engine, and children are unable to surpass their parents until well after the foundational primary development has been established. What tools will they have in their tool box? The more, the better.

My family takes care of me. My family is part of the community. Strong families make strong communities.

—ZACH, 1st grade

All successful families are willing to go outside the family for counsel when they are unable to solve their problems internally. The inability and unwillingness to ask for help is often a sign of deeper problems and concerns. Let's benefit our families by taking advantage of the available resources.

POINT TO REMEMBER

- *Clear, courteous communication is critical in the adolescent's family.*

Chapter 10

The Biggest Blockers of Healing Communication

WE HAVE SEEN FAMILIES PANIC during the period of adolescence and young adulthood, and in that panic both parent and child have become alienated. This alienation is rooted in pride, usually on both sides. As the parent (and/or child) becomes offended, an unwillingness to forgive surfaces. As a result, both go off in their own direction, hoping that they will find peace in the old adage "Out of sight, out of mind."

Boundaries and Bridges to Healing Choices

Years ago I came upon a fable about a bear. The author is unknown to me. The story is pertinent because it speaks so eloquently about the benefits of living life to the fullest.

BEAR HUGS KETTLE

It appears that a party of hunters, being called away from their camp by a sudden alarm, left the camp fire unattended, with a kettle of water boiling on it.

Presently an old bear crept out of the woods, attracted by the fire, and, seeing the kettle with its lid dancing about on top, promptly seized it. Naturally it burnt and scalded him badly; but instead of dropping it instantly, he proceeded to hug it; and so on in a vicious circle, to the undoing of the bear.

This illustrates perfectly the way in which many people amplify their difficulties. They hug them to their bosoms by constantly rehearsing them to themselves and others and by continually dwelling upon them in every possible manner, instead of dropping them once and for all so the wound has a chance to heal.

Whenever you catch yourself thinking about your grievances, say to yourself sternly, "Bear hugs kettle," and think about God instead. You will be surprised how quickly some longstanding wounds will disappear under this treatment.

Struggle Builds Character

It's okay to struggle. It's okay to hurt. It's okay to be confused emotionally. Most important, it's okay to ask for help. We're not failures when we have pain in our lives or our families. We're failures when we choose not to deal with the pain because we believe we can deal with it all by ourselves. Let's show our kids the benefits of talking with a counselor, a teacher, a coach, a youth leader, priest, a pastor, or rabbi.

We believe that the biggest killer of kids in the United States today is the family secret. "This is our secret, so don't tell anybody." In response, the child looks around and responds; whatever problem is surfacing is immediately stuffed inside. As a result, family members walk around ready to explode. Parental pride prevents us from allowing any family member to move outside the system in search of help. This resistance to outside assistance is then learned by our children and passed down to the next generation.

> *My parents try to listen, but I don't open up and talk, so I guess it is my fault not theirs. My parents sent me to a class about sex rather than telling me themselves. I felt better and more open to asking the strangers questions than my mom or dad. Then I had a problem over this summer because I got into a "lust" relationship with a twenty-year-old. After the summer was over and he left, I felt sad and confused. I wanted to talk to someone about it but I felt like my parents wouldn't understand or approve of me.*
>
> —STACI, 11th grade

Denial Blocks Growth

There is a good possibility that some of the material in this book causes you discomfort. This discomfort could, in part, be your resistance to face, embrace, and then openly work through painful areas in your life, breaking the denial.

Denial is a defense mechanism that occurs when we are uncomfortable working with or addressing an issue. It's when we turn our back and maintain the secret.

A year ago I got caught for drinking, and my mom blames my friends. It wasn't their fault, it was mine. They should blame the one who was at fault, me. Now I don't respect my parents as much because I feel they didn't face up to what really happened.

—JAMAL, 12th grade

The three most dangerous statements reflecting parental denial are, "not my child," "not my kid," "not our school." Problems happen, and problems can be solved — all problems — but nothing can be solved until recognition is first completed.

Discover → uncover → recover.

Enabling Blocks Help

"Enabling" happens any time we protect people from the consequences of their behavior. Addiction to alcohol or other drugs normally evolves out of a series of rewarding experiences that are directly or indirectly supported by a parent or somebody who really loves the substance abuser.

My parents encourage me when they tell me that they'll drop everything they're doing and put out as much money as they need to help me out.

—BRAD, 11th grade

Because the love is so great, denial surfaces, and the implications of certain behaviors are disregarded, rationalized, supported (enabled), and made to look insignificant. Examples that might sound familiar include: "Boys will be boys," or, "Oh, thank God, they only had two drinks," or, "At least it's not the heavy stuff." These kinds of justifications reinforce the negative behaviors.

My parents don't punish me — they threaten to punish me.

—JASON, 10th grade

Steps to Healing

Devastating events create intense pain. That pain either sits and festers or is understood and forgiven so that healing can proceed. Forgiveness involves a series of definable and predictable steps as we grieve the loss of something. Depending on the person and the issue, grieving can last minutes, years, or even a lifetime. The fallacy is stated as "Out of sight, out of mind," or "If I don't think about it, then it's gone." Many people actually shelter their problems, harbor their pain, and defend their hidden concerns for a lifetime. All pain that is buried is buried alive and will fester. You can deal with it when you're twenty-two, or forty-two, or sixty-two, or you can die with the pain still in you and pass it on to your kids, but eventually someone in the family will have to face the consequences of unresolved pain.

My dad and I get along great until my stepmom gets upset, then my dad has to get upset with me, too.

—JULIE, 8th grade

The Steps of Grief

The steps of grieving, originally articulated by Elisabeth Kübler-Ross, are well known in the mental health field. We have adapted that material to meet our needs for the topic of adolescence.

1. **DENIAL AND SHOCK.** The full realization of what happened or did not happen is not accepted. Being in denial is like being in a holding pattern around reality. It is the rationalization and excuses that we make for all behaviors that we are not ready to face or embrace. The breaking of denial leads to a shock that is a false acceptance. Some people in their rage say that they just have to accept. This is not the same as the peace-filled acceptance that comes at the end of the healing journey. This kind of acceptance is the introduction to ourselves about the realities of life. We let down our walls and let reality in.

2. ANGER. This is the letting out of festering repressed emotions. Anger is a healthy and natural response. No one *makes* anyone angry. People *become* angry, and it is like the flushing out of the poisons. As teens in the Boy Scouts, we were taught how to care for venomous snake bites. The wound was not covered with a patch; it was lacerated with a knife, and then the poisons and life blood were sucked out so that the venom would not remain in the system. Anger is like snake venom. Emotional dishonesty represses anger, and anger that is repressed long enough leads to stress buildup and possible mental illness.

3. DEPRESSION. This is anger turned inward. The poisons of anger that are allowed to remain begin to shut down the emotional systems, and then the physical systems follow right behind. Depression is a response to the regrouping that people go through after they have begun to face their issues. It's like a time of rest from emotional exhaustion. It lasts as long as it needs to.

4. BARGAINING AND REACHING OUT. These are the deals and promises that are made to get out of the responsibility and true consequences of facing issues. For adolescents, it is the promises they make to the principal or police officer so the authority figures don't call the parents. For adults, it may be the promises that are made to a spouse, or to God, when death or divorce is looming on the horizon. They are all the "if onlys" that are said to put off having to say good-bye, which naturally leads into the final stage of healthy, healing acceptance.

5. ACCEPTANCE AND PURE FORGIVENESS. It is in acceptance that we discover the pathway to legitimate peace. Anything can be accepted and forgiven. If we are unable to accept and forgive, then let's go back through the list. As we mentioned earlier, whatever we are unable to forgive has control over us and has the capability of destroying us.

We know we are truly on our way to complete healing when we are able to go discuss publicly our problem or concern rather than stuffing it inside and trying to cover it up.

Facing the Unfaceable

Forgiveness is a sign of strength. Forgiveness is a vehicle whereby communication is opened up. Forgiveness is the access point for moving beyond the present obstacles in life. Real love is founded in forgiveness.

I was giving a speech in the Midwest a couple of years ago. A concerned local merchant and member of the Chamber of Commerce had been generous and financially sponsored my trip to his community. He frequently supported programs that benefited young people, and he was the primary contributor to the community's "Say No to Drugs" clubs at the elementary schools. I was scheduled to speak at several schools that day and then to parents that night. The second presentation of the day happened to be at the high school. There, standing in the back, was the sponsor. He had slipped in to check out the message, the messenger, and the audience's response. I poured my heart out.

Commonly, after I speak, students will bunch up at the stage in an effort to get a hug or to share a problem. Those who don't get a chance to come up often write. That day was no different.

The first student to the stage felt the need to confess about his alcohol and other drug use and his need for ongoing support. The school counselor was standing offstage, and having won the alcoholic student's confidence, I immediately "bridged" the student to her. The next student in line fell into my arms sobbing. I suggested we move off to the side where we could sit down and visit. As we sat there, she timidly began to share the painful story about how she had been raped after the school homecoming dance several days earlier.

As we began her slow and methodical process of healing, I asked her if she had told her parents, and she responded that she had not. When I asked why not, she revealed her shame and how she felt very certain that her dad would be upset and disappointed if he were to find out about such a thing.

I told her that it was my experience that parents are normally extremely supportive of their children when they have been violated and hurt. Rambling, she went on that she had been drinking alcohol that night and that her father was the sponsor of the alcohol-free programs at the school and... Chamber of Commerce, and... local merchant, and... "he paid to have you speak here today. I really feel like I let him down. I can't tell him. Please don't make me."

"I don't make anybody do anything," I responded. "I just try to help people sort out their stuff so they can do what is best for themselves. Usually, when people are really hurting, they tend to do all the wrong things, so I try to act as a sounding board and offer suggestions, okay?"

At the same time that I was consoling this young lady, I glanced over her shoulder toward the side of the auditorium, and there was her father, who had come, basically out of his love for kids, to see how his investment (the speaker) was doing. I could see the anxious look on her dad's face as he probably wondered, "What are you doing to my daughter?"

The girl went on to tell me that after the rape she had called a local crisis line and then attended a meeting a few nights later at the crisis center. She had lied to her parents, telling them that she was heading for a friend's house when in fact she was heading off to a counseling session to deal with the rape. Keeping all of this from her parents did nothing but increase her confusion, which was now intensifying by the minute. Ironically, as she made efforts to hide this shame from her parents, she was at the same time feeling very distant from them. Lying only added to her loneliness and isolation, which broadened her confusion.

I said, "Do you feel closer to your parents or farther away from them right now?"

She said, "Real distant, and I don't like the feeling and I'm real scared and, and, and . . ."

I went on, "Do you feel like you're keeping a secret from them?"

"Yeah."

"When do you feel that you might get them involved in helping you, and tell them?"

"Maybe in a year or two I'll tell them," she answered.

"Do you think you'll feel good every time you see them during the next year or two, knowing that you have this deep secret?" In her silence, I went on, "If you do choose to tell them in a year, do you feel they might ask you why you waited a year?"

"Yeah."

"Knowing that, do you think in a year it would really be easier or harder to tell them?"

"Probably harder," she murmured.

I noticed a cross suspended from a fine chain that she was wearing around her neck. I asked what the cross meant to her. She told me that it meant that she believed in God.

Accepting what she already believed, I then asked if God would forgive her for anything that she ever did wrong. To which she responded, "Yes, he forgives."

"When does God forgive us?" I asked gently. "When he reaches out to us or when we reach back?"

"When we reach back," she said sheepishly.

"Is he always there and ready to forgive?"

"Yes," she whispered.

"All we have to do is embrace and accept all that we have done, be sorry in our hearts, and ask for forgiveness." (Keep in mind that though the rape was not her fault, the feelings of shame are tied into a need to know that she is not judged and thereby is accepted and forgiven. By not seeking forgiveness, many people hang on to their anger and block the opportunity for support and healing.)

"Yeah, I guess you're right."

"So, who determines when you get to feel forgiven, with God?"

"I guess...I do," she said with a little hope returning to her expression.

"Yep, you sure do," I affirmed. "Forgiveness is a gift you get to give yourself, but only on one condition."

She perked up. "What's that?"

I winked and whispered very slowly, "That you trust and ask."

I then made an analogy, telling her that a parent's job is similar to God's insofar as a loving parent is ready and willing to hear our problems and then offer encouragement and support as well as forgiveness. Parents are a child's human version of God as well as a child's first impression of what God is like. Caring parents are always reaching out to us; we're just not reaching back.

"Do you want to tell your dad now?"

"I don't know."

"I promise to help you," I said, squeezing her hand. "Will you trust and..."

"Ask?" she said, finishing my sentence.

"How 'bout if we have your dad come over, and we'll let him in on the secret so you can feel better?"

"Okay."

I motioned to the father to come in our direction. The young lady glanced up sheepishly as her father approached. With a look of concern, he slid into the chair beside her as she fell right into his arms crying. She then whimpered through the whole story about being raped and about how she'd lied to cover up her shame. Shocked, the father asked her, "Why didn't you tell us?"

I interrupted and suggested that she felt judged when he asked "why?" and that asking "what" questions beginning with "what happened?" might be more healing. The father responded with, "I'm not very good at this. I've never dealt with anything like this before."

I said, "Few of us have. You're doing just fine...just fine," and I got up and ventured out of the auditorium, leaving them alone in each other's arms, to hurt, to heal. Forgiveness, what a beautiful gift. A few weeks later I received a note from the father:

> My wife, daughter, and I thank you for the help you provided regarding the bad experience our daughter had two weeks ago. We are being supportive and letting her deal with it in the manner that she desires. Things appear to be "on the mend." Thanks again.
>
> —JIM, parent

This story shows that the work of healing needs to be done by the individual. Nothing is going to happen until that person reaches out and asks for understanding and forgiveness. The message for parents is found in the need that exists to set up an environment in which young people feel that they will not be judged or shamed as a result of their admission.

Slow to Forgive

Forgiveness is in reality a gift we give ourselves. The energy it takes to not forgive and to store anguish is tremendous. It is draining to hate and despise someone. To forgive somehow feels like submission. As individuals, it is healthier for us if we can eventually forgive others and not hold bitterness inside us. Bitterness tends to eat away at our own lives. Forgiving doesn't mean we have to accept what has happened as okay, or even forget; it just means we can move on from being bitter to a state of understanding and acceptance.

> In the past two months I have lost three people whom I loved very much; one was murdered, one a suicide, and one had AIDS. These

were senseless deaths that could have been prevented if they had only had the knowledge or asked for some help. I wonder how people can keep doing this to themselves and to other people. It's wrecking our whole society. If people respected themselves enough to say no to drugs, sex, or alcohol, many lives would be saved.

—RYAN, 12th grade

Healthy grieving can be a very painful process. The consequences of repressing the issues, maintaining the secret, and not grieving will always be greater. Making the commitment to honestly face and work through our problems as well as supporting our children through theirs is one of the greatest gifts we will ever give to our children.

Tapping Hidden Strengths

Weathering painful experiences takes support from others. Most important, though, it requires us to draw on our inner strengths. There have been times in my life when my inner strength pulled me through. I would tap my hidden strengths by taking time for myself through praying, exercising, walking, writing, reading, listening to some music that I enjoyed, or by spending time on something that really means a lot to me. The point in doing these things is not to forget our losses, but to remind us about what life is and what it can be.

Another thing that helps is to be available for others. For some reason, helping others seems to make the hurt and the pain a little more tolerable. It's based upon the principle that life is an echo. "Whatever we give away is what comes back to us." We seem to internalize what we project onto the world around us. Helping in the community is always needed and beneficial — to the giver and the receiver. Helping our family or parents, whatever the need, will facilitate our discovery of strength.

I also felt bad for all those kids who stood up and told about alcoholism. Now I know that I am not the only kid with an alcoholic parent and now I don't feel so alone and by myself.

—JASON, 9th grade

It also helps us feel that we're contributing to something, rather than feeling helpless and useless. We get back the energy and emotions we give away. To love others leads to feeling loved. If we feel angry or depressed, and we pass on that anger and depression, we may just get those same emotions back from others in return.

POINT TO REMEMBER

- *Parents need to stay alert and offer help in a low-key way when they suspect the adolescent is holding secrets.*

Chapter 11

Families Are Forever: Creating Lifelong Memories

I HAVE ALWAYS KEPT A JOURNAL. Writing in my journal reduces my level of stress and brings clarity to confusion. It is the vehicle that helps me successfully work through so much of the unresolved baggage of my past. It comforts me as I search to find security, to find love, and to find a sense of connectedness with the world around me. I thought it would be appropriate to include with this chapter an actual journal entry I made some time ago:

> Today I cried for the first time in seventeen years. What a rush of emotions came over me. There was a sense of holding back in embarrassment as I peeked through my tears looking for a sign of judgment or approval from my prodding counselor. I felt a relief of cleansing as the callused pockets of suppressed pain that had been fermenting in my heart and soul broke open for the first time in years. The wonderment of somehow being pushed passed a limit and into the unknown captured my curiosity. What's going on? Wow, I'm crying. Look, I'm crying.
>
> —JOHN CRUDELE, February 1991

Perhaps the significance of this journal entry is not immediately evident. My father committed suicide when I was fifteen years old. That event was so traumatic that my emotional system shut down. I actually went seventeen years without crying a tear. It's not easy to explain to anyone the effect of that death on me.

There I was, sitting on a therapist's couch, trying to work through the problems in my life that were getting me down. I needed to feel, to understand, to get over my loss, to move on, and to become a complete human being who could experience the full gambit of emotions. That was my goal. It was very important for me. Having put off the inevitable all these years, I knew it was not going to be an easy or a cheap process — emotionally or financially.

For some reason, men find it harder to seek counseling than women do. The emotional cost of doing nothing to change this pattern was tremendously hurtful, and the process to create this experience by seeking counseling went against all my basic decision-making instincts. Deep inside was the gnawing thought that "you're a loser if you can't figure stuff out for yourself." Such an attitude seems out of character for someone who has counseled hundreds of people himself.

As a boy, I developed mechanisms of protection so I could survive emotionally. I felt that my role in the family was to take care of everyone. I thought that if I had somehow been a better child, my father would not have died. Later, I convinced myself that if I could stay in control of my family, they would not get hurt, and all of us would live happy and satisfying lives. I wanted to be perfect and ensure that I never got into a relationship that put me at risk of being left or abandoned. Consequently, intimacy eluded me — or I eluded it. I compensated for what was missing in my childhood.

Those means of compensation, however, began to sabotage my adult life as I ventured out to engage in both professional and personal adult relationships. It was time to deal with everything that I had been running away from for so many years. I had challenged everyone else to seek counseling while remaining convinced that I could fix myself.

Though I played the events of my father's life and death over and over in my mind, I still felt trapped in the memories. I viewed the scenes of his death thousands of times, yet each time I tried to rewrite the script and change the past. I couldn't reach the happy ending that the movies and television depicted. Everything worked out fine in *Leave It to Beaver*; the Cleavers always seemed to end with happy solutions; what was wrong with me?

Today, some twenty years later, I can still picture the evening clearly — the night I discovered that my father had died. The police knocked on the door. "You need to call your Aunt Ang," I was told. At that moment I knew it had something to do with my dad, who was living with my Aunt Ang at the time.

My dad was a brilliant man with three post-graduate degrees. Then he suffered a stroke and lost most of his memory as a result of the shock treatments his doctors prescribed. He couldn't read and understand the academic papers he had personally written. He would pound his head on the refrigerator door saying, "I can't think. I can't remember. I can't think." In his mind, his dignity and value as a human being had been diminished. I often cried myself to sleep and prayed really hard, "God help my dad, please help my dad." That was twenty years ago; I was fifteen.

That evening, I walked upstairs and told my mom what the officers had said, and she called my aunt. Considering the message it delivered, it was a short phone call. Mom sat on the bed as her sister-in-law slowly explained what had happened — and then she slowly hung up the phone. My sister and two younger brothers stood behind me, but Mom talked as if I were the only one present: "Son, your dad died. He committed suicide." Dad had stepped off a chair in my aunt's basement and had hung himself. I was stunned, dazed, hurt — oh, but not angry. It wasn't fair to be angry at someone who died, or so I thought. I stuffed my emotions, and that's where I got stuck.

My mind locked into a cycle of thought: "Why me? This happens to other people — to other kids. Somebody else is going to lose a mom or dad because of death or suicide — but it's not going to happen to me. Not my dad. Somebody else is going to lose a brother or sister or friend because of a death or suicide — but not me!"

IT'S NOT GOING TO HAPPEN TO ME

It's not going to happen to me. Somebody else is going to have a friend or son or daughter get addicted to alcohol, but it's not going to happen to me. (...*and Nathan comes from such a good family.*) It's always going to happen to somebody else. Somebody else is going to have a girlfriend or daughter or sister get pregnant, it won't happen to me. (*You're what?*) One million teenage pregnancies last year in the United States. (*Not my niece!*) A half-million abortions to adolescents. (*Not my daughter!*) Thirty thousand births to girls under the age of fifteen.

(*My son? a father? He's only sixteen!*) We think it's going to happen to somebody else!

Did I tell my dad I loved him? Did I tell him I cared? What if I had called him? What if I had written him? I didn't get a second chance. I wouldn't get another chance to let him know. And I found out that life isn't always easy, and life isn't always right. Life isn't always fair. But life never gives us an excuse to be anything but the best we can be. We make up the excuses to compromise on our values, to turn our backs on truths, to take a drink or a drug, to let ourselves down, to fail. Life doesn't give us excuses; it gives us reasons. God doesn't give us excuses; God gives us reasons. We make up the excuses. But I want you to know something. I can now brag and not be bitter about my dad because I learned how to forgive.

Can we forgive? Our son wrecked the car two years ago, and every time we flip him the keys, do we remind him of how he wrecked the car? Do we drag it up again and again whenever we need to use that piece of history as ammunition? Can we truly let go, or do we continue to remind ourselves of the weaknesses and keep building on that? No relationship can move forward, including a healthy relationship with ourselves (the most intimate and significant relationship other than the one we have with God), unless we come to forgiveness.

Do we remind our spouse of mistakes made years ago? Do we burden our marriage with that kind of old baggage? Do we carry such a lack of trust into our intimacy? Only forgiveness can pave the way to trust, which leads to intimacy, which leads to growth. But forgiveness feels like submission, so we reject the fruitful possibilities it offers. Yet whatever we are unable to forgive has power over us. To gain control, we must let go of control — and forgive.

One of my friends at school may be pregnant. Her boyfriend is nineteen, and she is sixteen. She said she won't tell her mom, and she won't go to the doctor to find out, but she says that she will kill herself if she is pregnant because she doesn't want to have an abortion either. I don't know what to do. I'm so worried about her.

—TONYA, 9th grade

Have we forgiven ourselves? Maybe we've read something about life, parenting, or adolescence that reminded us of something we could have done but didn't. We did the best we knew how. We just didn't do the best possible. Can we forgive ourselves? It's okay to make mistakes. It's okay to accept, to face, to flush, to move on. My personal belief is that it's easier to forgive if we have God in our hearts. Forgiveness is a gift we give ourselves. I can brag, and not be bitter, now, finally, seventeen years later, because I forgave.

> *This is going to sound stupid, but how do you forgive yourself? I, like other people, have done some stupid things in my past and I tried to forgive myself, but I haven't been very successful.*
> —LAURA, 11th grade

I think of all the memories I have of my dad. What are the memories you have of your parents? Were your parents there for you or not there for you? Are you there for your son or daughter? How else will memories be created? What is ultimately important to you? I remember when my dad mowed the lawn; he had a little plastic lawn mower for me to push alongside of him. Why? Kids want to be like their dad; they want to be like their mom.

When my dad shaved in the morning, he would let me jump up on the stool next to him and dab shaving cream on my face — just as he did. He would wipe a big spot off on the mirror for himself, a little one for me, and with my fake razor, I shaved right along with him. Why? I wanted to be like my dad. Kids want to be like their dad; they want to be like their mom.

My dad would come home from work to four kids waiting to greet him. The first one there would give him a hug and stand on his feet, and he'd walk around with that little one standing on his shoes, arms wrapped around his legs in a loving embrace. I have so many memories of my dad.

I remember how my dad would wrestle with me on the living room carpeting, that long green shag carpeting, the kind you had to rake — remember? It came in two colors: green and orange. The only place it looked nice was up against the wall and under the furniture; otherwise it was all matted down. And you didn't replace that kind of carpet until a month before you sold your house. Remember that carpet? We'd wrestle on it and mat it down even more. My mom would get so upset, but we just loved wrestling.

I remember when my dad went to pick out a Christmas tree one year. Because I helped, it took hours. There I was in the Earl May tree yard, in Ames, Iowa, struggling to do the family proud. It seemed like a major decision at the time. My dad was always a perfectionist with our Christmas trees. He would saw off a branch in one place, drill a hole in another, and put that branch in the hole to give the tree greater symmetry.

I remember once when the electricity went off, and my dad said, "Son, the electricity is off." I said, "I can see that, Dad. No lights." He said, "You want to help your dad turn on the electricity?" I said, "Sure, Dad. Mom, stay here in the kitchen." Dad and I, we're a team. "We're going downstairs to turn on the electricity." Dad lifted me up, I flicked that breaker twice, and the lights came on. Running upstairs, I said, "Mom, I helped Dad turn on the electricity." Mom and Dad beamed with pride, and I basked in the light of their approval.

I remember how my dad would tuck me into bed at night. He would rub his whiskers up and down my chest to make me giggle and laugh. Then he'd lie down beside me, and I'd say, "Dad, why do planes fly?" And he'd tell me. I'd say, "Dad, why are there rings in trees?" And he'd tell me. "Dad, when you plant the little seed, how is it that the roots know they're supposed to go down, and the little plant knows it's supposed to come up?" And he'd tell me. "Dad, why is there war?" And he'd tell me. "Dad, why do boats float? I mean, boats are made out of metal and they float, but so are bee-bees made out of metal, and they sink to the bottom of the toilet, roll around for months, and no one ever takes them out." And he'd tell me. "Dad, what do birds think of airplanes? Dad, can you use a yo-yo on the moon? Dad . . . " And he'd tell me. He was a physicist. He could really tell me.

I remember how important prayers were at dinnertime — and they still play a major role in my life today. My father was the model. Wherever I am, when I pray, a little bit of my earthly father is with me.

I remember how at nighttime my dad would set me on his lap, slowly bounce me up and down, and sing, "This is the way the ladies ride, the ladies ride, the ladies ride. This is the way the ladies ride. Trot. Trot. Trot." Then, picking up speed, he'd continue, "This is the way the gentlemen ride, the gentlemen ride, the gentlemen ride. This is the way the gentlemen ride. Gallop. Gallop. Gallop." Thanks, Dad. I love you, Dad. I love you. You know, it's a shame, but I've said "I love you" to my dad more times since he died than when he was alive.

I live every day to be in the character of what I think my dad would want for me, based on the values in our home. I haven't seen Dad for twenty years, yet the impact he had on my young life was tremendous. As Dr. Alvera Stern, prevention consultant to the federal government, says, "I insist that we have underestimated the impact that we can have on our children." And where has that parental influence gone? Society, music, and peers haven't taken it away. We give it away! *We* give it away!

I remember him coming home from the bar drunk. I remember him cussing and yelling at us and telling us that we were useless and stupid. The most vivid thing that I would remember is when he would slam the ketchup bottle down on the table when he would get mad and get ketchup on the ceiling. When I was young and would cry, he would say, I'll give you something to cry about.

—ANDREA, 12th grade

Denying the Impact of Memories

To deal with the abandonment and grief surrounding my dad's death, I tried to hide by acting strong and burying all my pain inside, intending never to feel again, never to cry again, never to completely experience life again. Nothing was ever going to hurt me the way I hurt the night he died. Nothing!

There were times when others noticed certain things about me, indications that something was wrong. And I guess I noticed these same cues myself. But I spent years and years trying to ignore these cues, delaying resolution by procrastinating in my efforts to reach out and ask someone for help. My ego was just too strong and too stubborn. I remember one evening many years after my dad's death, sitting on the edge of my bed, thinking that something was missing in my life. I missed my dad fiercely, but there wasn't a lot I could do about that longing.

I used to ask myself, "Why am I unable to tear up and cry? Why can't I feel? Why can't I experience love?" I even tried to force myself to cry, but it never worked. I would think of something very sad, and I'd make crying noises, but I knew it wasn't real crying. I had no tears.

Finally, as a young man of thirty-two, this oldest, perfectionistic hero child ventured into counseling as a last resort. Little did I realize that my feelings of failure (because I needed to reach out for help) and my seeking professional help were the first steps on a profound journey toward healing. Isn't it interesting that we can help everyone else but are often unable to help ourselves?

Two months later, seventeen years after my father's death, I wept for the first time.

The experiences of my childhood are like those of so many adolescents. My passion to reach out to young people today, to listen to their stories and read their letters as they share their lives, has been as much my therapy as it has been my contribution. Though my world wasn't exactly fair when I was young, I can no longer blame the world. My inability to trust, find legitimate love, and feel a sense of connectedness had been set up by my childhood interpretation of what had taken place in my family. But now I am a volunteer of life and no longer a victim. If we are old enough to assign blame, we are old enough to do something about it.

Perception is always our reality. The skewed conclusions I reached from my childhood perception of the world needed to be reassessed and changed if I was to make my way through emotional adolescence and arrive securely at adulthood. Life is this kind of journey, and the paradox is that if we can just trust the process and let go of control, we will discover the peace we desperately long to grasp.

I still hold on to the memories of my father, and his influence is present in my life even today. January 21, 1974, my dad wrote me a letter wishing me a happy birthday. This laminated note is another of my treasured memories. It ends with:

> ...*I know you have trouble getting started to write but make an effort because we enjoy hearing from you.*
> *I love you and miss you very much. Dad.*

These are the last recorded words of my father. What will you be leaving behind for your children?

Exhausted Parents

Over the years, we have met parents who feel exhausted and who feel that they are being abused by their children because their children are not returning in kind the love, the time, the sacrifices, and the respect that parents have dutifully given.

Families and the situations of families affect people for a lifetime. Just by their very existence, families create memories; some are good and others are not so good. At one time or another the feeling of exhaustion is felt by both children and adults, and frequently thoughts of running away from the situation occur.

The Note Said: "You Win!"

A number of years ago, a sixteen-year-old boy was referred to me by a correctional institution. Terry was bright, handsome, and very intelligent. Terry's presence in the correctional setting was directly related to the shame that he felt in not being able to meet the expectations of his parents. His biological parents were divorced. Terry didn't get along with his stepmother, and he always was angry when his father told him that he wasn't doing things "good enough." "You could have made the [hockey] shot if you had really hammered that puck."

Terry just could never seem to get it right, or at least that was the message that his father gave him. Terry had good grades in school, and he'd made it to junior varsity status already by the age of sixteen, but his father was demanding more. For Terry, his response to divorce, his father's reaction to Terry's perceived shortcomings, and then a note Terry found one day taped to the refrigerator door sent him off on a self-deprecating journey of punishment that essentially brought him to the correctional setting. Terry came home one day, and at the age of twelve read this note from his mother addressed to Terry and his brother:

> *Dear Terry and Dave:*
>
> *You win! I can't take it any longer. I am sorry about the divorce that I know neither of you wanted, but then again, neither did I. You have made it very clear to me that you don't respect me and won't let me parent you. I can't stand the continued fighting, I hate the arguments, and I just don't want to live like this any longer. I am leaving and I'm not coming back. You can call your father and he can have you, and hopefully he will take better care of you than I could. As I leave I just want you to know that I love you and always have loved you, and this is the only way that I can*

see to stop this whole craziness that exists between everyone. No more! . . . You win!

Love and good-bye,
Mom

Terry's mom did disappear the day she left the note, and she had not resurfaced yet on the day of Terry's release from the institution where he had been committed for a string of house burglaries (all committed by himself, not with peers). Terry was released to go live with his father and stepmother. It is not difficult to see how the memories of this event will affect Terry for the rest of his life.

Self-Fulfilling Prophesies — the Story of Sheri

I was working in a junior high school as a school social worker about twenty years ago. In the course of my work I had a chance to meet Sheri, who at the time was a second-year eighth grader. Sheri was fourteen years old, already stunning in her beauty at that early age, with big brown eyes and long black hair. Sheri was the youngest of four children living in a single-parent family. Her next oldest sibling was a girl eight years older than she.

Sheri's mom existed on welfare, and the divorced alcoholic father provided no child support or involvement with his family; the dad had disappeared years earlier when Sheri was in kindergarten. Sheri never knew her dad except for the visual memories of a man who would frequently yell and hit her mom. Sheri and I talked about her dad a lot, and even though she never really knew him, she always talked in terms of what it would be like if she could find him and build a relationship with him.

Sheri and I got along very well, and she liked me so much that my office soon became the gathering place for a large group of eighth-grade girls, all close friends of Sheri (four of the six were repeating the eighth grade). I quickly got a reputation within the building staff ranks for my ability to deal effectively and gently with this group of six girls whom the school saw as major behavior problems. Staff considered it a benefit to have any one of these girls in my office, because they knew it would mean an opportunity to avoid hassles in the classroom.

The girls were well matched. All were quite attractive, all were right in the middle of full-blown adolescent rebellion, and not one of them considered school a serious priority. On a typical day, one or more of the group would get referred to the principal's office for skipping class, smoking in the building, using bad language, or being rowdy; if two or more got referred at the same time, it was clear to all concerned that the referral became a party.

Sheri was the leader of this group of girls. She was the most provocative, and without exception the most colorful. Sheri was our Jesse James and Al Capone, all wrapped up in a fourteen-year-old package of hyperactive energy, disrespect, incorrigible rebellion, and intolerable sassiness. All of the girls were very similar in their resistance to authority and disrespect as well as their provocativeness and seductive dress.

Arrogance and false bravado sometimes become a significant part of the equation in dealing with the adolescent's behavior, and it is not an unusual occurrence to see that this outward appearance is often accepted by the parent as genuine and thereafter interpreted as disrespectful. Always remember this concept: The greater an adolescent's front and false bravado, the greater the emptiness on the inside. So, regardless of what you see, always try to tell yourself that there is something else, something significant, going on behind the scenes and within the walls of the adolescent before you. By doing this, it will give you the opportunity to breathe a little easier and stay calm rather than responding with indignation at what would appear to be the insolence of the adolescent.

Over the months, Sheri and I spent a lot of time together, and she facilitated a bond between me and the "gang" (as they were called) such as I had never experienced in my life, nor have I ever since. I found myself becoming a surrogate dad to many of these young ladies, and a very close adult friend to them all, and that was particularly true of my relationship with Sheri. My first professional encounter with group therapy came in this setting as Sheri declared this activity "cool." In reality it was a "bitch" session. Everyone loved to come together in our weekly meetings to bad-mouth parents, teachers, authority, guys, other girls, and just about anything under the sun.

The group was obviously an important part of life for Sheri's gang, as witnessed by perfect attendance on the part of all participants for thirty-eight weeks of school. It was interesting to see how illness did strike often and required absence from school, but never on group day. Parents seemed to love their daughters' inclusion in this group, and from the sounds of parent input, it was the only place where the girls felt respected, listened to, and liked by an adult.

The school housed seventh, eighth, and ninth grades in a population of about eighteen hundred students. In this large student population almost everyone knew Sheri and the gang, and Sheri's attractiveness brought the attention of the elitist ninth-grade boys who were always out looking for the "big catch," as they referred to it.

Sheri was persistently defiant and was referred to the assistant principal's office on a very regular basis, and from there she would usually wind up being suspended. During the suspensions, Sheri's mom would be required to come to school, and so her mother and I became well acquainted. The mother was a delightfully patient woman. Each time that she would appear in my office, I would hear her ask Sheri, "When are you going to grow up?" Other times I would hear her mom say, "Sheri, you're going to be the death of me someday!"

One of the ninth-grade boys did make "the big catch," and Sheri ended up pregnant that year. This seemed to tip the scales of patience for Sheri's mother. Back in those days, pregnant girls were not allowed to remain in the regular school system and instead were remanded to a special school located in an apartment complex on the other side of the district. During Sheri's pregnancy, her school behavior deteriorated even further than the already outrageous level it had been earlier in the year.

Sheri's mom continued to come to school in response to suspension after suspension, and I would hear the repeated quote: "Sheri, you're going to be the death of me someday."

One afternoon in the middle of May, Sheri went home and, not finding her mom, looked into the garage to see if her car was around. Sheri found her mother dead behind the wheel of her car. In a desperate critical effort to help her mother, Sheri entered the gas-filled garage and tried to pull her mother from the car. Rigor mortis had already set in, and the stiffening of the body made it impossible to remove. In the process, Sheri herself got very sick from the inhalation of carbon monoxide. Sheri's memory of her mother in that car will never disappear.

The funeral was held three days later, and I was one of the congregation assembled. The casket was wheeled into the church followed by a parade of immediate family, each one coming down the center aisle in single-file formation, carrying a single long-stemmed red rose. I was immediately drawn to the presence of Sheri, who in her characteristic style giggled constantly, all the while holding her rose behind her back. Sheri continued to talk and giggle through the entire service, distracting and angering many of those assembled.

Sheri's story is a tragedy, to be sure, but more important it is a story of hopeless despair on the part of a parent. It is not uncommon to hear parents say that they are fed up and exhausted. Many talk about running away or jest about having a heart attack or stroke because of their children. Subliminally, as with Sheri's mother, this seemingly innocent venting of emotions may, in fact, predestine their future.

Running Away — a Solution With Harsh Consequences

In cases like Sheri's or Terry's, craziness abounds and chaos reigns. Understanding that this is a transient period of adjustment will hopefully help parents cope with the difficult times and not have to act out the need to run away, in whatever form imaginable. Waiting out the storm is the best therapy, and even with outside counseling, much of the craziness will still require time and patience, while at the same time testing intensely the coping ability of any parent.

If we take a close look at Sheri's life, we will discover all kinds of issues. Sheri felt she was getting her own way and was left with the clear message "You're going to be the death of me someday." Terry is left with the message "You win!" In reality, of course, both Sheri and Terry lose — and they know it.

Everything Creates a Memory: The Good and the Bad

Value the moment with your children and family. Your children will interpret this as valuing today. "This is it." Today is not a dress rehearsal for life. Value today and teach your children to do the same. Today is where life is lived.

> *When I was in the fifth grade, my dad took off work to come and talk to the principal because of a fight I was in. He was behind me the whole time.*
>
> —RON, 9th grade

Children remember the hugs that we give them, but they also remember the hugs that we don't give them. Children remember the time that we take with them, but they also remember the time that we don't take with them. They remember the "I love yous" — when it felt real and it felt close and it felt intimate — and they remember when the "I love yous" were distant, empty, and inconvenient.

They remember the consistency in our discipline, and they also remember the inconsistency. The memories that we give birth to are endless. Let's think about the memories that we are creating in the minds of our children through our use (or nonuse) of the following:

Behaviors	Setting limits	Compassion	Eye contact
Expectations	Words	Touch	Consistency
Physical contact	Example	Sensitivity	Values
What we say	What we don't say	Temperament	Judgments
Body language	Voice tone	Voice inflection	Availability

Let's consider these items when we are communicating and shaping memories within our family. How we say something is more important than what we say.

> *The next few months were hard ones for me. I relearned everything that I had lost. The emotional barriers were what was hard for me to conquer. The accident had left my face badly scarred, and I felt that I was ugly. So I stayed away from girls a great deal. One night when I was out with my mom, I met a girl who would change my life. At first I ignored her because I was embarrassed by my scars. She continued to call me, and one night she came to my house and told me that she liked me for what was on the inside. My hope for life came from my mom and my new girlfriend. I wish my dad could have lived to see the progress that I am making.*
>
> —MANUEL, 11th grade

Traditions Create Stability

More than anything else in life, it is family and the integrity of that family that will bring a sense of understanding and stability to our life and existence. Family is the springboard that individuals use as they embark on the challenges of life and the journey that becomes so important as a part of that life. Within family, doing things together, regardless of how dumb those things might be, fosters the creation of a solid foundation for people. With a solid foundation, just about anything will hold up and survive. It is the connection to family, not necessarily all family but people within family, that creates that bond of affiliation that everyone needs and thrives on.

The activities that surround and are identified by the word "tradition" support identity and connectedness. People without connectedness feel significant loss in life, and, conversely, people with connectedness have a strength beyond belief in dealing with life's adversities.

Traditions come in thousands of varieties. It is in the tradition that the family is remembered. Often with wonderful smiles we can look back on our family's traditions.

I heard somewhere that it is important to take traditions into marriage — not to wait until marriage to begin them but to establish our own, first. That way we will have more to offer the relationship and won't be draining as much from it. Who we are is found in the trademarks of our traditions and the rituals that accompany those traditions.

The Tradition of Family Christmas

At Christmastime, back home, I think it was a tradition to just have a Christmas tree magically appear. I never really knew where the trees came from. I had seen the Christmas tree lots selling them, but how one was selected and what considerations were important I was never told. Then, after our tree appeared, I can remember that my father would frequently get angry because one or two strings of light bulbs wouldn't work.

When the time came in our marriage, my wife and I decided that we would begin our own tradition by taking the children to a tree farm and carefully selecting the best tree in the world to stand before us in our relatively small apartment. I remember the activity, as do my children, because the day we went out the cold of winter was unbelievably harsh. As fate would have it, we couldn't reach consensus among the four of us, except we agreed that we were all freezing to death. Never having cut a Christmas tree before, I didn't realize that the saw I had available for cutting my household lumber wasn't my best selection for Christmas tree cutting.

The Christmas tree got to the apartment with everyone excited. As I stood the tree on end and my wife balanced it, we discovered that the tree's base was crooked and needed stabilizers attached to it. My wife and I thought for a time, and, considering our limited tool resources, we made the decision that I would attach an invisible wire to a tree branch and then nail the wire to the wall. It worked; the Christmas tree did not fall that year. What we did not anticipate, however, was that a newly cut tree needed to be nourished in a different way from the trees on the retail racks. Not knowing any different, we simply set up the tree and watered it. Before Christmas came, the tree had become so dry that the needles were shedding rapidly. We really didn't know what to do, and we were faced with the embarrassment of having a tree almost totally devoid of needles. By Christmastime the ornaments remained, but they were hanging pathetically on the raw, bare tree; the needles were gone.

The next Christmas, we bought our tree in a retail lot and have ever since. Nevertheless, I still struggle each year with a couple of light bulb strings that won't light. My father's story has repeated itself.

I am always saddened by the busy couple who are both working parents with little time for their families. What will they celebrate together in their later life? The children leave to begin their own lives and don't return because there is so little to return to. So often we give our children everything in life that they don't need. We give them everything to live with and nothing to live *for*. They become known for all the "stuff" that they have and not for who they are. It's great to have stuff. I'm not knocking stuff or successful careers, unless a person seeks them out to find identity there. But it's not the *presents* we give our children that let them know they are loved. It's our *presence* with them that lets them know.

A year ago I was thinking about suicide. Sometimes I would go to my room and just cry for hours because I really believed that I had no one to talk to. My parents went to counseling with me, and I have discovered a new life. As a result of counseling, my parents are spending more time with me, and I am feeling better.

—TAI, 9th grade

Making Memories

A friend of mine works for IBM and was telling me about a colleague who was consumed with work — very successful professionally, but his family never saw him. Well, the stress of the career eventually led to a premature death. His children went to clean out his office. As their father's colleagues stopped by to offer their condolences, the children would ask, "What was our father like? Did you know him? Did he ever talk about us?" They found family photos that they didn't even know existed. To have to ask someone to help us discover our dad or mom is a sad commentary on a "successful" life.

Ask yourself, "How will my children remember me?" If you can honestly say, "They will remember my love, my fairness, my patience, and my support," you have accomplished one of life's major miracles, transferring the beautiful gifts of stability, security, and self-worth to our children and grandchildren. Families are forever.

POINT TO REMEMBER

- *Running away never solves a problem, but it does create new ones.*

Part IV

LIFE BEYOND
ADOLESCENCE

Chapter 12

They'll Be Back, So Don't Sell the Bedroom Furniture

Each of us has only one life and one opportunity to make a difference. It is our belief that the most important difference to be made is the one made within the family. Over the years, I have counseled powerful corporate executives who have successfully led magnificent growth patterns for their companies. They have supervised and directed the activities of employees, thousands in number. Without exception, I have heard these same very powerful people say with regret, "I wish that I had put the same kind of energy and creativity into my family that I put into my work at the office."

The purpose of life is really defined in four elements:

1. Whom have I loved?

2. Who has loved me?

3. What have I done with my life to make a difference?

4. What have I done with myself to be real and truthful?

All of us at one time or another grapple with questions related to purpose. Several years ago I heard James Kearn, a motivational speaker, close a seminar with a story he called "The Parable of the Eagle." Reflect on this parable and see if it helps you to put into perspective your own purpose.

The Parable of the Eagle

There was a mother eagle whose nest in a tree was collapsing and her babies were going to be endangered. There was a secure nest across the lake. She carried her babies one at a time to the safety of the secure nest.

As she carried the first one, she asked the question, "How will you treat me when I'm old?" The baby eagle replied, "Mother, when you are old, I'm going to treat you just the way you've treated me." The mother eagle opened her beak and dropped that eagle into the lake.

She picked up the second baby — wiser still — and as she carried him, she also asked the question: "How will you treat me when I'm old?" This eagle said: "When you and Father are old, I'll treat you both just the way you've treated me." The mother dropped that eagle into the lake also.

The third eagle — the wisest of the three — was asked the same question. "How will you treat me when I'm old?" This eagle responded with, "I don't know how I'll treat you when you are old, Mother, but I know that I'll treat my children just the way you've treated me." The mother carried that baby to the safety of the new nest.

Living by example, personally demonstrating what we have done with the questions of purpose, is a lesson that becomes our legacy. The end comes for all of us. The memories we create will affect generations of people who will follow us. I think often about the question, "How will they remember me?"

As parents we do the beautiful things that we do in the hope that there will be a generation that follows us that won't have to live in a world of fear, hatred, bigotry, and prejudice. We hope that our children will know the joy that we've sought, will know the happiness we keep searching for, and will be able to live a life so fulfilled that love and laughter are ever-present gifts.

Love in Reconciliation

There is something about the power of the subconscious mind that will not permit the permanent burying of any material related to family. Family is sacred, and once family has been created, it can never be permanently eradicated from the conscious mind. The yearning for reunion and the love found in reconciliation will always be there. Unfortunately for some, by the time the need for forgiveness or the willingness to give forgiveness surfaces, the realities of our existence have interfered with the process, and death has prevented true reconciliation and consequently blocked true peace.

It is our contention that regardless of how a hurt is caused, the lack of forgiveness has a negative impact, both psychologically and spiritually, on individuals. Lack of forgiveness essentially erodes the very foundation of the family, which for generations and generations has been the source of love and stability for all people. If family is going to survive and restructure itself as an important entity in the life of America, the very people who call themselves family will have to return to a new and revitalized understanding of love and its importance. Consider seriously the message of the following four very prestigious authors:

> Love cures people. Both the ones who give it, and the ones who receive it.
>
> — Dr. Karl Menninger

> In psychology, we have only begun to realize the tremendous power of feeling loved: it can promote the growth of mind and body, and it is probably the most effective therapeutic force we know for repairing both psychological and physical damage.
>
> — Dr. Thomas Gordon

> Love is the most powerful immune stimulant in the body.
> — Dr. Bernard Siegel

There is no difficulty that enough love will not conquer,
No disease that enough love will not heal,
No door that enough love will not open,
No gulf that enough love will not bridge,
No wall that enough love will not throw down,
No sin that enough love will not redeem....
It makes no difference how deeply seated may be the trouble,
How hopeless the outlook, and how muddled the tangle,
How great the mistake.
A sufficient realization of love will dissolve it all.

If only you could love enough,
you would be the happiest and most powerful being
   in the world.

—Emmett Fox

A scriptural reference from 1 Corinthians 13 sums it all up: "Faith, hope and love abide; but the greatest of these is love."

"The Twelve-Word Rule" for Parents

Our best advice is twofold. The first and most pragmatically helpful is "The Twelve-Word Rule." Let's keep our comments with our children (this applies to children of all ages, including adult children) to twelve words at a time or less, especially our answers to questions. This prevents deafness while at the same time causing confusion in our child (and the confusion provokes questions). The confusion relates to prior conditioning wherein we have probably taught our child that every time we open our mouths, there will be a long dissertation about nothing (their opinion).

By using "The Twelve-Word Rule," we actually encourage communication with our children. Because we haven't worn them down with too much talk, they will be willing to ask more and more questions. Each time they ask a question, we are then entitled to answer again with twelve more words. See how it works? The reason we lose our ability to communicate effectively with our children almost always relates to our need to talk and talk or to drive them absolutely crazy by asking question after question.

In the event that nothing seems to be working and we are going crazy, let's feel comfortable moving into the second part of solution options. I will have to admit that "The Twelve-Word Rule" isn't perfect and without flaw, so in times of real-life crisis, I would suggest a couple of alternatives. First, we can call 911 and exit the house until the police arrive, or, as an alternative, my favorite over the years has been to take two aspirins and head off to the Dairy Queen for a Turtle Sundae or to the local movie theater. I have always had a theoretical belief that I would rather have my stroke because of an ice cream overdose or excess ingestion of trans-fatty acids in the buttered popcorn rather than because of fights about how the car always seems to run out of gas or have a flat tire exactly at curfew time.

Heng

I've heard parents talk about the unexpected child. In our particular case our first three were well planned, Kathy and Kurt biologically and Peter through adoption from Korea. Heng was our unplanned child, and he came to us on impulse as a result of an ad in our church newspaper.

My wife and I were sitting in church one Sunday a couple of years ago. The minister was making the weekly announcements and preparing the congregation for prayer time. I was reading the outreach section of our Sunday bulletin and was drawn to an ad that read:

> Heng is a 12-year-old
> Cambodian refugee looking
> for a stable, loving home.

I leaned over to my wife and pointed to the ad and whispered to her, "What would you think of giving this kid a look?" My wife responded with a somewhat startled, "Are you crazy? Let someone else do that...we're through with that part of our lives...be quiet and pray!"

My wife was certainly accurate: We were past our parenting prime and had enjoyed the previous year as empty nesters. My prayers were disrupted by thoughts of the ad and this kid named Heng. I became obsessed with thoughts of this kid who was actually pleading with anyone to take him in and give him a home. I thought about him night and day and eventually bugged my wife so much that she agreed to give it a try. We had the room and we had the experience, but the question remained, did we have the energy?

We decided to go for it and invited Heng to live with us. Heng hadn't even arrived yet when we got word that both of our adult sons would be moving back home by the end of the month. Within a period of ten days we went from empty nesters to a full house — all boys. The house was not only full, it was full of noise, music, and ringing phones. I was expecting a note simultaneously from the gas company, the electric company, and the phone company thanking me for all the new business.

Heng fit in well and relished the opportunity to be around his new brothers. My wife and I were actually surprised with the degree of involvement that all our children (now all adults) put forth. They seemed to like the idea of having a truly "international family."

Heng had only been in America a year when he came to us, and he was assigned to the third grade. During immigration his age had been falsified so that he would be placed in what appeared to be an appropriate school grade level. It was soon discovered that he was not nine years old as the social worker said on his immigration papers, but thirteen.

We were able to verify his age through X-rays. Our son Kurt made a big deal out of the age disparity and liked to announce at dinner from time to time that Heng would be the only kid in the fifth grade who would be driving if some paperwork changes weren't made and his grade changed.

The first three years of Heng's experience in America were turbulent since he went from grade three to grade six; now he is in the ninth grade, where for the first time he is with age-appropriate peers.

Heng is a real adolescent in the sense that he seems to be addicted to television and has memory loss when it comes to garbage and piano practicing. Nonetheless, the most noticeable difference between Heng and our other three is found in his compliance. My guess is that Heng is (and was) so desperate in his search for a family that he can't afford to be rebellious to the extent that other teenagers might. We don't experience very much of that with Heng, and his short tenure at our house and in America would probably be the reason for that.

Heng is a young man who keeps his room neat and always does what he is told. Maybe that will change, but in the meantime, it is certainly fun having him around and sharing the love of our family with him. Please don't misunderstand — Heng is not totally compliant. He has developed the capacity to tell us that as parents we are old-fashioned when we insist that he not wear his hat to dinner and when we require a clothes upgrade for church. I guess we've seen and heard this all before. What do the kids say nowadays — been there, done that? He makes perfect sense — for an adolescent. Heng is bright, handsome, and loving. What a gift to our family! He has captured our heart.

They Have to Leave So That They Can Return as Adults

One of the most significant "rites of passage" that adolescents experience is the need to grow up and move out of the house and away from their parents and siblings as soon as they possibly can. Away from the family is where independence and the perfect tranquillity of "nirvana" are to be found; and it is away from the family that the "dharma," the true teaching about the purpose of life and the complexities of life, can be discovered.

Their departure is both sweet and sour. As parents we understand that it's time for the baby eagles to fly on their own, but the heart of the parent is filled with fear for the safety of their journey. The journey outward has a biblical base, but in my readings I have never found the appropriate references suggesting that they would return once again to stay. They do, however, return in their own time, and it is in that return that parents discover the growth and the maturity in their children that they had so long hoped for.

In their quest for the perfect tranquillity of nirvana beyond the doors of the family homestead, typical adolescents find some of the stark realities of life. Exorbitant rents, food costs, transportation problems, insurance requirements, health care, designer clothes, entertainment, utilities, toothpaste, soap, and shampoo, even the real cost of those video games in restaurant foyers — these factors and a multitude of others bring to the average adolescent the first "wake-up call" of life. Colliding internally within the brain's billions of neurons comes a message that essentially says, "Oh, that's what they were doing with all their money, and that's what they were talking about." The realities of life surface and help in the rather quick development of an appreciation for the commitment of parents and the significance of clichés worn out through the years.

Sometimes it takes one or two passes at "reentry" for the parents to discover that their kids have "finally got it" and matured and truly do appreciate all that has been done for them over the years. Hopefully that time will have come before they cart you (and me) off to the nursing home where we will spend our own time contemplating life and its true purpose.

Whose House Is This Anyway? Whose Rules?

When our kids land in their family-of-origin household reentry, it is important that the friction of adolescence not be rekindled. We would strongly suggest that everyone sit down and negotiate a "lease agreement" of sorts that articulates in writing very specifically the rules of this reunion. It can really be a treat to have the children, adult children, back at home, but everyone involved needs to understand and accept the new rules that come with the territory. We have found it helpful at our house to charge rent as a way of avoiding the insanity of game playing that was characteristic of adolescence. As a result of the rent stipend, the children can be free of all labor obligations that used to cause the big philosophical discussions and the horrendous fights pushing us toward the long-awaited stroke.

With the rent payment it is fairly easy to contract the lawn to a professional service, which will cut the grass on the day we desire rather than after it has gone to seed. With the rent money we can avoid the old sermons to the effect that "everyone in this family has a responsibility for its maintenance." With the rent money (which includes meals) we really don't have to worry about whether they show up for dinner on time or not. At our house, dinner is served at 6:00 p.m. If they are "no-shows," that's okay — they can eat out and discover the cost of restaurant food. We use the leftovers for the next night, thus reducing our food costs for the month.

Can you see how this is working out? Without saying a word, we are teaching the kids about life — that there is no free lunch, anywhere — but without preaching and without nagging. The most effective communication is developed in the form of real-life experience. It is important to experiment with situations, both good and bad, as a way of learning. Experiencing firsthand the relationship between cause and effect can be an immensely helpful and maturing experience. Doing too much for our children does nothing more than create dependency, blocking them from developing the skills to survive in the world.

One of the other luxuries of life at this time can be found in our ability to go to bed at 9:00 p.m. if we feel like it, maybe even at 8:00 p.m. if we are deserving of such treatment. No longer do we have to wait until they get home forty-six minutes after curfew with an excuse that suggests their belief in parental stupidity and naiveté. Now with these adult children around, we just go to bed, and if the kid comes home at 4:45 a.m. we just hope that he has the courtesy to pick up the morning newspaper from the driveway so that we don't have to get our feet chilled by the nippiness of the morning air.

The transition patterns of late adolescent children (adult children) in America today are moving more and more in the direction of reentry visits to the homestead of parents. Let that be a message to you: "Don't sell the furniture just yet, and unless you move with no forwarding address, expect that they will be back, if for no other reason than to use the washer and dryer — 'no coins are required.'"

Eventually, they do grow up and move on, unless they are what my kids refer to as "lifers." I once saw a family who came to counseling in an attempt to get their thirty-two-year-old son to move out of the house. These are very rare families, so don't panic, and when I helped these parents understand that it was okay not to give their son lunch money and provide him with other perks, their son decided he could get a better deal someplace else and decided to move out.

Yes, it is a good life, all in all! Put your mind to it, change your paradigms to reflect that "life can be great with children," and discover that your blood pressure goes down as the gift of family and the love of family come into your heart and your life.

Good luck to you as you continue the journey of "making sense of adolescence." May you find peace and understanding.

POINT TO REMEMBER

- *The Twelve-Word Rule will enhance communication within family.*

Afterword

IN EARLY SPRING of this last year, I took my three sons on a fishing trip into the beautiful boundary waters of Minnesota. I had been in that region before and therefore knew of its beauty and serenity. Reflecting on my previous visits to this land of blue skies and ever-present loons, I was eager with anticipation. I looked forward to getting away from my office and to relaxing in one of the truly miraculous centers of creation. As I remembered the towering majestic beauty of pine trees and the abundance of wildlife and fish surrounded by the beauty of fresh water separating the land boundaries of Minnesota and Canada, my expectations soared.

The trip I had excitedly anticipated turned into three nights and four days of horrendous rain and wind such as I had never experienced. Our tents were ripped to shreds by the vicious winds and the constant downpour of a cold spring rain. Tarps that normally protected us from the elements were wind-whipped and destroyed. Our gear was soaked, and our boats were filled with water. In fact, the rain came so fast and furiously that we couldn't bail water quickly enough to keep our boats afloat. The rain ruined our food, and everyone was miserable and wet. Building a fire was impossible. Without a fire, our meals were messy, soggy, and tasteless. A trip designed for relaxation and rest became an ordeal in survival.

The rains destroyed our meager human comforts and provisions. All I could think was, "Please, God, get me out of here." I fantasized about death and what the funeral was going to be like. I saw the local newspaper headline: "Father and Three Sons Die in Boundary Waters." It was a demoralizing experience to be trapped on an island while nature's harshest elements thrashed at our campsite hour after hour. Even the best of outdoor enthusiasts can become depressed, if not downright angry, at the lost opportunity for a wonderful vacation.

Looking back on the trip is completely different from actually

257

experiencing the problems. Now I have fond memories of under-going — and surviving — a difficult circumstance with my three kids by my side. Sure we caught only six fish, and many of our personal possessions perished, but we survived. The destruction of our camping gear was the only permanent and lasting casualty of the storm. My kids were safe, I was safe, and now we are planning another adventure. We all agree that because of our struggle for survival during that trip we learned a lesson; this time we will approach our trip with better planning and more refined techniques to ensure our safety and comfort. Today my sons and I refer to that experience as fun, as a challenge. At the time, however, it was simply misery, helplessness, and discomfort. It was a time when life was totally out of control.

That fishing trip is similar to the unexpected challenges, frustrations, and turbulent times that families experience, especially during adolescence. Often families meet with unexpected pressures and chaotic downpours that they never anticipated as they embarked on their journey of a dream home and sweet children underfoot. The gratification parents enjoyed with their lovely babies can change — sometimes quite suddenly. We think about the canoeist who enjoys the flow of calm waters but suddenly experiences significant stress when the canoe comes upon the churning waters of a river's rapids and strong current. The push and pull of the river's force is a metaphorical paradigm for all families because it very closely resembles the daily push and pull by both parents and adolescents.

Wherever you are on your journey in this life, be aware that others have gone before you. We hope that this book has already served as a guide for you as you navigate the turbulent rapids of life.

Thanks for sharing your experiences and letters. I now know that I am not the only one.

—JENNIFER, 9th grade

Notes

Chapter 1:
Smile, It's Only Adolescence, and It's Not Contagious

1. R. Demski, "Rock Music and Today's Youth," *Journal of the American Academy of Child & Adolescent Psychiatry*, July 1986.

Chapter 2:
Psychological Dynamics of the Adolescent

1. William Glasser, *The Quality School: Managing Students with Coercion* (New York: HarperPerennial, 1992), 14.
2. John Powell, S.J., *Why Am I Afraid to Love?* (Allen, Tex.: Tabor Publishing, 1967).
3. Dorothy Briggs, *Your Child's Self-Esteem* (New York: Dolphin Books, 1975), 137.

Chapter 3:
Adolescents: What Do They Look Like?
What Makes Them Tick?

1. Jacques Ives Cousteau, *Marijuana Legalization and the Shadow Pushers* (Drug Watch Oregon, 1993).
2. William J. Bennett, *The De-valuing of America* (New York: Simon & Schuster, 1992), 42–43.
3. Quoted in "Up Front: The Best Contraceptive," *People*, October 24, 1994, 56.
4. Dorothy Briggs, *Celebrate Yourself* (Garden City, N.Y.: Doubleday, 1977), 18.
5. "Parents Told: Get Involved," *USA Today*, February 19, 1990, 1A.
6. Anita Manning, "Marrying Age Higher Than Ever Before," *USA Today*, June 7, 1991, 1D.

Chapter 4:
Teen Motivation: Uncovering the Mysteries

1. Stephen Glenn, *Raising Self-Reliant Children in a Self-Indulgent World* (Rocklin, Calif.: Prima Publishing, 1989), 121–23.

2. Family Research Council, *Free to Be Family* (New York, 1992), 25.

3. Bo Jackson and Dick Schaap, *Bo Knows Bo* (New York: Doubleday, 1990).

4. David J. Wilmes, *Parenting for Prevention* (Minneapolis: Johnson Institute Books, 1988).

Chapter 5:
Why All the Rebellion?

1. William Cobbett, *Advice to Young Men and to Young Women, in the Middle and Higher Ranks of Life* (London, 1829), letter III, 83.

2. Cyril S. Smith, *Adolescence: An Introduction to the Problems of Order and the Opportunities for Continuity Presented by Adolescence in Britain* (London: Longmans, 1968), 2.

Chapter 6:
Helping Our Adolescents Make Responsible Choices

1. Debra O'Connor, "A Virtue-a-Month: One Way Schools Can Put Values Back into the Classroom," *St. Paul Pioneer Press*, September 1993.

Chapter 7:
The Biggest Concerns of Parents

1. Armand M. Nicholi, Jr., "The Impact of Parental Absence on Childhood Development: An Overview of the Literature," *Journal of Family and Culture* (Autumn 1985): 19–28.

2. Parents' Music Resource Center, *Let's Talk Rock* (1990), 9.

3. Ibid., 8.

4. Ibid., 15.

5. Nielsen Television Research.

6. Carnegie Council on Adolescent Development.

7. The Monitoring of the Future Project, Institute for Social Research, University of Michigan, *Trends in Prevalence of Various Drugs*, Table 1, 1993.

8. J. Klenk, Speech to the National Conference on Youth Suicide, Washington, D.C., June 19, 1985.

9. Eighth Special Report to the U.S. Congress on Alcohol and Health, October 1993.

10. Gregory F. Sanders and Ronald L. Mullis, "Family Influences on Sexual Attitudes and Knowledge as Reported by College Students," *Adolescence* 23, no. 92 (Winter 1988).

11. Up Front, "Teen Pregnancy: A Special Report," *People*, October 24, 1994, 45.

12. Stanley Henshaw, Lisa Koonin, and Jack Smith, "Characteristics of U.S. Women Having Abortions, 1987," *Family Planning Perspectives* (March/April 1991).

13. *U.S. News and World Report,* July 17, 1989.

Chapter 8:
Rites of Passage and Assets That Create Identity

1. U.S. Bureau of the Census, U.S. House of Representatives.

2. Peter L. Benson, *The Troubled Journey: A Profile of American Youth* (Minneapolis: The Search Institute, 1993).

3. Ibid.

4. Search Institute survey of 47,000 adolescents. Minneapolis, 1993.

Chapter 9:
Enhancing Self-Esteem Through Communication

1. Jerry Johnston, *Why Suicide?* (Nashville: Oliver-Nelson Books, 1987), 103.

2. Special Report, "The Baby Trap," *People,* October 24, 1994, 48.

3. Sandra L. Hanson, et al., "The Role of Responsibility and Knowledge in Reducing Teenage Out-of-Wedlock Childbearing," *Journal of Marriage and the Family* 49 (May 1987): 241, 244, 250.

Appendix

Resources

Alcohol

Al-Anon/Alateen Family Group Headquarters, Inc.
P.O. Box 862
Midtown Station
New York, NY 10018-0862
1-212-302-7240
1-800-344-2666 (U.S.)
1-800-443-4525 (Canada)

Alcoholics Anonymous (AA) World Services, Inc.
475 Riverside Drive
New York, NY 10115
1-212-870-3400

Children of Alcoholics Foundation, Inc.
Box 4185, Grand Central Station
New York, NY 10115
1-800-359-COAF
1-212-754-0656

National Association for Children of Alcoholics
11426 Rockville Pike, Suite 100
Rockville, MD 20852
1-301-468-0985

National Clearinghouse for Alcohol and Drug Information
11426 Rockville Pike, Suite 200
Rockville, MD 20852
1-301-468-2600
1-800-729-6686

National Families in Action
2296 Henderson Mill Road, Suite 204
Atlanta, GA 30345
1-404-934-6364

Marijuana, Hallucinogens

American Council for Drug Education
204 Monroe Street, Suite 110
Rockville, MD 20850
1-301-294-0600
1-800-488-DRUG

Families Anonymous, Inc.
P.O. Box 528
Van Nuys, CA 91408
1-818-989-7841

Nar-Anon Family Groups
P.O. Box 2562
Palos Verdes Peninsula, CA 90274
1-301-547-5800

Narcotics Anonymous (NA)
P.O. Box 9999
Van Nuys, CA 91409
1-818-780-3951

National Council on Alcoholism and Drug Dependence
12 West 21st Street
New York, NY 10010
1-212-206-6770
1-800-622-2255

National Families in Action
2296 Henderson Mill Road, Suite 204
Atlanta, GA 30345
1-404-934-6364

Center for Substance Abuse Treatment
Information and Treatment Referral Hotline
11426-28 Rockville Pike, Suite 410
Rockville, MD 20852
1-800-662-HELP

Inhalants

International Institute for Inhalant Abuse
799 E. Hampden Avenue, Suite 500
Englewood, CO 80110
1-303-788-4617

See also the groups listed in the previous section

Smoking

American Council for Drug Education
204 Monroe Street, Suite 110
Rockville, MD 20850
1-301-294-0600
1-800-488-DRUG

National Cancer Institute
Cancer Information Service
Johns Hopkins Oncology Center
550 North Broadway, Suite 307
Baltimore, MD 21205
1-800-4-CANCER

National Clearinghouse for Alcohol and Drug Information
11426 Rockville Pike, Suite 200
Rockville, MD 20852
1-301-468-2600
1-800-729-6686

National Families in Action
2296 Henderson Mill Road, Suite 204
Atlanta, GA 30345
1-404-934-6364

Office on Smoking and Health Center for Disease Control
Mail Stop K-50
4770 Buford Highway, NE
Atlanta, GA 30341-3724
1-404-488-5708

Index